ADMINISTRATION
of
CRIMINAL LAW

ADMINISTRATION
of
CRIMINAL LAW

By

Ernst W. Puttkammer

THE UNIVERSITY OF CHICAGO PRESS

CHICAGO & LONDON

International Standard Book Number: 0-226-68665-5

THE UNIVERSITY OF CHICAGO PRESS, CHICAGO 60637
The University of Chicago Press, Ltd., London

FOREWORD

THIS BOOK has been written with two different types of reader in mind. One is the law student (and, to a less degree, the lawyer). The other is the layman who, for one reason or another is interested in obtaining some information on how the criminal law functions. While these two groups are very different, it is hoped that the difficult task of adjustment to both groups and their needs has been met.

The student in our modern American law school is usually confronted with a single but required course in criminal law. In a comparatively limited number of hours he is given his entire classroom contact, not only with substantive criminal law, but also with its procedure and administration. The result is a constant pressure to economize in the use of time. Much of the procedural and administrative part is purely descriptive and lends itself well to that type of treatment. Where problems are raised, classroom discussion can be easily focused on them. (For this reason in many of the more contentious matters there is a special effort at brevity.) For the rest, economy in time can be achieved, at not too high a cost in adequacy of information, by the reading of a descriptive text. If more thorough treatment of the purely legal topics is wished, it can be obtained in such excellent treatises as Orfield's *Criminal Procedure from Arrest to Appeal* and the same author's *Criminal Appeals in America.*

Even the practicing lawyer who normally has no professional contact with criminal law may welcome a brief and rather elementary description of what, very often, is terra incognita to him. The community looks to a great extent to the lawyer for guidance in matters of this sort, even though they may not in the strict sense involve rules of law. It is he who is expected to know the answers to a great many questions of criminal-law administration. How is the police department organized and functioning? Is the prosecuting attorney acting properly in waiving a felony and allowing a plea of guilty of a misdemeanor? Should we abolish the grand jury? These are illustrations of the field that he may wish to have quickly surveyed for him. Thus for both the law student and the lawyer it may make somewhat easier the assumption of his responsibilities as a citizen.

What has just been said will also largely indicate the type of lay reader the author has had in mind—sociologists, social workers, justices of the peace, and any other person who finds it desirable to know how the law functions and how lawyers look at its problems. A detailed legal treatise not only would wholly fail to meet their needs but, on the contrary, would bog them down in a mass of minutiae. Yet anyone in the field must have noted how often even an intelligent layman's assumptions and suggestions rest on a complete misunderstanding of the law or, at any rate, of how lawyers look at the law. These difficulties could be largely overcome with the aid of a comparatively brief and nontechnical description of how the legal machinery works.

These comments as to the type of reader envisioned will show that the author has chosen to confine himself to a limited task. Only the conventional area of criminal prosecution is dealt with. There is no attempt to examine the changing and expanding functions of criminal law in the social structure or even its history, except as this may at times be needed to understand its present status. Detailed discussion of controversial matter is avoided. It need hardly be said that so limiting the scope of one's design was often neither pleasant nor easy. But in the author's judgment it was absolutely necessary to do so in order to keep the book's size within bounds. The contrary course would necessarily have defeated the author's primary purpose.

The material is taken up in the chronological order in which it would actually arise in a case. In some chapters, notably those on "The Trial" and "Appellate Review," the treatment is incomplete in the sense that there is no discussion of those matters that are identical in criminal and civil law. Inevitably the result is a somewhat jerky treatment, but this seemed preferable to adding still more pages containing matter not needed by the lawyer-reader and not significant for the lay reader.

These comments, it is hoped, will make clear what may fairly be expected from this book and also what should not be looked for.

E. W. Puttkammer

Chicago, Illinois

CONTENTS

I

INTRODUCTION: THE PURPOSES
OF THE CRIMINAL LAW

To PUT our subject in its proper setting, some preliminary general remarks are necessary. The title of this book indicates that we are dealing here with "Criminal *Law*"; but it may be well to point out a fact which, no doubt, will have been observed frequently elsewhere, viz., that the same word may mean very different things according to the context in which it is used and according to the background of the user and the purpose he has in mind. There is no better illustration of this than the word "law."

A few illustrations will suffice. The theologian or moralist would give a definition of law that spoke in terms of rules that determine what is right morally. He might phrase it in technical and religious terms, or he might speak of abstract ethics, but his definition would certainly deal with the morality of certain conduct and the immorality of other conduct. If the physicist were to be asked to define law, he would almost certainly put it in terms of certain principles believed by him to be immutable and unchangeable, certain cause-and-effect relationships that are necessarily so in the kind of world we live in or necessarily so as a consequence of certain more fundamental assumptions that he chooses to make. And he would find as an illustration of law as he used the term such propositions as that two and two are four, or he might cite the law of gravitation. Or, if we were to ask the anthropologist for a definition, he in turn would give something entirely different. He would not concern himself with morals or immutable physical principles. He would speak of racial or tribal customs, which he would analyze for their underlying meaning and for the interesting point of how they came to arise. To him, law is a formulation of tribal or racial beliefs, values, folkways, etc., and his definition would concern itself entirely with expressing that viewpoint.

These are ways of looking at "law," but they are not, any of them, the way in which the term is usually used by lawyers. In a broad sense the definition which we should give would clearly indicate that we are basically, whether we realize it or not, social scientists or that we try to be. We are concerned with the way in which people get on with each other, with the relationship that they hold toward each other—how those relationships are working out so as to produce or to hinder smooth and satisfactory human relations. And so the social scientist, in which classification we include the lawyer and judge, would define law along terms that suggested its function as something by which such satisfactory relationships might be set up and secured so far as possible. Obviously it is true that what would be regarded as a satisfactory social relationship will change from age to age and from society to society; and social relations that were regarded as of real use, and as highly desirable and therefore to be furthered by law in feudal Europe or in a slaveholding economy or in a totalitarian state, may perhaps not seem such in a democratic society or, indeed, in any society other than the particular one that is setting up a particular law.

But whatever the goal may be—totalitarian, feudal, or democratic—the lawyer and the judge are trying to set up rules that will seem socially desirable to those to whom those issues count and who are in a position to make their wishes prevail. Always the sociologist's view of law is that it is a means to bring about that pattern of conduct on the part of those people who are at the receiving end of the law which will be then and there regarded as desirable. That certainly is the way in which we look at law in this volume. It is a social tool to influence human conduct along the lines that we regard as desirable by encouraging certain kinds of conduct and by discouraging other kinds of conduct, viz., the contrary ones.

It is important to remember, but too often forgotten, that law is only one of the ways by which we hope, and try, to influence human conduct so as to get people to do the things we regard as desirable and not do the things we regard as undesirable. The layman, especially, tends to forget that there are other ways also of thus influencing human conduct. Education in the schools, setting up certain ways of behavior as being wise and approved, is an obvious example. The influence of the church is another. The law is only one of three or perhaps more tools that society has at its disposal in this effort to influence conduct. But it tends to be the tool that a layman especially is most likely to look to when he sees some type of conduct of which he disapproves.

It is understandable why the layman should want to have recourse first of all to this tool called "law" rather than to the tools called "education" and "religion" or to still other tools. Education and religion, if they are to accomplish the results, will only do so slowly and gradually, and we are all impatient to see those goals that are very important to us achieved more quickly. Thus it is entirely natural that, casting about how to achieve a result that he wishes, he will feel most inclined to use the tool that will bring about a result in a hurry. We see this in his almost instinctive reaction when he sees something that he does not like: "There ought to be a law against it." He does not stop to ask whether he is wise in trying to put so much of a burden on the law. No doubt it is very flattering to lawyers that the layman should have such an almost childlike, innocent confidence in what we in our profession can accomplish. But, unfortunately, however flattering it may be, it is important for him to realize that he may be giving us a little more credit than we really deserve and that it may be decidedly wiser not to ask the law to do a given job or, at any rate, not to trust simply and solely to this tool but to accompany it with the use of the other tools that are, of course, not in the least inconsistent with the legal tool.

This abstract statement may be brought down to earth by citing an example of a case where the community—or at least a large enough segment of the community to get its wishes incorporated in law—put too much confidence in what the law could do. The reference is to the prohibition experiment. It was believed that alcohol was a very serious evil. True, to some people it did not seem as great and outstanding an evil as it did to many others, but whoever was right on that is beside the present point. What was obviously proved by the prohibition experiment was that, even if matters needed correction as badly as the more frightened members of the community felt they did, it still was a job that very plainly was beyond the powers of the law to accomplish. Whether or not it is wise and desirable to eliminate entirely the use of alcoholic drinks, it certainly was shown that legal prohibition was not the best way to accomplish this result. It would seem obvious that it is very valuable for the citizen-lawyer, or lawyer-citizen, to be in a position where he can realistically appraise the limits of achievement that are possible to the law in influencing conduct, so that he can help accomplish the very real and constructive goal of discouraging this too great, too flattering, confidence in what we in our particular line of specialization can accomplish.

A very definite thread, therefore, that will run all through this book will be that of pointing out the human limitations that exist in regard to the effectiveness of the law in general and of criminal law in particular—limitations we tend all too easily to forget. Though we speak in abstract terms of the law accomplishing this, that, or the other goal, what must not be forgotten is that what is really meant is that a certain group of human beings, intrusted with certain definite responsibilities, are to accomplish certain goals. Those human beings whom we make so abstractly impersonal by describing them simply as "the law" are such individuals as, for instance, police officers, state's attorneys, judges, laymen serving for a while as jurors, penitentiary officials, probation and parole officers, etc. By and large, they, like all the rest of us, are willing to work or can work about eight hours a day. They are capable of so-and-so much work output; they have so-and-so much capacity, which may be higher or lower according to the effectiveness with which the citizens are selecting their government. They have, in other words, very definite limitations on their capacity. If we could realize those limitations, we should realize also that, by putting on them more work than they can handle, one or the other of two consequences will result. Either we will make them spread themselves so thin, and do the work so superficially, that they will do nothing really well; or we will force them to do something that we have not the slightest justification to ask them to do—to exercise their own discrimination as to the part of their job that they are going to neglect and the part of their job, on the other hand, that they are going to try to accomplish. Actually, the way things will work out, the police, at least, are going to strike a compromise by partly using both of these methods of getting out from under the dilemma.

They will probably spread themselves pretty thin and will also neglect certain jobs entirely. And, incidentally, to make matters worse, the jobs that they choose to neglect will tend to be a fluctuating group which will be made up of those particular offenses that for the time being are not in the public eye. Let us suppose that there is a crusade on to eliminate drunken driving, a very worthy purpose. Very well, the police department, which is anxious to please—as all public agencies normally are—goes all out against drunken driving, neglecting for the time being numerous other offenses and cutting into the manpower available against burglaries, for example. Drunken driving is getting the kind of attention it deserves, until the public becomes aware of the fact that the curve of burglaries is going up. This is proclaimed to be monstrous and terrible. The police department agrees that it must cut down burglaries; and it does so, but now it neglects perforce still another job. It is a salutary and valuable thing to look realistically at the human beings that make up the machinery of the law, and to see just how much they can accomplish, so as to discourage putting more on them than they are capable of handling.

Or another illustration might have been used. We may feel that it is desirable to develop ever minuter distinctions in law, say, in murder and manslaughter. And so we have murder in the first degree and murder in the second degree and manslaughter in the first degree and manslaughter in the second degree. One state even had murder in the fourth degree and manslaughter in the fifth degree, or nine kinds of criminal killing. What was the net result? It was such a multiplicity of minutely fine distinctions that they all broke down as far as the capacity of the jury to differentiate was concerned.

In sum, if we want law to modify human conduct, we must realize that it has limitations and that it is not a universal tool that can accomplish everything instantaneously but a very sharply limited one with capacities that will enable it to do so much and no more.

How, then, does the law try to influence human conduct? How does it set about its objective of inducing people to do things that are regarded as desirable?

There are three principal ways by which law tries to accomplish this purpose. One of these ways of encouraging society-approved conduct (and by the same token discouraging the contrary variety of conduct) is by the method that we call the suit for damages. In effect we say: "John Doe, you have done this undesirable thing, resulting in disadvantages and losses to Richard Roe, disadvantages and losses that on the whole seem to us to be about the equivalent of $1,000. We will remove from you, John Doe, the incentive in the future to engage in this kind of conduct by taking away from you the financial gain that you have achieved by this undesirable conduct and transferring it to Richard Roe; or, even if it has not resulted in any financial gain to you, we will make you compensate Richard Roe for any amount that he has been forced to pay." This, in a nutshell, is the suit for damages. The conduct itself that we desire to discourage may be in violation of an express agreement entered into with suitable formalities, so that we call it a contract, or it may be conduct that, even without any specific agreement on John Doe's part as to how he is going to behave, is obviously not desirable (a tort). But, in any event, from the standpoint that we are now pursuing, whether it is a bit of desirable conduct that we seek to induce or, on the contrary, undesirable conduct that we wish to prevent, our method of achieving this result for the future is by this device of monetary damage. That constitutes the great field of the civil law.

Another way in which the law achieves its goal of bringing about results that it regards as desirable is by specific performance —a method much more rarely used, indeed so rarely as to make many wonder why the common law made so little use of it— viz., those rules and doctrines that say, in effect: "We will make you, John Doe, do a certain thing that you ought to do, or (in the more modern version of it) we will regard you, John Doe— whether or not you did a certain thing that you ought to have done—as though you had actually done it." In short, the law achieves its goal by arbitrarily, willy-nilly, telling John Doe that the result has been achieved and that from now on everybody will behave as though it had been done in its more ordinary way.

These, then, are two ways by which pressure is put on people to modify their conduct. The third method of pressure that the law may use is that of applying to the doer of an undesirable thing certain experiences, usually unpleasant, that we call punishment (incidentally, what is now said will, of course, have to be partly recast in so far as we try reformatory methods). These experiences, standing as they will as an object lesson, will, we hope, make him, and other people who have heard of his undergoing these experiences, less inclined to engage in conduct of this sort in the future.

So criminal law, historically at least, aims to modify future conduct neither by the method of taking away the financial benefit of engaging in undesirable conduct nor by saying to the offender, "We will not pay any attention to your action or inaction." It tries to meet the problem by direct pressure on the *doer* of the undesirable thing. It should be apparent that there is neither a theoretical nor a practical reason why we cannot simultaneously use any combination of these methods, as, for instance, a suit for damages against the wrongdoer and also criminal action. John Doe hits Richard Roe in the eye and inflicts painful injuries. Normally, that will give rise, without any feeling of inconsistency on our part, to the simultaneous prosecution both of the civil suit for damages and of criminal action. Today at least they can be simultaneous. To guard against possible misunderstanding, it must be recognized that in the past if the event was a very serious one, so serious that it was the kind of crime called a felony, then historically the two actions could not be simultaneous. The criminal action had to be carried to its conclusion first. (The explanation probably lies in the very realistic view that the king took. In the days when felony was limited to one of the very serious matters, conviction of a felony meant the confiscation of the felon's property by the king. The king did not propose to have the injured citizen collecting damages first. He wanted everything without any diminution even by the person who had after all suffered.) In any event, today we feel no difficulty about the simultaneous use of both the criminal and the civil action.

There may, however, be certain kinds of conduct in which we feel it expedient to use only one method; for example, trespassing on real estate. We do not regard that as a crime, but we do give civil rights to the owner of the real estate. There we have a situation where for reasons that seem wise to us we use only one of the two methods. On the other hand, if a man drives down the street at eighty miles an hour, no civil damages are collectible by anybody against him, so long as he does not hit anybody. But a criminal action will lie. In this book we shall, of course, concern ourselves only with situations where, as a matter of substantive law, it has been decided to use the criminal action.

It was stated above that the purpose of the law, as visualized in this book, is to modify human conduct. Obviously, the criminal law hopes to do this by the achievement of one or the other of two very different, and more or less inconsistent, goals. One of these goals is deterrence by means of punishment. We punish in order to deter people from engaging in the undesirable conduct which we call a crime. The other goal is reformation. We hope to build up in the individual (by means of a wisely planned treatment program) modified habits of conduct that will make his future behavior less likely to be antisocial. The former of these goals, deterrence, addresses itself, so far as its look at the future is concerned, both to the individual himself—we hope he will be deterred in the future—and to the entire community. We hope that others will be deterred by being made aware of what happened to him. In other words, deterrence operates, insofar as we conclude that it does operate, on all the members of the community. Reformation, on the other hand, has a narrower hope. It addresses itself only to improving the particular individual who is subjected to the improvement program. And, realistically considered, it probably will not be claimed even by its advocates to be accomplishing very much so far as remoter persons are concerned.

Before proceeding to more detailed comment on deterrence and reformation as goals of treatment, it should be added that there is a third goal that is very important and that does not fit into our picture at all. This third goal of punishment is historically the oldest; it is the goal of vengeance. To it punishment exists primarily, or perhaps solely, for the purpose of satisfying the very human desire to inflict hurt on that person who, or even that thing which, has done us a hurt. This primitive goal does not fit into the scheme of things which was laid out above, because it quite frankly is not concerned with modifying future conduct. It concerns itself only with getting even with what has taken place in the past. "You hurt me, and I am going to hurt you." It seems safe to say that vengeance represents an utterly unconstructive outlook upon punishment and one that we shall not devote much time to, but nonetheless there are some points that must be made.

One concession that must be made is that there are certain persons who argue, sincerely no doubt, and to themselves more convincingly than to most others, that vengeance, too, is entitled to the credit of holding a more progressive viewpoint, namely, the viewpoint of trying to modify future conduct, and that it is not merely destructively concerned with the past. It is said by people who hold this view, mainly the psychoanalyst group of thinkers, that punishment is a means of regulating, and thus reducing to control, what would otherwise degenerate into unregulated and unlimited feudism. Their position, to put it in very homely terms, is that we are all in our inmost natures not much more mature than savages, and pretty poorly restrained savages at that, and that the criminal has had the fundamentally supreme satisfaction of breaking himself free from all the unpleasant inhibitions that all the law-abiding rest of us have been chafing under and observing. He has achieved a pleasure that we have denied ourselves, and the balance can only be redressed—with restored peace of mind to ourselves—by forcing him, in his turn, to suffer. And so society finds it well to satisfy and channelize that desire on the part of the rest of the community by taking charge of the function of getting even with one's criminal associate, thereby following the only course available to avoid the Kentucky feud or Sicilian vendetta pattern of conduct.

Another version of what is perhaps basically the same kind of argument can be found in earlier apologists for vengeance who recognized the need for explaining and excusing and justifying it and who maintained that vengeance was constructive in that the

gods were angered by the wrongdoer and that through punishing the wrongdoer society would allay their wrath—take the curse
off. Thus the community's well-being would be helped by such
punishment, and, therefore, vengeance did modify the future.

Whatever one's appraisal of the value of these arguments, it
would seem that it does not seriously shake the feeling that, by
and large, it is not unfair to the vengeance goal of punishment to say that it is mainly concerned with the past and that
with those minor qualifications it is an unconstructive purpose
of punishment. It is no wonder, then, that modern criminology
concerns itself very little with vengeance as a goal and purpose
of punishment. But yet another word of caution is necessary. We
like to pretend to ourselves that not only the criminologist but
also the modern man on the street, who is not a criminologist, is
advanced beyond vengeance. Unfortunately, this is wishful thinking. The modern man on the street is, in this sense at least, as the
psychoanalysts claim, a good deal closer to the savage than it is
pleasant to contemplate. He, just like his ancestor, is still profoundly moved by the desire for vengeance, and, while he may
get over it quicker than his ancestors would have and be brought
to a point of comparative reasonableness, there are very few indeed of the genus man-on-the-street who can truthfully claim
not to be influenced at all in their thinking by the vengeance mo-
tive. We all know that, when we read the story of some particularly revolting crime committed in a particularly selfish, heartless
manner, we are scarcely ever entirely immune from the desire to
have the treatment given the doer reflect, in part, at least, our
passing hatred. At best we can only hope that we are able to get
over it faster than other members of the community, and, much
as we may regret it, we must concede that, realistically, the vengeance purpose of punishment, unconstructive though it may be,
is still an extremely important one; and in moments of discouragement we might be willing to concede that it is still *the* most
important purpose of punishment, at least in the initial stages of
the entire criminal proceeding. There is no point in belittling the
importance of vengeance, no matter how much we may dislike it.

For our purposes, however, there is much more to be said
about, and thought about, deterrence and reformation as goals of

punishment, and, therefore, with the caution that we should not disregard the importance of vengeance, we pass on now to these two more constructive goals. Their discussion can only be extremely general and superficial.[1] We shall deal first with deterrence. Discussion of its effectiveness is almost always in the hands of extremists, both pro and con. One set of enthusiasts will claim that deterrence is the solution of the entire criminal problem and that we can solve the problem of the antisocial behavior of a criminal completely by the mere effective use of deterrence, since people, being enlightened and selfish, will not engage in such conduct if the only result to them is going to be a very unrewarding experience, more unpleasant indeed than if they had not engaged in it. The group which is entirely in favor of deterrence is met head-on by another group of individuals—a group which has come into origin in more recent times—who argue equally vehemently that deterrence never deters. We cannot, they say, punish a child out of being naughty, and we cannot punish the grown person into becoming a law-abiding citizen. We are slowly but more and more definitely coming to realize this truth so far as rearing our children is concerned, and, sooner or later—the sooner the better—we shall realize this also in regard to our adults. For this latter group there is no hope whatsoever in deterrence. It is not necessary, or even possible, to agree completely with either of these viewpoints, since they are both guilty of overlooking one highly important factor, viz., that the applicability of deterrence is a variable and that we are getting off to a mistaken start at the very beginning if we feel under obligation either to agree, without more ado, that it is going to work or to say that it is not going to work. It is completely impossible to give any one answer like that. The chance of its working will vary greatly from crime to crime.

Here are some illustrations of factors that, as we study these problems more carefully, we may find will have a great weight in determining whether or not, in any given situation, deterrence is going to deter—factors whose weight we are only dimly aware

1. John B. Waite's *Criminal Law in Action* (New York: Harcourt, Brace & Co., 1934) and the same author's *The Prevention of Repeated Crime* (Ann Arbor: University of Michigan Press, 1943) are valuable supplementary reading.

of now or even, so far as some of them are concerned, not at all aware of. Suppose that the crime in question is the very minor one of driving through a red light. Is deterrence going to be an effective factor there? If we see a police officer standing at the corner, are we going to drive through the red light? Probably we would not even drive through the orange but will wait until the light is fixed green. One would say that deterrence there, especially if the officer is on a motorcycle, works with absolutely complete effectiveness. Contrast that situation with a crime at the opposite end of the scale. Let us suppose that it is a crime involving an immense amount of emotion of one sort or another. Typically, let us suppose that it is a question of a mother who is facing social problems that make it impossible for her to see any way to support herself and her very young child and who is also aware that the child is a hopeless idiot. Under the stress of tremendous emotion she decides that she cannot stand it any longer, and she proceeds to kill the child. Or some member of a family sees another member suffering horrible tortures from an incurable illness that will result in death in a few weeks or months in any case and proceeds to relieve the sufferer by killing him. When we have a situation in which the emotional stress is so terrifically strong as to break down all the inhibitions that a whole lifetime of living in a law-abiding way has built up and so great that all these inhibitions completely disappear, how much influence will the thought, "If I do this, I may be punished," have? It must be very obvious that that factor will have little influence if any.

Again, there is another type of factor whose importance must be great but where, in our present state of knowledge, it is difficult to determine what its influence will be. Suppose that the crime is one that is more or less coldly calculated, such as operating a confidence game and swindling innocent people. It is not at all the consequence of emotional stress; possibly there is no person under less emotional strain than the gentleman who makes a fortune marrying gullible women. Emotional stress is completely out of the picture, and in that sense this person falls into the category of the one who drives through a red light. On the other hand, in the coldly calculated crimes, especially crimes like picking pockets or blowing a safe, or, even to a less extent, burglary, there may be a degree of slowly acquired, perhaps even professional, skill and know-how that is a factor in minimizing deterrence and in urging continuance in this kind of conduct. After all, just from a business standpoint the pickpocket has a large amount of invested capital in his occupation. That capital is represented by a long, slow, and difficult course of training in which he has learned how to carry on his highly skilled profession. The safeblower too has acquired a capital that is invested in his business—in the form of knowledge of explosives and of how to appraise the desirability of a potential victim. Even the successful burglar has more professional skill invested in training than one would think. Those who just break into a house without any background of training at all are usually caught very quickly. Perhaps a better illustration than any other is that of the expert engraver who can use his invested capital either as a legitimate worker or as a counterfeiter. But in either case he is using his invested capital of skill.

It would seem clear that this factor of invested capital of skill is a powerful one to minimize or overcome the factor that one is proceeding in a cool, calculating manner; and, whereas the cool, calculated result might make deterrence more effective in his case, his investment in that form of business is going to make deterrence less effective. In the present state of our knowledge, where the balance lies we cannot know. All that we can be sure of is the inadequacy of an approach that simply and sweepingly says that deterrence works or, conversely, that deterrence does not work. We do not know how far it works, but, whatever the answer is ultimately going to be, we may be convinced that we shall find that there is not merely one answer—there are many answers—and that it would be very unwise for us at this point either to pin all our hopes on deterrence or, on the other hand, to reject it as utterly valueless.

With this word of caution against either absolute acceptance or absolute rejection of the value of deterrence, and assuming from now on that we are in an area where deterrence is at its most effective point, how right are its advocates in making the easy assumption that humanity always with enlightened selfishness follows that course of conduct which will bring long-run happiness, or, at any rate, the greatest chance of it? Are all of us really such coldly calculating managers as to see everything in this methodical way and to single out as best we can what is going to make us most likely to be happy and then follow that course of conduct? The answer would have to be "No." Or, at any rate (this is very much the same as the "No" answer), the course that we choose will very often take into account a vastly greater number of factors than the comparatively very simple ones that deterrence advocates believe we do. Deterrence advocates assume that we consider factors of long-term and short-term well-being and financial gain and that that is about all. But all of us, in making all kinds of decisions—decisions that do not have anything at all to do with criminal law—take into account a great many more things than that in determining whether or not to engage in certain conduct. The more exciting the crime is, and the more emotional the factors involved are, the more factors there are to consider.

An illustration is available that comes right out of the past experience of many of us. How much cool calculation was there in the thoughts of substantially every one of the servicemen who saw service in the army, the navy, or the air force when they were first inducted or when they first went into a position of danger? Theoretically, according to the deterrence advocates, when each such person was summoned for service, he weighed in his own mind the prospects pro and con of future happiness if he adopted the course of following orders, going into the service, entering an area of danger, obeying commands, enormously increasing the prospect of danger, etc., against the prospects of future happiness involved in saying, "I won't serve; I claim to be a conscientious objector, and they can sentence me to prison. After all, I ought to be able to count on a pardon three or four years after the war is over, and I can stay home and be safe. I won't go." How many people engaged in that type of thought-process? Not one in a thousand.

We are all influenced by a vast number of other factors which the deterrence advocates simply do not take into account, such as factors of habit, of conformity, factors that we are able to put under a catch-all term called preserving one's self-respect, one's group values, that is, values felt by the group that one belongs to. These factors are entirely disregarded in the oversimple approach of the out-and-out deterrence advocate. In fact, one of the greatest and most complex problems of criminology is that of dealing with people who have set up socially undesirable values. We may take as an instance the typical gang of young delinquents that we will suppose a juvenile officer is trying to break up or to bring to a better pattern of conduct. One of the most important elements influencing the conduct of each member of this juvenile gang is the factor of his conforming, at all costs, to the values that his gang has set up; and the sad thing is that those group values that are so important to the gang are antisocial values, but that does not modify the fact that to this youngster and to the adult criminal as well conformity to them is a tremendously important factor in motivation. We see it every day in the refusal of a fatally wounded gangster to tell what he knows about those who assailed him. Of course one can tremendously overplay the importance of loyalty among thieves. There is precious little loyalty as such among thieves. But the dying man is nonetheless still under pressures of tremendous importance to him. And the important thing is that they are important to him, dictating his silence. He may, of course, keep silent because he feels that his associates may get worse treatment if he talks. But there is also a curiously perverted feeling that "we will settle this among ourselves; keep the police out." If such conduct is to be regarded as cold-blooded calculation of pros and cons, it can only be by giving a tremendously extended meaning to the term "cold-blooded calculation."

At any rate, we shall find that, at the operative moment when the decision is made to commit the crime or not, the actor is influenced by values of an intensely complicated nature that may comprise many elements which in the narrow sense, at least, do not have anything whatsoever to do with the supposedly simple choice of future happiness: Which way will I be more happy? Which way will I make more money? Which way will I suffer less? Which way will I lose money?[2] Thus it would seem that deterrence is open to the very serious criticism that its advocates take far too simple a view of the elements that go to make up a decision, that the decision is the end result of far more variables than they will admit, and that much more enters into it than just a relatively simple cold-blooded calculation.[3] In fact, it can fairly be said that the case for deterrence has not yet been made or unmade and that we do not know enough about it because we have tended to forget that its effectiveness is a variable according to the crime involved and also because we have left out of account far too many factors that go toward the making-up of the decision.

At this point our uncertainty is still further increased by the seeming paradox that in a very real sense deterrence can be said never yet to have been really tried. It has never been given a really fair and just chance to demonstrate how much it can accomplish. Certainly this statement needs to be justified, because, as will be recalled, it was also remarked that we have been going for a considerable length of time on a deterrent theory of punishment. What is meant is that we have tended to confuse two separate things under one heading: deterrence, which is one thing, and severity, which is another. We have tried to suppress crime by means of extreme severity, and our reaction has been, when we saw that severity did not work, or rather that crime did not go down—whatever the reason might be—just to add still move severity. If a year's confinement as a threat did not deter, we made the threat two years. If two years did not deter, then we locked them up for ten years. In short, we have visualized deterrence as necessarily involving severity. To some extent that is no doubt true. If we are hopeful of the curative effects of a threat, we have to make the threat unpleasant, which is another

2. A factor of tremendous importance, too, is the publicity given in our newspapers to an accused person. It is no answer to say that to a normal person it would be unpleasant publicity. To the accused it may be highly gratifying and eagerly sought for and highly valued.

3. An excellent illustration of the slight importance of mere fear in the entire situation is afforded by the old-time public hangings at Tyburn. Though picking a pocket was itself a capital offense, the greatest period of activity by pickpockets was when a hanging was taking place. It was a heaven-sent opportunity to carry on one's business, and the pickpockets never missed it.

way of saying that we have to be severe. But we tend to lose sight of a factor which is at the very least as important as severity and which is probably more important. That factor is certainty of punishment.

If deterrence is to be given a fair chance to show what it can do, we must have the punishment not merely severe enough to be unpleasant but also certain enough definitely to enter into the calculations of the persons whom we are seeking to deter. It is largely unimportant how severe the punishment is if we are to assume that only a small number of persons are ever subjected to it and that the great majority get away with their crime. Then deterrence is not in fact given a fair chance. A survey made some time ago in Cook County, Illinois, disclosed that in a given type of felony only one out of every twenty-six ever resulted in anybody's being tried. By no means all of those who were tried were convicted, but only one in every twenty-six was ever brought even to the trial stage. If, then, one puts one's self into the position of someone who is coldly calculating whether to commit the crime or not, as the deterrence advocates believe one does coldly calculate, he is going to figure out not only *what* he stands a chance to get but also *how big* the chance is that he is going to get that. And if there is only one chance in twenty-six against him, he will probably not be worried too much, no matter how bad the fate for that twenty-sixth chance may be. An illustration of the way in which we in daily life almost unconsciously take account of not only the danger that is involved to us but of the likelihood of that danger happening is the matter of riding in an airplane. The penalty for guessing wrong as to the safety of a plane is not a sprained ankle; it is a good deal more severe than that. It is probably a matter of life or death. Yet we all indulge in flying when it is expedient and convenient for us, because we know quite well that the chances of something going wrong are very small indeed.

So it can be said that deterrence has not had a fair chance, because we have thought only in terms of severity, and not in terms of certainty, of punishment. Deterrence will really be tested only if we can so far increase the efficiency of our machinery as to produce, if not absolute certainty of punishment, at any rate, a high degree of certainty, by improving our police forces, by improving our judicial machinery, by improving our jury system, by improving the whole line of procedure. And, in analyzing how far such an improvement is possible, we should never forget that to some extent at least severity and certainty tend to be mutually exclusive—not absolutely mutually exclusive, but that they tend so to be—because the more severe punishment is, the greater the precautions that have to be taken to make sure that an innocent person does not undergo that punishment. If the punishment is only a five-dollar fine, we can be relatively crude in our mechanism of proof of guilt. We can, for example, take the traffic officer's word for it without further investigation of the factor of guilt or not. But our United States Constitution itself recognizes that if the crime involves very serious punishment, as does the crime for treason, then the proof must meet certain more severe requirements as to the number of witnesses, the overt act, etc.; and all the way through, quite properly, as the punishment scale goes up, the difficulty of conviction goes up, too.

But when we say that the difficulty of conviction goes up, we are only using a different form of words to say that the certainty of conviction goes down. In short, in gross unfairness to the deterrence theory, we have tended to load it down with far too great an increment of severity; and, as a result, we have not given it the amount of certainty that it is entitled to have. By way of proof of this, it is only necessary to pick up almost any of our newspapers. Whenever there is a so-called "crime wave," there is an immediate outcry. Police action should be stepped up; court action should be harsher; there should be quicker trial and more severe punishment all the way down the line. If need be, the legislature should set up a new punishment scale. And there the matter rests. Yet it is often stated—probably correctly—that, on the whole, not only does the United States lead the civilized world in severity of punishment but also that Illinois is one of the most severe states in the entire Union. But it would be decidedly rash to insist that Illinois is particularly outstanding for its law-abiding nature, and certainly Chicago's reputation is not that of being the most orderly city in the country.

Thus one winds up with the feeling that we are far, as yet,

from knowing just how much betterment deterrence as a method of handling the crime problem really is going to give us. Maybe it will do much for us; maybe it will not do so much. We shall have to know a great deal more than we do now before we can be too dogmatic about our answer.

We can turn now to the other theory, according to which the criminal law is to be used to modify future conduct, the theory of reformation, where our attention is not centered upon scaring the wrongdoer and all other persons into behaving themselves but is centered instead almost solely on the wrongdoer and only incidentally on other persons, in the hope that it may be possible to devise some sort of program for him, or treatments for him— to use the broadest term possible, some sort of experiences for him—that will modify his conduct in the future. Obviously, this reform theory is in point of time the newest of the various goals of punishment; and, incidentally, it becomes questionable whether one is justified in continuing to use the word "punishment" when one speaks of the reform purpose of treatment. It may or may not mean punishment according as we feel that unpleasant experience is, or is not, likely to lead to better conduct patterns. That is a problem on which there is considerable disagreement; probably the majority feel that punishment as such is not the cure-all by any means that the old axiom of "spare the rod and spoil the child" would indicate. There is no need to assume from that, however, that there is no value whatsoever in punishment as a curative mechanism; it is conceivable that there is some. The reform theory merely constantly stresses the importance of modifying conduct patterns by fundamentally changing the individual. We can accept that theory and still be uncertain as to what the most effective ways are of accomplishing that purpose.

Here, too, we are confronted by a phenomenon strikingly similar to the one discussed under deterrence, namely, the exaggerated claims for the theory made by its overenthusiastic advocates and the equally exaggerated contempt of it by its opponents. Just as in the case of deterrence, reformation is a very slippery variable, which in certain areas may probably work very well and in other areas not at all. With the first offender who has committed a crime of a crude, unplanned nature, typically, let us say, the first offender who has committed a robbery, one's guess would be that the possibilty of reformation would be rather high. On the other hand, at the other end of the scale, if we are dealing with a person who has been repeatedly arrested and convicted—and who, in addition, was engaged in committing a kind of crime in which he had invested a considerable capital of time to learn how to accomplish it effectively (as the pickpocket has invested time and capital in learning to be an effective pickpocket)—then one's guess is that the chances of reformation would be rather poor. We shall probably be able to make much more progress if we do not let ourselves fall into the temptation of being all-out enthusiasts, either pro or con, but instead cautiously recognize that here, too, we are face to face with a variable and that it is not easy at all times to know exactly what in any given case the chances of success will be. Certainly the excessive claims made for the possibilities of reformation by overenthusiastic advocates have done more harm than good as far as the adoption of a reformation program is concerned.

Probably one of the strongest arguments for trying out, wholeheartedly, a reformation program is that in any event such a program cannot fail much more thoroughly than the deterrence program has, under the conditions in which the latter has been tried out in the past. Reference has already been made to the prevalence of picking pockets at a public hanging. There can hardly be any better illustration of the failure of deterrence than that; and if we are not prepared to revise out deterrence program, but propose to keep on with the program exactly as it has been applied in the past, then it is submitted that a strong case for trying something else has been made, simply on the score that one or two or three or a dozen mistakes are enough, and it is high time to try something else. It is, therefore, rather amusing that so often the advocates of a reformation program are plastered with the obviously contemptuous label of being nothing but "long-haired enthusiasts" and "theoreticians" by those on the other side of the fence—the "treat-'em-rough" deterrence advocates. The latter apparently consider themselves as the only hardheaded, practical citizens. Those who take any other view are the theorists! This may be so, but it seems at least equally plausible that the theorist is the one who, without profiting from experience, insists on blindly perpetuating the mistakes that have been made for two hundred or three hundred years and is so wedded to the belief that his method is going to produce results that he pays no attention to its failures. That certainly is riding a theory into the ground and is being a theorist to the *n*th degree.

There are, however, certain underlying obstacles to the really large-scale adoption of a program of reformation. Some of those obstacles are rather obvious; others lie beneath the surface. The obvious obstacles are ones that do not need extended attention here because of the very fact that they are obvious. Our concern is rather with the obstacles which are not so obvious and which, perhaps for that reason, are even more serious, because there will be greater difficulty in clearing them out of the way.

One obstacle to a widespread institution of a reform program lies in the attitude of the layman toward problems of criminal-law administration. On the whole, the layman is likely, at least in the first blush when a crime has been recently committed and when by that token the convicted person's fate is decided upon, to be so moved by emotion and desire for vengeance as to be wholeheartedly on the severity side of the fence. It is hard at that moment of emotion to persuade him of the importance of a reform program. That view only comes with sober second thought, when the decision has been made. And the layman's viewpoint is extremely important in deciding what the program is going to be, partly because the layman is personified in the jury and partly because all law in every area reflects public opinion and does so particularly in the more emotional areas of law. The layman is especially likely to have opinions and to insist on having those opinions effective and decisive as to what is going to happen, simply because he does feel a strong emotional pull.

This can be brought out by a comparison with some other area of the law in which there is no emotional pull at all. Let us suppose that a proposal is before the legislature to change the insurance laws with reference to the type of investment, or the percentages of given types of investment, that insurance companies may hold. The general run of citizens, feeling no excitement about it, are perfectly willing to turn the decision of that question over to experts, recognizing that they are not themselves experts in the field. There is no public hostility toward the use of expert guidance in problems of that sort. But is that the reaction of the layman about problems of criminal-law enforcement? It is not! He knows the answers and knows them better than anybody else does. For experts in this and experts in that he has only dismal contempt. Who are *they* to tell him what the answers should be?

In a sense, the layman is right, because the answers that he arrives at are answers dictated by emotion, and he is likely to have a great deal more emotion about the thing than the relatively cold-blooded expert. Thus what we have here is an area in which the layman insists upon having the last and controlling voice, and, since the layman will be influenced by his emotion rather than by expert opinion, we must take lay opinion into account to a very high degree in deciding what the future is likely to be. And the layman is by no means as yet generally convinced of the effectiveness of a wide-scale program of reformation. This will long remain a great obstacle to its general adoption.

Another difficulty that a reformation program encounters is that it calls for much more skill and flexibility of thought and originality on the part of prison officials and the administrators of such a program than the deterrence program does. After all, a deterrence program need not concern itself with such questions as: "Why did this man commit this crime at the time when he committed it?" "Is he likely to commit it again?" "Are these circumstances likely to be repeated?" All those questions can be rejected by deterrence with the simple statement: "They are irrelevant. What we are out to do is to make a lesson of him so that others may learn. It is too bad if in his particular case it happens that there is no danger of any future crime, but he has to be punished just the same in order to deter others; we are not interested in what made him do it."

Life is much more complex to the practitioners of the reformation system. They must, perforce, interest themselves in all these questions of the background and personality of the individual offender. And they must be in a position to adopt an infinitely variable program of treatment for the various persons whom they are handling. Any program that calls for greater skill, greater ingenuity, and greater thought on the part of the administrators of that program than they have been applying in the past will be resisted bitterly by the people on whom these greater claims will be made. Thus to a very large extent it is unfortunately possible to say that the less able members of our law-enforcement setup (particularly those who have to do with prisons) are likely to take a very dim view of a reformation program. And their opposition is by no means to be lightly dismissed.

A third obstacle—and an ally to the one just considered—is the inertia imposed on us simply by the physical fact of the huge prisons that we are afflicted with in almost all the states. Typically an American penitentiary is an institution that houses a thousand or more inmates The very biggest penitentiaries, in fact, house a great many more than a thousand. The largest penitentiary in the United States has an inmate figure of somewhere around five thousand. These huge institutions make impossible any real adoption of individualized programs for inmates. There are a great many reasons for this. Partly it is because they have great industrial factories inside their walls—textile mills, broomworks, soapworks, etc.—needing large numbers of men all doing more or less the same thing. Partly it is true, also, because in an institution of that size we must, in self-protection, require of the inmates uniformity of conduct that is so drastic that any departure from the normal will at once stand out and be noticed by the prison administrators. After all, when we are dealing with inmates of penitentiaries, we are dealing with a highly selected group of citizens. Though we can be as sentimental as we wish about the "poor boys," the fact remains that a high percentage are very dangerous human animals, and we simply cannot afford to disregard that danger. If, then, there is a concentration of some five thousand persons of that sort, where danger may emerge at any moment from any one of them—no one knows where or when—with a guard personnel that is, let us suppose, set at some five hundred, with eight-hour shifts, with a relative manpower strength of inmate versus guard so overwhelming in mere numbers in favor of the inmates, we must set up rigid rules to be conformed to so exactly that any deviation of conduct can be noticed at once. True, we do not go so far any more as to require the lockstep; that has been abolished. But there can be no doubt that the original idea back of the lockstep was of making absolutely sure that there would be noticed, the instant it took place, any abnormality in the conduct of offenders. In short, we can individualize only when the units are small enough so that we can safely let differences of conduct emerge—differences of conduct that are part and parcel of the individualization program.

What, then, are the chances of getting away from these "white elephants" of excessively large penitentiaries? One would say that they are very poor indeed, because we have them; there they are. They represent a costly investment in stone, steel, mortar, and many other things. And it would be a rash prison administrator indeed who dared to advocate a program that would result in the junking of such a large investment. The average citizen is not going to be very cordial toward discarding something that tax money paid for, and it takes a terrific amount of convincing that it is really a step in the right direction before he will stand for it. And that is precisely what reformation on a large scale does involve. True, prison administrators of the enlightened sort do what they can to institute specialized programs even in the large institutions under them. But they would be the first to recognize that it is a very stiff task.

Lewisburg Penitentiary, a federal prison where the less serious offenders are sent—and therefore the offenders with whom there are the greatest chances for reformation—was deliberately designed to have great flexibility of treatment. Its architecture and its entire setup are so designed. In that sense it might be thought of as a collection under one roof of a number of different institutions. If the institution is so designed, it is a different story. It should also be pointed out that in the Anglo-Saxon system of law the most successful institutions of confinement, as far as curative results are concerned, have proved to be the Borstal institutions in England. They are small, with only a hundred and fifty to two hundred inmates per institution; and the program in each is different from that in any of the others. The work setup, the kind of treatment—the whole program—differ, and a careful analysis is made of each of those who are to be committed to a Borstal institution to determine which of the various ones would best fit his needs. Recently a report was issued by a royal committee in Sweden, charged with the duty of recommending a revision of Swedish penal treatment, which went so far as to recommend that no institution house more than a maximum of sixty inmates. That was the product of careful thought. We do not need to worry about setting the figure too low; but we can readily see how completely that supports discouragement with our "white elephants" of three, four, and five thousand inmates.

There is still a fourth hidden obstacle to the adoption of a reformation program. Like the problem of capital invested in a huge prison establishment, it is a financial one. If we are going to have a really worth-while reformation program, it is plain that one of the starting points to emphasize is the type of day-by-day work that the inmate does. The work program, in short, will have to be adapted to his particular needs, not he to the work program. Yet, in our big prison institutions, it is exactly this latter—his adaptation to the work program rather than the reverse of that—that has to take place.

A typical big prison has a certain number of industries that it carries on. These industries normally require a big invested capital in the way of complex and very valuable machinery. The number of industries maintained in any given prison is, therefore, limited by the ability to provide the necessary machinery equipment. Take the two branches of Joliet Penitentiary in Illinois as illustrations. The old prison in Joliet itself is very largely confined to textile work and has elaborate equipment for that purpose. The new prison at Stateville does some textile work. It also has a furniture factory, a soapworks, and a few other industries. Or, again, the Pontiac Branch of the Penitentiary has a large-scale establishment that does work in metal products of various kinds—the manufacturing of road signs, etc. It is easy to discover that the kind of industry that is selected will depend upon the financial return to be obtained from that industry rather than on the reformative possibilities it holds out for the people who do the work. The state gradually, and more or less unconsciously, tends to emphasize the making of brooms, let us say, not because brooms are good character-builders, but because brooms are useful in the financial structure of the institution. A great many brooms are needed by other state institutions, and therefore there is a ready market for them. (We say "needed by other state institutions," because under the usual state laws prison products are not allowed to be sold generally in competition with non-prison products. It is permissible only to dispose of prison products to tax-supported institutions.) Thus the work program will have been really determined purely on financial considerations.[4]

Left to the last is a difficulty that calls for some explaining. It is not a difficulty that is apparent on the surface, but for this very reason it is one that ranks among the more serious ones. That difficulty lies in something that has the rather cryptic name of "the principle of less eligibility," so named by Jeremy Bentham. Under this term he refers to the widespread (and understandable) feeling that the wrongdoer who has been convicted and who has thereby shown his social inadequacy, and in that sense his undeserving character, should not, as a result of and thanks to his conviction, secure any benefits that are withheld from the honest, law-abiding, good citizen. Says this principle: "It is a monstrous thing that by reason of having done a wrong you should get a benefit that your good and worthy neighbor does not get. You should in all respects be less eligible for social benefits than the man who has fairly played the game with his neighbors."

That is a very understandable attitude to take. It may or may not strike us as a justifiable one, but we can at least understand the viewpoint of the person who does take that attitude, whether

4. A striking example of this is supplied by the Menard Branch of the Illinois State Penitentiary, in the southern part of the state. Some time ago it was decided that this was to be used for offenders who were of the slow-thinking type, the border-line cases who have been held responsible by juries as not being too feeble-minded to be guilty of a crime but who are more or less hopeless cases—hopeless either because they had committed so many offenses that it was thought nothing could be done about them or because of their mental inadequacy for competition. That is a thinkable and practical way of classifying offenders. But it also happens that at Menard there are some extremely complicated textile machines that take intelligence of a high order to operate. The machines are too large and too costly to move to Joliet. So, a certain proportion of the Menard inmates must be men of rather exceptional intelligence, capable of operating these machines. One can see what is left of a reform program when it is confronted by fiscal necessities.

we share it with him or not. But it is also obvious that its adoption is utterly and necessarily inconsistent with a real adoption of a reformation program. We will use a concrete illustration. An individual has been subjected to whatever reformation program the local prison setup makes possible. His time for discharge is approaching. It is clear that a genuine program of reformation will require us to see to it that, when released, a job is waiting for him, because the time immediately following his release will be the critical one for him. If he is turned loose with a new suit of clothes and $10.00, it is almost certain that that critical time will produce the maximum danger of a relapse, if he has nowhere to go and no further resources. It is, therefore, simply common prudence to provide him with a job to take care of him. Yet, we are up to now very far from having adopted the view that it is the state's duty to provide everybody who wants a job with one —there are many law-abiding members of the community who in periods of recession or depression are looking for work and cannot find it. This wrongdoer is thus getting some kind of benefit that the law-abiding citizen does not receive. The upshot is that we must make our choice—either we shall apply the principle of less eligibility or we shall carry on with our program of reformation; but we cannot have our cake and eat it, too. Unfortunately, there are a great many people who as yet fail to realize that we must make a choice and that that choice may at times involve doing something for offenders that we are not yet prepared to do for the community generally. Are we willing to do that, or are we not? We must not delude ourselves into believing that we can do both at the same time.

These, then, are some of the principal difficulties that a wide-scale adoption of a reform program will encounter. Allied to them is another point that does not present precisely a difficulty but leads many people to feel that reformation has failed where, in fact, it has not. Because of that mistaken belief, it leads them to oppose reformation where a more adequate understanding would leave them with a more open mind. The reference is to the phenomenon of discharged persons who have been subjected, let us suppose, to an adequate reformatory program, so that they come out reformed, as far as we can judge, but, nonetheless, a year or two or three later, commit another crime—perhaps of precisely the same sort as the one they committed before. People very often make the quick inference that this is proof that reformation does not work. There is a surface plausibility to that. Actually, it is completely unfair toward reformation. The person who is discharged from a penitentiary or other institution may genuinely be a better person, with a better adjustment; but if he is returned to the same old environment, and (even though he has the desire to go straight) if nothing is done to aid him in implementing that desire, but, on the contrary, he is subjected once again to the same stresses that made him go wrong in the first place, then of course there is every chance in the world that he will go wrong again.

The point can be likened exactly to its corresponding one in medicine. Suppose that a person suffers from a case of pneumonia, owing to the fact that he works in an extremely damp room with alternating currents of cold and hot air. He is sent to the hospital, is subjected to certain treatments there, and in due time is discharged as cured. He resumes work in the same place where he worked before. In a few months exactly what might have been expected to happen does happen—he comes down again with pneumonia. Would any of us think of analyzing his case by insisting that this demonstrated that there never had really been a cure? On the contrary. We recognize that the cure was successful but that the same kind of environment and the same stresses produced the same result as in the first instance. That is the fault not of the curative measures but of what happened after they were entirely successful. We shall thus not be giving a reform program a fair chance unless and until we realize that there is going to be no permanent change in the individual unless there is likewise a permanent change in his environment[5]

5. It is this idea which lies back of the fact that in some of the more advanced penitentiaries in the United States wardens are likely to insist that inmates who are assigned to some sort of vocational training program should not be allowed to select a vocation that is at all similar to the one that they previously practiced, in the belief that the more sweeping the change in work program is, the greater the likelihood—not the certainty but the likelihood—that the individual may go out to an environment different from the one that he was in before.

II

POLICE ORGANIZATION

WE ARE now at the point where the sequence of events begins which will occupy us throughout our subject. The first item in this general sequence is usually an arrest.[1] Historically, any citizen had (and has) the privilege of making an arrest under certain circumstances. It is possible to go further, indeed, and say that historically the private citizen was the only person who made arrests, because the rise of police departments is a comparatively recent phenomenon in the law. Since there were no police departments, the private citizen occupied the field all by himself.

It is only some two hundred years ago that a very rudimentary police department was established in London, known as the Bow Street Runners. They were very few in number, and there was no thought of their taking over the entire task of arresting wrongdoers and suppressing crime. That remained a citizen activity and responsibility—so much so that there was even a crime known as misprision of felony, consisting in the citizen's failure to perform his actual duty to arrest a felon when he had the opportunity to do so. In the modern sense, therefore, the Bow Street force can hardly be regarded as a genuine police department. It was only in 1828 that Sir Robert Peel, the Secretary for Home Affairs, organized a real police force. The officers that he recruited and put into uniform were nicknamed after him and were originally called "Roberts." Finally the name was shortened to "Bobbies," and of course to this day the London police officer is referred to as a "Bobbie."

The idea was so obviously a good one that, like the idea of the

1. The term "usually" is used because the arrest may be made on a court-issued warrant. In that event, obviously, the issuance of the warrant would constitute the opening event. This step will be considered in chap. v, "The Magistrate."

postage stamp, which arose in England only some nineteen years later, it very soon began to spread to other countries. New York was the first city in the United States that had organized police, its force dating back to 1841.[2] How rudimentary it was is indicated by its structure along ward lines, with as many separate police forces as there were wards. Another indication is the bitter resistance, on the part of the members of these various forces, to the requirement that they wear any sort of distinguishing uniform. The idea was still so strong that policing was a function of the citizen that members of the police force felt—quite logically— that they were merely doing general citizen work, for which they were paid and for which there was a special obligation on their part, but that that was not sufficient reason why they should dress differently from other persons.

In line with this idea, for a long time and to a considerable extent even today, the view prevailed that, as far as their legal status was concerned, police forces were not, and are not, different from the private citizen. The only difference between the police officer, according to this thinking, was that he was paid to do what anybody had the privilege of doing and that he was, therefore, under a duty to do what the ordinary citizen might or might not do as he saw fit. One may say "might or might not," because by this time the crime of misprision of felony—that is, the failure to make an arrest when one saw a felony being committed—had already disappeared. Police officers, it was thought, were under special obligations, but they had no rights, when they did act, which the citizen, if he chose to act, would not have. The officer could not make an arrest under circumstances where the private person could not make an arrest. He could not do so without a warrant where the layman could not. He was on exactly the same footing that all of us were and are on, except that he could get himself into trouble if he failed to act.

Gradually that notion has tended to disappear; very slowly, but very surely, the law has been moving in the direction of giv-

2. For details on the early history of European and American police forces see Raymond B. Fosdick, *European Police Systems* (New York: Century Co., 1915) and *American Police Systems* (New York: Century Co., 1920).

ing police officers actually greater legal privileges than nonpolice have—not only greater duties but greater privileges in the exercise of those duties. So that today, when we analyze under what circumstances an arrest may be made, it will be necessary to distinguish between cases involving a police officer as the arresting individual and cases where it is a private citizen. Similarly, also, the extent to which the arrested person may use force in resisting an improper arrest will vary according as it is a private person or a police officer who is arresting him. All the way through we find, increasingly, a distinction between police officers, on the one hand, and private citizens, on the other.

To the author's way of thinking, this tendency is sound. We insistently demand of the police that they accomplish certain purposes; that they produce certain results. In the long run they—like all public agencies—will produce, or try to produce, what their public demands.[3] They are going to do it in a lawless manner if we put the lid on too tightly. They are going to do it in a law-abiding manner if we give them a certain freedom of action. To cut down freedom of action too much will not result in the elimination of certain undesired conduct on the part of the police. It will result simply in engaging in that type of conduct in an unlawful, irresponsible, and therefore thoroughly demoralizing, way. We can sit on the safety valve for a certain length of time, but, if the safety valve does not have any possibility of allowing the steam to escape, sooner or later there is going to be an explosion. If, then, we demand of the police certain results and yet deny them the right to do those things in a controlled, regulated manner that they need to do in order to achieve these results, the only consequence is going to be not that they will fail to achieve these results but that they will achieve them in a thoroughly unregulated, arbitrary, and therefore extremely dangerous manner. It is far better for the law to increase the authority of the police and then subject them, very definitely, to

3. "What the public demands" is not necessarily identical with "what the public should demand." In the long run our government is as good and as bad as we, the majority, wish it to be.

answerability and the requirement that they live within the authority that has been conferred upon them.[4]

What, then, are these police forces, as we have them typically in the United States, as of today? Our present-day police structure falls into one or the other of three categories. The third category—the state police—will not be dealt with until the other two have been disposed of. These two other categories, which had the field to themselves until the recent rise of state police forces, are the urban, or municipal police forces, on the one hand, and the rural police organization, on the other. (When the term "urban" police structure is used, reference is sometimes only to city police structures, sometimes also to the one-man police "department" of a small village. The context will make it clear in which sense the term is at the moment being used.) Numerically, and in every other way, urban police forces have long been the major element in our American police setup, and among them the big-city forces have been the most important. There are certain structural and policy problems connected with these forces that every intelligent citizen should be aware of, because they are recurrent policy problems that are met with all over the country, from one coast to the other, year after year. It is the more impor-

4. Here is a typical example: The police are under the obligation to suppress the carrying of concealed weapons. It is also true in a great many of the states that, if a police officer suspects someone of carrying a concealed weapon and then searches him and finds that there is in fact one, the courts will say when the case is before them, "You had no right to search this person without a warrant to that effect. The discovery of the concealed weapon was therefore part and parcel of an improper search, and, being part and parcel of an improper search, we will not allow the introduction into evidence of the results of this improper search." Therefore, there can be no showing that there was in fact a concealed weapon, and the case falls. Consider the dilemma into which that puts the police officer. If he cannot see the weapon, he is not allowed to make a search. If he can see the weapon, it is not concealed, and therefore the individual is not guilty. Thus either way he is on the horns of a dilemma. How, then, will he handle that situation? The one way open to him is by this thoroughly lawless but very understandable method: He will assert to the carrier of the weapon, "Aren't you John Doe, who is wanted for murder in Seattle? I suspect you are and arrest you." Then, having arrested him on suspicion, which he may properly do if the suspicion is a reasonable one, he proceeds to search him, because it is proper to search a person who has been arrested, and he finds the concealed weapon. Now the concealed weapon has been found in pursuance of a lawful search, and, though afterward it turns out that this man is not John Doe of Seattle at all, the charge of carrying a concealed weapon can be made to stick. But, to make it stick, the officer must commit perjury in asserting his belief that he was arresting Doe.

tant of these problems which will be considered briefly here. There will be no reference to what might be called the professional problems of the police.[5] But there are certain nonprofessional problems having to do with policy in the larger sense of which every citizen should very definitely be informed and certain possible shortcomings of his local police force that he should be on his guard against.[6]

One of the most frequently encountered inadequacies of urban police organization in the United States consists in the shortcomings of the headship of the police force—whether we call him a commissioner, a superintendent, or a chief, or whether we have as the head a professional patrolman who has risen through the ranks to the top, a civilian, or, even, perhaps, a board of three or five members. Whoever or whatever is the head, there is all too often the accepted practice in a given police force of frequent changes in headship. The citizen takes in stride, without any qualms, a constant succession of changes of chief. (The term "police chief" is used to indicate the headship, whatever the local title may be.) He would not for a minute dream of investing his money in the stock of a corporation that hired and fired a new president or a new chairman of the board of directors every six months or every year. If that corporation is unable to make any better selection of the personnel to run it than that, it is not a fit resting place for his investment funds. He takes it for granted that he will only intrust them to one which selects the right man and which then keeps him in office and gets the advantage of his increasing experience and training. Yet, by a strange inconsistency, that same citizen is perfectly willing to intrust the headship of this highly responsible organization to a chronically inexperienced man. Indeed, more than that, in his thoughtlessness he even

5. By "professional" problems would be meant such questions as whether there should be patrol sergeants or whether control of the patrolmen on the beat should be done entirely by callboxes; whether motorcyles should be used or small-sized squad cars; whether the detective force should be a part of each district station or be centrally controlled. All such are professional problems that obviously the citizen has nothing to do with and where his views cannot and should not count for anything.

6. Nothing will be said here of the supreme importance of separating the police from politics. That is a truism sufficiently explored in many other texts. In any event, the achievement of this goal is primarily a matter of political science.

applauds changes that he should look on with the utmost misgiving. He finds that conditions are, let us say, not improved, and he vigorously applauds the mayor when the latter announces that he had given the incumbent six months to show results, that results were not shown, and that he is changing to a new (and therefore better) man. So a new chief comes in. A few months later it is his turn to go. In they go, and out they go, chronically inexperienced in the very specialized tasks that confront the head of the department. Indeed, it is worse than that, because, if a city is once committed to a program of constant changes in the headship of the force, it is demoralizing even beyond the chronic inexperience of the head. Why? Simply for this reason: Put yourself in the place of one of the captains who is under the command of a new police chief. He is a realist. (He would not be a captain if he were not.) He knows very well that this new chief will almost certainly be out of office in a few months. Is he going to be such a fool as to tie his particular kite to this man's star too closely—to be known too definitely as "one of Chief John Doe's men"? No, because when John Doe goes out of office and Richard Roe comes in, Roe will represent some other group in the department, and if one is known too definitely as one of John Doe's adherents, he will suffer along with Chief Doe. So he refrains from being too outstandingly co-operative with the head of the force. The poor incumbent is faced not only with inexperience but with a situation that almost insures the failure of his principal subordinates to give him wholehearted support.

Again we can compare the resulting situation with practice in the world of business. How far could the president of an industrial organization go if he did not have the support of the vice-presidents and the various department managers? We take that all for granted there. Why should we not take exactly the same line of reasoning in our police structure? It is no unconnected accident that one of the best policed cities in the United States—if not the best of large cities—had, until a recent change, two police chiefs in fifty-one years. They got a good man, and they kept him. We must improve the tenure situation for our top police executives.

At the other end of the scale, the recruitment end, we are like-

wise normally guilty of very unwise programs, which we uncriti-
cally take for granted. The particular reference is to our normal
American insistence that police recruits come exclusively from
the city or town, or even the village, in which they are to serve.
We take that requirement absolutely for granted. We do not
even give it thought. We apply it even when the area is so small
as manifestly to cut down our choice of possible candidates to
practically the vanishing point. But the harm is worse than that
resulting merely from the reduced choice. This insistence on local
men only for the local police force means that we have voluntarily
insisted on taking into our police force only those persons who present the maximum likelihood of having conflicting loyalties—loyalties toward other community groups than the police department;
loyalties that may very likely bring them into sharp conflict with
their police obligation. Contrast that with the state of affairs in
England (and England is mentioned because again and again we
find the British system held up to us as being so superior to our
own). If we encounter a London police officer, we may not know
where he is from, but we can be sure of one thing—he will not
have been a native of London originally. If we meet a Manchester
police officer, he may have come from Birmingham or from
Liverpool, but he will not have been born in Manchester. No
local person is even eligible to serve on the local police force.
Take even an American police organization that we quite properly regard as the extreme in efficiency—the famous Federal Bureau
of Investigation. The FBI seldom permits a man to enter service
in his own home town. He normally commences to serve elsewhere. True, this sacrifices thereby the local information which
he may have and which may be definitely valuable, but it is believed that the price is worth paying, in view of the disadvantage
of his possibly having too many conflicting local roots. Yet, while
applauding the FBI, we take it absolutely for granted that in our
city police forces completely the contrary policy must be followed. We do not even question it. In a few instances, civil service commissions that had a wiser outlook indicated that they
would throw open the possibility of recruitment to outsiders;
and it has been interesting to see what a storm of disapproval
immediately arose from the local community at the thought of

local jobs going to nonlocal people. In most of these instances the civil service commissions then rather contritely admitted that they were guilty of a serious error; in effect, they apologized and backtracked.[7]

A further problem connected with recruitment, to which the citizen might well devote more attention than he does, is that of police training—the recruit training program, the scope of police schools, and, allied to it, the problem of promotion. The average American police force is wholly unequipped to give its recruits adequate training in what has now become a profession. True, fifty or seventy-five years ago it certainly was not a profession. Whatever it was then is unimportant. It is a profession with a high degree of professional knowledge necessary to it as of today; and we cannot simply equip a newcomer with a nightstick and a revolver, turn him loose, and tell him, "Now you're a police officer."

We do have so-called police schools in most American cities; but too often the schools are such in name only. They are normally scarcely more than travesties on schools. Recruits enter upon a program; they pursue it for the required number of weeks; and at the end of these weeks they have finished their police training program. It is absolutely unthinkable, in such a school, that any recruit police officer should ever fail in his schooling; no matter how lax in his attention, no matter how slow his thought-processes, if he once gets by the civil service examination, he does not have to worry about any more weeding-out processes, so far as the school is concerned. True, for six months he is a probationary officer and may be discharged without benefit of civil service. True, also, that that probationary period is made use of to weed out certain men. The point now being made is that the school is not part of that weeding-out process; and it is easy to imagine how seriously the recruit officers are likely to take a school program in which they know that the only thing

7. A further criticism to which most civil service commissions are open is that their examinations are not so much as to the fitness of the candidate (his alertness, judgment, speed of reaction, etc.) as to items of knowledge—the law of arrest, the duties of the police, city geography, etc. These latter are matters that he can and should learn about in the recruit school. They are not matters of information bearing on his fitness or unfitness to become a police officer.

that is necessary to successful passing of the course is the ticking of the clock.

Even if the school were used for weeding-out purposes, the typical American training school is so inadequate as hardly to make it possible for anybody to fail to meet its limited requirements. It is true that certain cities have set up better police schools. New York City has a police academy that is the real thing and not merely a name; and one of the best police training schools in the country is operated by the Chicago Park District Police Force. Thus there are brighter spots. But it still remains true that in the main these schools are a travesty on what should be provided for recruits to so responsible a position.

In a way it is not such a surprise that police training schools have had no easy time of it, because it is, even with the best of intentions in the world, difficult for the police heads of all but the very largest cities to operate a school. Take even a good-sized city of, let us say, a quarter of a million population. That city will have a sizable police department, it is true; but it will not be such a huge police department as to make it feasible to operate the school in any but very irregular, occasional periods. So that, aside from the big cities of a half-million or a million and over, the operation of the school is bound to be a sporadic sort of thing; and this fact quite naturally has had a big share in the responsibility for the inadequate training that we have. More will be said further on about the many disadvantages that we face through our accepted policy of fragmentation, viz., the breaking-up of police forces into a huge number of small units; this is simply the first illustration of a point that we shall return to on several other occasions.[8]

There is comparatively little to say about the problems of promotion inside the police department, because, when we deal with them, we shall probably find that they are problems of what was referred to above as of a "professional nature"—that is, too inten-

8. To some extent the difficulty or even impossibility of operating training schools town by town and certainly village by village has been met by smaller cities' using facilities set up by police organizations in a neighboring large city or, more likely, facilities for which the state police organization is responsible. These improvements will be considered below while dealing with the topic of co-ordinating our police agencies.

sively a matter of police administration for the general citizen to concern himself with. Of course, in so far as promotion is determined by political consideration, and at the worst even by dishonest compulsion to pay in order to secure a promotion, it is of citizen interest. If no time is spent on this point, it is, of course, because it is so obvious as not to need any comment. But there is one thing which we should be on our guard against and which should not be practiced in an ably managed police department, viz., making promotion in part or largely the result of some sort of personal bravery or personal exploit by the police officer who is being promoted. The spectacle of the brave patrolman who has just made a highly dangerous arrest and is rewarded by being made a sergeant is not one of good police practice, because the qualities that made him a brave officer do not necessarily mean that he will also be a good sergeant. Of course, this does not mean that there should not be special rewards for meritorious performance. There may be all kinds of rewards. But it is not wise to make the reward consist, necessarily, in promotion to a different type of work. We are most likely to run into this phenomenon of promotion as a reward for bravery, where the promotion takes the milder form of assigning the officer to the detective bureau. Every uniformed police officer hopes some day to be assigned to the detective bureau, where he will get out of uniform and have the greater freedom which that kind of work carries with it. But detective work calls for—or should call for—a very special and particular aptitude, with which certainly the lucky accident of a brave deed need not have any connection at all. To make promotion into the detective bureau the result of personal bravery is to give away the fact that the chief does not have any concept of what the detective bureau is really for and of what kind of aptitudes it really requires.

We come now to a danger that confronts many of our police forces, especially the smaller ones, and that may constitute a growing one—the danger of overequipping a police force or, perhaps one should say, of making the physical equipment advance at a more rapid rate than the advance in the manpower to handle that equipment. With more and more machinery, more and more instruments of scientific detection, we are facing a real danger, in many of our small police forces, that the fine equipment, the very tangible tools of the profession, may take forward steps at so great a rate as to produce the likelihood that the net output of results, by the combination of physical equipment plus human beings to run that equipment, may actually go down. The point may be illustrated by the experience that many of us have had in using a camera. We began by using one of the old-fashioned box cameras, where we just pushed the lever and the picture was taken; we did not have to measure any footage; we did not have to go to work with a light meter; we did not do anything but push the lever, and then, if we could, we remembered to turn the film so as to bring a new film into place. And almost always the pictures were good enough for one's purpose. Then we acquired a really good camera, and footage, light, lens speed, and all had to be carefully considered. And for most of us that was the end of even passable pictures, simply because of overequipment. The equipment had advanced at one rate, and the human being who ran it had not advanced at all. Very possibly we face somewhat the same danger in those police forces that are functioning, let us say, in a community that is wealthy enough to buy them the best and public-spirited enough to be willing to do so. Such a community ought, always, to be well aware of the fact that it must make simultaneous forward steps in both equipment and manpower if it is to be sure of real progress and not possible deterioration.

Finally, a mass of problems arises from the excessive decentralization—the actual fragmentation—of our police forces. It is almost incredible, until we break down the figures, to see to what an extent our police forces are fragmented and broken up, not only into the forces of the big cities, the towns, and the small towns, but even into the individual villages. A generation ago the city of Chicago alone had four large forces and innumerable small ones. Some years ago a count was made of the number of separate police forces in the United States and the manpower in them, and their average strength was found to be four men. With New York's twenty thousand and Chicago's seven thousand, the median must be much lower even than that. And when we realize these four work on eight-hour shifts, that would mean that the average police force had one and one-third men on a patrol, or on duty rather—which is a wider term—at any one time. The implications as to police efficiency are obvious.

An obvious one is that the "force" operates over so small an area as to be almost crippling; almost immediately, in the pursuit of an offender, the police officer will pass the city or village limit. Unless legislation has remedied this shortcoming, as it has in some states, he will become a mere private citizen. In any event, even if he still retains his police character when he is in hot pursuit, it is a very real and practical question for him as to how far he is justified in passing beyond the boundaries of his city or town or village. In short, either legally or practically, or both, he is likely to have sharp geographical limits set on his activity. It is enough to contrast that with the high degree of mobility that his opponents, the criminals, equipped perhaps with a motor vehicle, have at their command.

Another disadvantage has already been mentioned—the impossibility of maintaining a training program. Indeed, almost every aspect of police activity has its efficiency weakened or broken down. It is small wonder, then, that the last quarter of a century has seen an effort to achieve some degree of integration. That effort at integration received its first stimulus when fingerprinting systems of identification came into wide use; and it was, of course, obvious that it was impossible for every separate police department, from the one-man village force on up, to have its own fingerprint files. The sensible thing was for the smaller forces in the neighborhood of a big city to turn over to the big-city force the keeping and administering of a centralized fingerprint file. (We are not speaking of the still higher degree of centralization that at a later time came in, viz., the state bureaus, and, overshadowing them all in importance now, of course, the centralized bureau maintained by the federal government in Washington.) But, confining ourselves to municipal forces, there was a very considerable and increasing use made of the facilities of the neighboring big-city force. That operated as an entering wedge toward co-operation and a breakdown in fragmentation.

Another factor that operated in the same direction emerged from the growing use of radio for squad cars. It is, of course, impossible to assign a separate wave length to every single municipality in the United States that chooses to have radio-equipped cars. A wave-length was assigned to the large-city force, and the forces of the neighboring small cities and towns used the same wave-length. Again, that is a step in the direction of co-operation, made necessary by physical conditions.

The practice of the small forces' availing themselves of the big city's police recruit school and sending their recruits to the city school against a certain money payment for the tuition also took root.

Those are three illustrations—the most important, no doubt, but by no means unique—of ways in which, by sheer necessity, the smaller forces in the neighborhood of a big city tend to co-ordinate themselves with the big-city force, while still preserving all their independence.[9]

This type of co-ordination has proved very important, useful, and encouraging wherever a large city serves as a focal center. Where that is true, we may have the phenomenon of what might almost be called a more or less integrated metropolitan police setup; but in its very nature it is a solution which only partly meets our problems. It is a method that presupposes the existence of some overwhelmingly much larger urban force and then in its neighborhood a mass of small forces. But that is a state of affairs that is by no means necessarily to be found everywhere. In fact, it is probably more accurate to say that it is the exception rather than the rule. There are many states, for instance, Iowa, that do not have a single huge metropolitan force within their entire boundary. Our problem as a whole will not be solved for the entire country by this metropolitan police development, nor will it do anything for progress in policing completely rural areas.

What is the law-enforcement machinery that historically we have used for rural policing? It is the county sheriff, aided by such deputies as he may care, and be financially able, to appoint. As the only law-enforcement officer in the county, the county

9. A fourth one that is worth pointing out and that is often in the public eye is the development of road-block systems whereby, if a crime is committed in a particular city, neighboring forces can be notified and can immediately set up a widespread road-block network.

sheriff could, we shall assume, do a tolerable job in the days preceding quick means of transportation—in the relatively simpler
days, that is, before the automobile. Rural law enforcement, then,
was a rather simple job. Crimes, typically, were limited to crimes
of violence. The identity of the perpetrator would usually be
known. In every way the problem was a comparatively simple
one, and the county sheriff, with his deputies, could fairly well
handle it. All that was completely changed when modern inven-
tions came into the picture, and (again) particularly modern
rapid transportation. County lines that at one time had had a real
meaning—it will be recalled that the county was supposed to be an
area of such a size that anybody could drive to the county seat
in a day's time—and that had seemed to be rather wide-flung con-
tracted in practical fact, and the county sheriff's jurisdiction, that
at one time had been wide enough to enable him to have elbow
room for his work, became anything but wide enough. He was
faced with a problem that was growing rapidly more complex.
At the same time a condition continued to operate to his disadvantage that became more and more serious as time went on. This
was the problem of his continued inexperience. In many states
(of which Illinois was until recently one) the sheriff normally,
as a law-enforcement officer, was and for that matter is, inexperienced, because the law forbids a sheriff to succeed himself
in office. True, he may be re-elected sheriff after an interval, but
that is not very likely to occur. Normally, not only will he
go out of office at the end of his term, but he will not at a later
date come back into office.[10] Thus, by this requirement of rotation in office, we have produced what might almost be described
as a state of compulsory inexperience during a considerable
share of his time in office.

   That group of disadvantages ultimately led, in some counties,
to conditions that became perilously close to a breakdown in
rural law enforcement. Various expedients were tried to get away
from these difficulties. County sheriffs' associations have been
formed, in which information is pooled, and co-operation, to

   10. Occasionally, when the sheriff is a dominant political figure, this difficulty is overcome by his allowing his principal deputy to succeed him in
office, and henceforth, perhaps for years, maintaining a regular rotation in
office with him. But this is bound to be an unusual situation.

some extent, encouraged; but obviously a voluntary association is not the answer to the problem. It can do but little toward integrating the various sheriffs' offices. As another expedient we occasionally find that county police forces have been set up in more populous counties; these forces have a jurisdiction throughout the county and are supposedly on a permanent basis in order to get away from the changes that successive sheriffs would produce. County police forces, however, have not been satisfactory. For one thing, a new sheriff, if he is a "spoilsman," may throw the old county force completely out of office, and then we have a final result that is in no wise different from the old setup of a new sheriff and new deputies. The only difference is that the people who had been dismissed were called "county police" instead of "deputies." Furthermore, it is only rarely that counties have chosen to set up county police, and rural counties have perhaps never done so.[11] Finally, it must be remembered that the county police are geographically just as handicapped as are the sheriff and his deputies. In an area that is now too small they offer no real solution.[12]

Perhaps, however, the two movements that have been spoken of—metropolitan organization, on the one hand, and some sort of improvement in the county sheriff's organization, either by improved county police or by some other development—might have gone further and achieved more than, taking the United States as a whole, they have if it had not been for the increasing use made of a completely new device to meet the requirements of integration and of rural policing—a device that has worked so well wherever it has been tried as to have become apparently the final and long-sought solution to this entire problem. The reference is, of course, to state police organizations.[13]

The state police movement had its beginning in the last years of the nineteenth century in Pennsylvania. It has since spread so that now probably the majority of the states have state police

11. In Illinois only two counties have done so. One is Cook, in which Chicago is situated, and the other is a county involved in the crime enforcement problem of Peoria, the state's second city.

12. Illinois has no less than 102 counties. Many states have more.

13. For a detailed and authoritative treatment of this subject see Bruce Smith, *The State Police: Organization and Administration* (New York: Macmillan Co., 1925).

forces, although this term may cover anything from a mere highway patrol body to a force having and exercising full police authority. Originally, the movement grew out of the realization that there was one kind of turbulent situation in which the sheriff and his deputies were particularly (and even more obviously than usual) unable to handle the potential trouble. This was in the event of industrial disputes and possible industrial violence emerging out of strikes or lockouts. Prior to the existence of state police forces the only way of coping with industrial disputes that were beyond the power of the sheriff that had been worked out was by means of the use of the state militia. It is hard to imagine any body of persons less fitted than the prewar state militia to handle an industrial dispute of any magnitude.[14] For one thing, the state militia is completely unprepared psychologically to do the job. It was, and is, made up of civilians who, for all the fact that they have drilled in close-order formation a number of evenings a week and have been doing so for a number of years, are still basically civilians. Put these civilians into uniform, send them to a high-tension area, and you would be subjecting them (and this applies not only to the enlisted men but to the officers as well) to pressures, stresses, and decisions that have to be taken in moments of excitement for which they have had absolutely no training and no background.

It is not an accident that the veteran police officer, who perhaps for years has been giving orders and has been expecting obedience to them, is levelheaded and calm in circumstances where the man who has no such background would either be completely helpless and inadequate or inordinately tough and authoritarian. Power is a very intoxicating thing. Not only were the militia most unfitted to handle the job, but, as if to make absolutely sure that their output of law enforcement would be as undesirable as possible, we equipped these militia groups with the most unwise of weapons for that kind of a problem of peace preservation. We equipped them with rifles and bayo-

14. The reason for limiting the statement to the "prewar militia" is that, for the time being, while the state militia is made up of veterans who have seen active service, some at least of the arguments in the text will not be so effective or apply so widely as they did in the past and as they will again in the future.

nets and later on with machine guns, and as a result they were completely over- or underweaponed, as you choose to look at it. The militiaman equipped with a rifle and a bayonet would have the choice either of using his weapon and inflicting human damage far beyond what that type of trouble called for, or of not using his weapon and simply being bowled over as a non-entity. What could he do with his rifle and his bayonet? He faced the choice of one or the other extreme, and, no matter which choice he made, he would be damned for it. So that, psychologically and materially, the militia were the very worst kind of peace weapon to use in industrial disputes. As industrial disputes grew in number and violence, there was increasing popular demand for some sort of new tool to handle this type of situation; and, as has already been indicated, the state police was the answer.

It got off to a very bad start. The first state police to be organized was an early force in Pennsylvania, and under the guise of building up a law-enforcement, order-preserving agency, what actually occurred was that a reactionary group used the device as nothing more or less than a state-paid and state-authorized organization of strikebreakers. That development was met quickly and properly by the disbanding and abolition of the Pennsylvania State Police.[15] But it produced a result that has plagued us ever since, because it made organized labor supersensitive on the subject of state police forces and basically hostile to any and every suggestion of the establishment of such a force. It is interesting to note that, so far as the author knows, without exception, in each state where a state police force has been established, often against the active and more or less bitter opposition of organized labor, the impartial attitude of that force and the useful results achieved by it have ended by completely overcoming that hostility. But the mere fact that it has been overcome in one state will not modify in the least degree the hostility that a neighboring state, at the time it seeks to establish a force of this sort, will also have to overcome, so that this

15. The present Pennsylvania State Police is a wholly separate and more recent creation.

initial distortion of the purpose of state police in Pennsylvania is still plaguing us even though in constantly diminishing degrees.

These state police forces have achieved a success and an efficiency that have surprised even their advocates. The state police in such states as New York, New Jersey, Massachusetts, and Michigan are outstanding, but it would be hard to mention any state police force that is not signally better than the level of urban policing in its own state. Probably this is due, in the first instance at least, to the fact that to a large degree each successive state police force has emerged from public demand for improvement. There has been great public interest in the creation of the force, public attention has been centered on it, and the public has refused to endure the things that it has become so accustomed to in urban policing as to accept without question. It has demanded a higher standard of performance by its state forces. That has shown itself notably in the way in which the best of the forces have been headed by men of outstanding ability who have been allowed to carry on as autocrats in their own force.

Some of the best state police forces have no tenure of office for their personnel, whatsoever. If that were true in a municipal force, it would mean the chronic raiding of the force by spoilsmen—the throwing-out of office of all the old incumbents and the installing of a wholly new force. Actually, in these forces, it has meant that the disadvantages of civil service in freezing a person into his job have not been present, but the political independence of the chief, and his personal stature, have been effective in securing, in fact, complete tenure for the subordinate members of the force. Similarly the chiefs themselves have often had no legally guaranteed tenure, though the statutes under which state police are organized very often provide that a head is to be removed only after a public hearing on charges filed against him. Some give him not even that protection. Yet, in the main, police heads have been pretty safe and certainly have been so in the best of the forces.

In the leading state forces a fairly uniform policy has been followed of enlisting men for definite, fairly long periods and starting them on initially low salaries with rather frequent raises in pay in the opening years. Obviously, the purpose of such a measure is to add to the enlistment period by increasing the inducement to stay, once the job has been obtained. Many of the forces limit recruitment to unmarried men and provide that marriage shall operate as an immediate discharge from the force, if the officer marries within a certain number of years after his first recruitment, the idea being that there is greater independence of action and greater devotion to police duty on the part of unattached men. In the same way practically all the leading forces follow a policy of assigning a man not to his home district but to a district in some other part of the state. Like the FBI, this policy is often supplemented by routine transfer from time to time.

The state police not only have been free from political interference and pressure, because of public interest and attention, but have also, for the same basic reason and starting as they do with a clean slate, been able to begin with the establishment of a professionalized tradition. One of the most baffling problems in raising the level of police work from a mere job to a skilled profession has lain in the hostile attitude of old-line police veterans themselves. Consciously or unconsciously, the old-time officer resents the introduction of new methods into his force. It is understandable why that should be so. For one thing, the introduction of new methods puts upon him the obligation to learn these methods. It jars him out of the comfortable state that he is in by putting up to him entirely new problems and entirely new procedures. Nobody likes that, unless he is very alert mentally! Furthermore, the introduction of new methods is a reflection on the effectiveness of the old ones. For both of these reasons, the leading obstacle to the improvement of police technique is likely to center around the existing members of a police force. In so far as these members are merely patrolmen, that resistance may not be so effective, though the dead weight of hostile public opinion is likely to be as discouraging in police circles as it is in any other aspect of life. But the dead weight of opposition to new methods is especially an obstacle when the resistance comes from commanding officers, the captains, who, if they have been promoted from the ranks, often share to the full the run-of-the-mine belief that the old methods on which they were brought up are good enough. What was good enough for them is good enough for the young sprigs that are coming into the department. They learned the hard way; let the newcomers learn that way too.

Thus, from all the grades, both the rank and file and the higher ranks, city police administrators often face a great mass of intradepartmental hostility toward modernization. The state police, starting as a new broom, have not been faced by that difficulty. Whether in the course of time they will harden too is something that only the future can disclose. But, at any rate, so far as this generation is concerned, we shall not face that difficulty with them. We started afresh, and, therefore in that sense, all methods were new methods.

It is no wonder, then, that because of all these points state police forces have been effective in more ways than such obvious ones of efficiency as, for example, the circumstance that they are not cramped by jurisdictional lines that limit them to the county, the municipality, or the village. In fact, the success of the state police has by a curious inversion operated to become one of the possibly major dangers that they face, so far as continuing to be successful is concerned. Very often the state police, with a record of efficient performance of their duties, have found that that very efficiency has resulted in their receiving any and every new job that some organization of the state government has to assume; and when it is a question of who shall do it, George, who always does his job well, is always selected, and in this connection George means the state police. Thus, there is a real danger that state police forces may be loaded down with a mass of duties that merely by their volume will cut down this initial efficiency.

By way of illustration, some of the nonpolice activities that particular state police forces have been given in various states may be cited.[16] The list does not characterize any one force, nor does any one force have all these obligations. They are merely illustrations of the duties that some forces have received. In one of the states they are under the duty to run ice-breakers

16. For more details see Smith, *op. cit.*, pp. 67–69.

in order to keep highways open when these are near a lake or unbridged river. In many states they have the duty of inspecting elevators for safety conditions. They also have the duty in some of the dairy states of discovering and destroying diseased cattle. Very often they are charged with the duty of censoring movies, and, farthest afield of all, one state puts upon them the duty of Americanizing aliens. What time does the performance of all or even a substantial fraction of these, strictly speaking, non-police duties leave for police work? Add to that the circumstance that probably without exception state forces are very small in point of numbers compared to the areas that they are responsible for.[17] Is it to be doubted that this presents a real danger?

The state police themselves have not been so active as one might suppose in resisting this tendency to put too many jobs on their shoulders. Rather, on the contrary, they have understandably but unwisely at times even welcomed additional jobs. It is understandable when we realize the setting in which the police organization finds itself. Typically, it is one of the newest, one of the youngest, of the state agencies. All state agencies, from the state university on down, are in ardent competition with one another for appropriations. While it is, of course, true that the appropriation for the state university will not hang directly on the amount of money that is assigned, say, to the mine-inspection service, it is also true that the legislature will be harder and harder to convince that an appropriation should go through the bigger the total gets. In this indirect sense all state agencies are, therefore, more or less in competition with one another. And the newcomer who was not present at all before is going to fare like every other newcomer. He will find a great deal of opposition to his "muscling in" on some of the funds. The state police have not been immune from that difficulty, and unquestionably they have been anxious to make friends in other parts of the state government. What is a more effective way of making widespread friends than to do jobs for

17. Incidentally, their smallness has uniformly led them, even when this is not required by law (as it is in some states), to refrain from assuming any patrolling obligations inside municipalities that maintain their own police forces. Thus, in Illinois the state police has washed its hands almost entirely of Cook County and entirely of intra-Chicago activities.

as many Toms, Dicks, and Harrys all through the state government as possible? It will make one's position that much smoother
when one is competing with the said Tom and Dick and Harry
for some of the wherewithal. As a consequence they have themselves been somewhat at fault in showing an ill-advised willingness to take on assignments that are occasionally more than
they wisely should carry.

Basically the state police movement is inconsistent with the
continuance, in unchanged ways, of the sheriffs and the deputies
as county law-enforcement officers, because it is in competition
with them. It is, perhaps, the realization of this that accounts
for the fact that sheriffs' associations have been among the
governmental agencies[18] least friendly, if not actually hostile, to
the state police movement. Similarly, opposition has been met
at times from municipal forces, though this has been a less important factor, because the state police themselves have uniformly refrained from intra-municipal policing, as has already
been stated.[19] In addition, the state force has often strengthened
itself with small city forces by the extremely useful idea of
maintaining police schools for the latters' recruits—a most valuable contribution toward solving the whole school problem.
Other forms of co-operation with municipalities consist in
maintaining state-wide identification bureaus and furnishing
crime laboratory facilities for forces not able to afford their
own. Thus to a very considerable extent state forces not only
are providing better rural policing but are proving an important
factor in bettering intra-municipal work.

It will be noted that nothing has been said so far about federal
police agencies. One of them, the Federal Bureau of Investigation, is of tremendous local use because it maintains the world's
largest identification files (as well as crime statistics). It has also
stepped into the school program by operating the nation's most

18. Accurately speaking, the associations are not themselves governmental
agencies, but their members are.

19. An interesting exception to this has been Connecticut, where a municipality may make a contract with the state police whereby the state police will take
over the function of policing within that municipality. The municipality pays
a set amount per patrolman, and the state police enlarges its personnel so far as
the contract payment permits. Whether this is a development which will spread
is a question that only the future can answer.

efficient police school. By way of caution, however, it should be pointed out that this school is not (and is not intended to be) a direct factor in the recruit-training program. It manifestly would be impossible for the FBI to take on this burden. Its school is a highly advanced and specialized one, and the local officers who attend it are a selected lot, who will influence local conditions only by themselves becoming the examples and the teachers for the members of the local force. In that indirect sense, no doubt, the FBI school will be a factor in police training, but only in that indirect sense. Without detracting from the excellence of the FBI as a single, though very important unit, it is still true that the federal police setup too, to some extent, suffers from the same fragmentation that the city and town and village forces suffer from. In the case of the federal setup, however, it is not along geographical lines but along functional lines. It is only necessary to mention the principal federal police agencies.

There is the Secret Service, which is charged with two wholly separate tasks. One is that of watching against counterfeit money and the counterfeiting of federal securities. The other, utterly unrelated to the first one, is that of watching over the personal safety of the President, the presidential nominees, important foreign visitors, etc. In addition to that, there are the Post Office inspectors, whose duty it is to detect and suppress crimes against the Post Office and the postal system, such as mail robberies, counterfeiting of postage stamps, etc. And then there is the Border Patrol to guard against illegal immigration. Likewise there is another border patrol to guard against smuggling across the border. In fact, there is a third federal police force that also is concerned with border smuggling, viz., the Narcotics Bureau. The name will indicate its function. And there are a good many other less important federal police agencies, to say nothing of the one already mentioned and the most famous of all—the FBI—which, being the direct police agency of the Department of Justice, has a responsibility and a jurisdiction that cover the whole area of federal offenses.

It must be apparent what a waste of energy it is to have no less than three police forces watching the border, while two are checking on engravers who go wrong (the Secret Service, when the engraver makes a false piece of paper money, and the postal inspectors, when he makes a counterfeit stamp). That, too, is fragmentation, and because of the universal persistence with which all governmental agencies are able to cling to life, it is not easy to see any great promise in the early future of breaking it down. Based simply on present indications, if integration is to be achieved, it may perhaps be most easily obtained by the overshadowing role that in recent years has been played by the FBI. While, of course, over a longer period of time it is always questionable whether such a development will necessarily continue, the favorable strategic position of the FBI relative to the other federal forces is of course obvious, since it is the agency of the Department of Justice and thereby necessarily has an interest in the whole area of federal law enforcement and is not limited to any particular functional aspect of it. Perhaps it may ultimately be the only federal police agency.

There remain for comment a few miscellanious matters concerning the police, which are unrelated to one another, except in the fact that they are all of general citizen interest and concern. The first of these is the so-called "crime wave." It is, of course, true that there may be a sudden and surprising upsurge of crime not to be explained by the usual causes such as economic dislocation, the suggestive effect of a highly publicized crime,[20] etc. But in the great majority of instances citizens should be on their guard against accepting "crime waves" at their face value. It is not a matter of accident that crime waves almost always occur when there is no war scare going on, no sensational divorce just taking place, no earthquake anywhere. In other words, the crime wave is in most instances a reflection of the lack of news of a sensational nature of a noncrime kind. It supplies the lack of news items of reader interest along other lines. In short, crime waves are often entirely synthetic so far as the newspapers are concerned and can largely be constructed out of any kind of situation. Indeed, there are certainly in-

20. Advertising is effective not only in furthering legitimate business. Some of its most striking achievements have been in inducing suggestible individuals to imitate crimes receiving wide public attention.

stances in which crime waves were reported with much fanfare, when actually the statistics showed a diminution of the crime rate at the very time that the wave was supposed to be in progress. At other times, it is true, the statistics may show really rising figures, and hence there is, superficially, substance to the wave. But here again it should be remembered that the amount of crime that is apparently going on is in the first instance measured by the number of crimes that the police in their statistics announce as taking place, and the announced amount of criminality may or may not bear a definite fixed ratio to the amount of actual criminality. A particular district or a particular city may be very adept at concealing the amount of crime going on in its boundaries and may as a consequence show a much better figure than a district or a city or a region that frankly faces the problem and comes out with the facts. Notoriously certain police departments are anything but complete and accurate in their reports on crimes of violence when Negroes are both the perpetrators and the victims. Thus an entirely distorted picture of a local situation may emerge, and this is particularly serious because it is entirely possible that there may be a real improvement in policing at the very time when the statistics show an increase in crime. The old regime that was more concerned with brushing the dirt under the carpet than it was with repressing crime may have made in the statistics a much better showing than the administration that is frankly and honestly trying to remedy the situation and that recognizes that its first obligation is to bring the truth out into the open.

A better source of information as to local conditions is the local crime commission. The value and significance of this organization can best be shown by a brief description of the Chicago Crime Commission—the oldest and most successful. It was established in 1919 and is a citizen group maintained from such resources as may be derived from voluntary contributions by private persons. Its object is to gather together and make available all kinds of information bearing on how effectively and in what manner law is being enforced in its particular locality. Its basic assumption is that public knowledge of how the public officials are doing their work is the major factor in getting a good, efficient, and honest output of work from these officials. It is obvious that in a big community it is no longer possible for the individual citizens to gather this information for themselves solely on their own resources and hence that it is the responsibility of some sort of organized piece of machinery to supply them with the information. The typical crime commission is that piece of machinery. Normally a crime commission then is entirely privately supported. To have it financed even in part by the government is, to that extent, to risk destroying its very purpose.

In Chicago the only connection that the Crime Commission has with any governmental agency is that its files are so much more adequate and full, and its index is so much better than the public records, that the Crime Commission is referred to by the parole authorities to supply them with data on all convicts who come to the penitentiary from Cook County, and for that service the Crime Commission does in fact receive a certain fee, but it is entirely based upon service rendered and leaves the commission wholly independent so far as any governmental affiliations are concerned. It would seem safe to assume that the idea of an organized and reliable observer group to furnish information to the public generally as to good and bad methods and procedures of criminal-law enforcement is so obviously a sound one that the mere description of it will sufficiently make the point.

The subject of publicity suggests, in turn, the topic of improper relationship between the police and the newspapers. It is far from the smallest of the many problems that face us in police organization. And it is far easier to point to the many serious abuses than it is to suggest cures or even to apportion blame. In its most obviously undesirable form the disadvantages to the community are best shown in a phenomenon that every reader must have observed and wondered about many times. The reference is to this type of thing: A crime has been committed and is spread all over the front pages of the newspapers. A day or so later we read a newspaper item that perhaps states that the police have discovered certain clues. These clues are then minutely described—just how many there are and what they

are—and, by an easy chain of inference, exactly what the police
do not have as well as what they do have. And then the story
goes on and tells how the police therefore now suspect that
John Doe is the person who committed the crime and have spread
a net of detectives around John Doe's residence and the residence
of John Doe's parents, and so on, in the hope of picking him
up when he appears.

If you have had that experience (and it seems safe to say
there is no reader who has not seen items like that), you will
surely have wondered at the folly of the police in making so
completely sure that their efforts will come to naught, or, if
not sure that they will come to naught, at least make their
efforts so much less likely of success. Why in the world should
they tip off their hand in this way and give John Doe all this
valuable information by which he may protect himself? The
answer obviously is not that the police are so stupid as to be
unaware of the harmfulness of what they are doing. They are
not only as aware of it as we are; they are even more keenly
aware of it because they have to work under the consequences
of their own disclosures. Why, then, do they do it? They do
it because they are under terrific pressure on the part of the
newspapers to make disclosures of this sort—all sorts of pressures on them to "play ball" by disclosures of this kind. If
they resist such pressure and refuse to hand out releases, there
are various ways by which the newspaper which is willing to
be unscrupulous to this degree can make life miserable from
then on for the individual officer who is so unfriendly as to
withhold the desired information from the reporter. From then
on he can become a marked man and can be sure of publicity
for every unfavorable act he does. Conversely, the officer who
co-operates can be sure of protection in everything that he
does, with the best light thrown upon every doubtful circumstance that he may be involved in, and every chance given to
him to explain his side of the story. Thus, to the individual
officer seeking promotion or betterment in any way, newspaper
favor or newspaper hostility is by no means a factor of small
importance.

But, to emphasize how hard it is to apportion blame, it is not so easy either to be convinced that this condition is the fault of the individual newspapermen. The newspaper business, in general, and the job of crime reporter for a large newspaper, in particular, are both highly competitive enterprises. Results—perhaps even occasional scoops—must be produced. If not, then for the newspaper it means the well-known diminution of circulation and therefore of advertising, in favor of the successful competitor. For the individual reporter too great a frequency of scoops by the other fellow means a lost job. It is easy to be abstract and say that the reporter should not squeeze the police for all he is worth to get what he can out of them and that he ought to be more solicitous of the repression of crime and the detection of criminals and so on. It is easy, unless we are in the position of the individual reporter, and then it probably is not anywhere near so easy to adjust one's conduct to the best interests of society.

It is interesting to compare our practice with the rigorous restrictions on crime reporting that the British have put upon newspapers and the extreme care that the British newspapers must use in selecting the publicity that they will give to pending criminal cases. This, too, may be an important factor in the greater British success in crime repression. Yet if we jump from this conclusion to the inference that we ought to repress our newspapers' exuberance and cut down on their freedom of publication, then we are opening up questions of the freedom of the press where we are on very doubtful ground and where the resultant harm may well be greater than the benefit. Unfortunately, the harms of newspaper publicity and newspaper police are far easier to describe than the cures or corrective measures that should be adopted.

There are other ways besides the premature disclosing of clues by which the harmful effects of publicity on police work may be shown. There is the tendency, on the part of publicity-conscious officers, to measure their interest in a case on the basis of its publicity value and to let this determine how much attention it is to receive. Thus a murder in a socially desirable neighborhood looms much larger than one in a poor one. The result is a complete imbalance in police attention, not only as to individual crimes, but as to whole groups of crimes, those that make the front page as a group getting more attention than many less spectacular but very serious ones. We may also find, for the same reasons, that where a crime has high publicity value, the supervising officer, who should be a supervising officer and nothing else, and who should be a desk man marshaling the efforts of his field organization, tends to become the detective himself and to be on the scene as much as possible in the actual investigating of leads. That, in turn, at its least harmful, leads to disorganization of the investigation with nobody really directing it. At its worst and most harmful, it even means that the viciousness of struggling for publicity may result in various branches of a given police force competing with one another for the spotlight. That competition for the spotlight may result in actually hiding from one another useful leads or useful clues so that the lucky obtainer of a particular clue will be sure that all the attention will be directed to it alone.

In police force after police force the feeling is chronically strained between the uniformed force, on the one hand, and the detective bureau, on the other, because of the belief on the part of the uniformed force that, whenever there is anything that "breaks" that is worth noticing, the detective bureau takes over, and it leaves the uniformed force to hold the bag with all the unpromising cases. It is easy to imagine the amount of helpful co-operation that such an attitude produces between the two groups. Also, all this stimulates the use of spectacular, and not necessarily efficient but possibly even highly inefficient, detection methods, as against quiet, unspectacular ones that get somewhere.

As the most frequently encountered instance of that sort of thing, we may cite the relative prevalence of two types of gambling raids—the quiet, unspectacular getting of search warrants, and then the entering with the search warrant, and the discovering of all the evidence of what is to be discovered, all in a perfectly legal, effective manner—a most unexciting performance—on the one hand, and, on the other, the raid with all sirens going, the breaking-down of doors with an ax, and a tremendous amount of publicity for it all, which probably will get nowhere. The only feasible means to counter and control this publicity-seeking is by the issuance, and rigidly enforced observance, of an order by the head of the police force, confining the giving-out of information to the public (including reporters) to a certain part of the force. Such an order is as difficult to get as it is difficult to enforce, because all kinds of leaks may come out, and who is responsible for the leak is known only to the giver of the information and the reporter who gets it. But it is a step in the right direction.

A particular practice that once was more in vogue than it is now and that has not made for good policing has been the giving of rewards to police officers for the discovery of the perpetrator of a particular crime. It should be noted that we are not referring to the giving of a reward to police officers for particularly brave conduct after the conduct has taken place. That type of reward is an entirely different one. We are speaking of the reward offered in advance for the doing in the future of a particular piece of work, which is an entirely different thing. That is harmful because, if it is a widespread practice, it may result in the officer's allocating his time and attention rather on the basis of the financial implications than of the police implications. The problem has to a considerable extent been met in many forces by requiring that such rewards be turned in to the local pension fund, for the general benefit of the whole force. That seems to be a fully effective means of meeting this particular difficulty at least.

III

ARREST AND SUMMONS

IN THE chronological sequence of legal steps in enforcing the criminal law the first is the issuing of a warrant of arrest, to be followed, as the second step, by the arrest itself.[1] We shall, therefore, commence by describing the procedure of obtaining a warrant.[2] The process is begun by the appearance before a judge of a person whom we call the "complainant"—that is to say, the person who lays before the judge his desire to have the warrant issued and his reasons for it. Any judge, broadly speaking, may be asked to issue a warrant, but in fact this work is usually handled by the judges of lowest rank who, while engaged in this task or in the tasks described in chapters iv and v, are commonly called "magistrates." The information given to the magistrate by the complainant is referred to as the "complaint."[2a]

In many of the larger cities much of the magistrate's time is saved by requiring would-be complainants to go first to a police officer assigned to the magistrate's court and usually referred to as the court's "warrant officer."[3] His presence is a recognition

1. In certain situations (described below, p. 63) an arrest may be made either with or without a warrant. If, in such a case, no warrant is obtained, the arrest itself will be the first step.

2. In strict accuracy the expression used should be "warrant of arrest," to distinguish it from other kinds of warrants. In its original usage the word "warrant" signified, in general terms, any kind of authorization to do a thing which, apart from the authorization, there was no right to do. This meaning survives in such an expression as "By what warrant are you acting in this way—what warrants it?" Any branch of the government could, conceivably, issue a warrant. Thus the Navy might authorize an enlisted man to perform certain functions usually reserved to officers. Such a man is then referred to as a "warrant officer." But most frequently warrants emanated from the courts. Of them, two are part of criminal-law enforcement—the search warrant (below, p. 83) and the warrant of arrest. This latter is, of all warrants, so far the commonest that, quite naturally, it has come to be referred to simply as a "warrant," without any further term of description.

2a. In New York it is known as the "information." This departure from general usage is particularly unfortunate, since the word "information" has a very different meaning in most other states (see chap. ix).

3. Of course it is obvious that this use of the term has no connection with the Army or Navy meaning.

that a great many persons come to court for a warrant when there is no legal basis whatsoever for the issuance of one. Their speedy elimination is a great convenience to the magistrate, and this the warrant officer is able to do for him. Or, again, the party who wishes a warrant may be in such a state of excitement as to have considerable difficulty in telling a coherent story or may be so uneducated as to make it rather hard to tell from the confused story what it is really all about. With the magistrate having a full calendar every day, he is naturally anxious not to be the one who has to untangle all the involved bits of information; so for this reason it may be extremely convenient to have this buffer as the first person whom the complainant sees and who takes down the story in its first stage and draws up the complaint in understandable form. This draft is then taken to the magistrate.

At common law it was entirely proper to make a complaint orally, but today it is usual to require that it be put in writing. It must then be sworn to by the complainant. If not sworn to, the magistrate is not justified in taking any further steps. Views differ as to whether the complainant is restricted in his complaint to facts that he knows of his own knowledge or whether he may include in the complaint statements made to him or information obtained by him from others, with the added statement by him that he believes this information to be true. (Such a complaint is referred to usually as one "on information and belief" because the typical way in which the material will be presented in the complaint will be that the facts following are obtained "on information" from such-and-such sources and "are believed" to be true.) But whether the complaint is adequate if made merely on information and belief or must be based upon facts known to the complainant himself, in any event the complaint must be on oath.

Incidentally, complaints on information and belief would typically be the kind of complaints that police officers, when they seek a warrant of arrest, will make, because ordinarily the police officer would be acting simply on information furnished to him. In a jurisdiction recognizing a complaint on information and belief, that would be satisfactory. In a jurisdiction that did not recognize such a complaint, it would be necessary for the police officer to have the person who wants the warrant issued come himself and make the complaint. Indeed, a cautious police officer even in a jurisdiction that permits complaints based on information and belief might well prefer to have the aggrieved person come in and himself take the responsibility of making the complaint.

Assuming, now, that the complaint is in proper form and sworn to, the magistrate will then look it over[4] to determine whether, if it tells the truth, it does in fact charge an offense. If his conclusion is a negative one, then the magistrate will refuse to issue the warrant. But if the complaint, assuming it is true, states an offense, then the magistrate proceeds to the issuance of the warrant, which likewise is a written document. The warrant is directed to a designated person, now normally a police officer, but originally anybody whom the magistrate might choose. Indeed, unless the common law has been modified by statute, it is still perfectly proper for the magistrate to direct the warrant to anybody whom he desires. He can arbitrarily pick out a private citizen and direct the warrant to him. However, by statute in some states he must direct it only to a peace officer, and, in any event, whether he is so restricted by law or not, warrants nowadays are always directed to police officers. In the typical urban setting the warrant will be directed to the chief of the department, and this is regarded as in effect directing it also to all the members of that department. The warrant orders the person to whom it is directed to "bring in the body" of the designated individual. This rather gory way of phrasing it is a survival of the fact that the warrant in its original form was in Latin and that the Latin term used was to bring in "the *corpus*"; and *corpus* was literally translated as "body." A warrant of arrest, contrary to a search warrant,[5] is valid for an indefinite length of time. It may be retained by the police, where for one reason or another they are incapable of

---

4. As a matter of fact, if there is no warrant officer (as would be the case in all but the biggest cities), the magistrate has no doubt assisted in the drawing-up of the complaint himself by indicating what statements are necessary, etc.
5. See below, p. 83.

making the arrest, for an indefinite length of time and be used when the individual is available.

At common law a magistrate could properly issue a warrant only in connection with an offense which had occurred in the area in which he had jurisdiction. Furthermore, the warrant was valid only in that area. If the person to be arrested had meanwhile gone to another county, then the procedure was the cumbersome one of going to the magistrate in the county where the offense had taken place, getting his warrant, and then taking it to a magistrate in the county in which the accused person was then to be found and having the magistrate countersign it (a step known as "getting it backed"). Today very frequently we find statutory provisions permitting a magistrate who has the authority to issue a warrant (and this is usually limited even today to magistrates who sit in the jurisdiction where the crime was committed) to direct it to any police officer throughout the state, thus obviating the necessity of having local backing.[6]

We come, finally, to the contents of the warrant. It must state the offense with which the person to be arrested is charged —not the detailed evidence to back up the truth of the charge but information so that one may know what the offense is. It must state that the complaint was sworn to, and it must identify the person who is to be arrested. It is not sufficient to leave the identifying information blank and thereby in fact attempt to confer upon a police officer the right to do his own picking as to the person whom he will choose for the arrest. How is it most feasible to identify one human being from another? Obviously, the normal manner is by putting in his name, so that typically the warrant will specify the person to be arrested by name. But it is not absolutely necessary. If the magistrate and the complainant do not know the individual's name, they may do the next best thing—describe him as minutely as possible. In such instances it is well, or perhaps requisite, for the magistrate to supplement the description with the affirmative and definite statement that the name is unknown, because whenever we diverge radically from the accepted way of procedure,

6. Any such general statement regarding the authority to issue a warrant and the area of its validity must, however, be checked against local variations.

whether it is law, or social conduct, or anything else, it is just as well to explain why we deviate. Curiously enough, however, the law has fallen into the habit of not omitting a name entirely. When we do not know the name, legal tradition has led us to the curious practice of inventing a name; and we say that the warrant is to arrest "John Doe, whose other or better name is unknown." Indeed, warrants that do not identify the person with particularity are even typically referred to as "John Doe warrants."[7]

If the warrant meets the foregoing requirements, it is technically "fair on its face" and is a complete protection to the person serving it against any claim of false or improper arrest. Social policy will not permit requiring a police officer to examine into the truth of what the warrant states. He may properly and safely assume its truth.

It is not, however, uniformly and always necessary to secure a warrant before making an arrest. There are situations where an arrest may be the first step taken.[8] Little generalization is possible as to when on-view arrests are permissible and when not, since there is great diversity of view in the various states. (Nor is the question primarily one of criminal-law administration, since, even if the arrest was an improper one, the arrested person is nonetheless held to answer to the charge. The impropriety of the arrest merely gives him ground for an action for damages—probably valueless—against the person who thus improperly arrested him. It affects criminal-law administration only in that a strict rule may make an officer more hesitant to make on-view arrests.)

Perhaps the only completely safe general statements are that anyone—police officer or private citizen—may make an arrest to stop the commission of a felony or to apprehend one who has just committed a felony. Probably the same could be said when

7. The statement that the person to be arrested must be identified seems to be contrary to occasional decisions upholding arrests where there was no identification or where simply "John Doe" was entered. It will be found, however, that these decisions were in cases in which no warrant was necessary at all and in which, therefore, its validity was immaterial.

8. In police slang such arrests without a warrant are known as "on-view" arrests.

the crime is merely a misdemeanor but involves a breach of the peace. Beyond this point generalization ceases to be safe. When the crime being committed is a nonviolent misdemeanor, the local holding may continue to accord the right of an on-view arrest to all or may limit it to police officers—an instance of the tendency to give greater rights to police officers.[9] When the offense is completed, the officer may arrest where it was a felony. But there is no unanimity that the private person may. Still further complications may arise from arresting the wrong person, owing to a reasonable mistake, or when no crime has in fact been committed. Broadly speaking, when there is a felony, a police officer can excuse the fact that he made an erroneous arrest by showing that he reasonably and honestly supposed that a felony had been committed and reasonably and honestly supposed that the person whom he was arresting was involved in its commission. If the arrestor is a mere private citizen, that will not be enough to protect him from a successful suit for damages. He must show, according to the general viewpoint, that a felony was in fact committed by somebody and will only be allowed to show, so far as the mistake was concerned, that he was honestly and reasonably mistaken in his belief that the man he seized was the one who really had committed that felony. He cannot extend the area of his excusable mistake to the fact of the commission of a felony by someone. It would seem, however, to be inexpedient to endeavor here to examine more closely into these questions.

Just as there may be a civil wrong[10] in making an on-view arrest, so too there may a civil, and even a criminal, wrong in using excessive force in making an arrest. Here, too, in defining "excessive," generalizations are dangerous. In any event, it will not include more force than is, or reasonably seems to the arrestor to be, necessary. There is likewise probably agreement that it is "excessive" to kill an escaping misdemeanant, even though this is "necessary" in the sense that by no other means

9. The difference between a felony and a misdemeanor is variously phrased. In the main it may be assumed that a felony signifies any crime which is punished by either death or penitentiary imprisonment; misdemeanor, one punished by jail imprisonment or fine.
10. I.e., a wrong giving rise to a suit for damages.

can his escape be prevented. And—general police belief to the contrary notwithstanding—it is of course unlawful to shoot to prevent the escape of one not suspected of any crime but whom the officer wishes to question. Further particularization, however, is not possible.[11]

From what was said above,[12] it was shown that the police officer is in various ways in a more favorable position than is an ordinary citizen in making an arrest. What then if the officer, in trying to arrest, follows a fleeing wrongdoer out of the city or county in which he is an officer and hence into territory in which he holds no official status? About half the states have enacted a statute known as the Fresh Pursuit Act, which confers on an officer in fresh pursuit of an offender the continuing status of an officer even outside the local limits.[13] In these days of motorized police and criminals such a provision is highly necessary. The same continuing authority should, of course, exist where the purpose in crossing the city or county line is not to make an arrest in the first place but to follow and recapture someone who has been arrested and is now seeking to escape.[14]

A police officer may be under a duty to perform an official act inside a house (for instance, he holds a warrant to arrest someone who is in the house, or he hears sounds indicating that a breach of the peace is being then and there committed in the house). Under these circumstances he should identify himself as an officer and demand admission. If thereafter he is still not admitted, he is permitted to break his way in.

Finally, a police officer may call upon other persons to render him such assistance as he needs in making an arrest (as, for instance, in letting him use an automobile to follow a fugitive). To refuse the help demanded will itself constitute a violation

11. The use of handcuffs on an arrested person where it is evident that there is no need for them may constitute "excessive force."

12. See p. 64.

13. Of course this presupposes that all that occurs is in the same state. The act does not apply to an "officer" coming in from another state.

14. In this general connection Illinois has in its statutes a little-known provision that, where two or more municipalities are both adjoining and also in the same county, they shall form a single "police district" and that the police of any one of the municipalities are officially such (for most purposes) all through the district (*Illinois Revised Statutes*, chap. 24, § 8 [5] and [6]).

of the law. This doctrine is, of course, a survival of the old law that made it the general duty of all citizens to participate in making arrests, when it was the normal thing for the sheriff to recruit his necessary manpower by a general call for help. The group so recruited was known as a "posse comitatus," a term that has survived almost into the present day in our western states.

Another privilege which, to an increasing extent, is being given to an arresting officer (and which, indeed, he may already have had in some states, under the common law) is that of requiring witnesses of a crime to identify themselves and, if they fail to do so to his satisfaction, of permitting him to detain them and take them before a magistrate.[15] Technically this does not constitute an arrest; it is referred to as a "detention" only. In fact, this concept of a "detention" that is not an "arrest" (and hence does not go down in the man's record as such) is extended in the Model Arrest Act, beyond mere witnesses who are "detained," to suspected offenders.[16] Within a maximum of two hours the detained person must either be released or be formally arrested. The great argument for such a provision is that it would legalize, and therefore bring under control, steps that are already in fact being taken and that, because of their illegality, present the maximum danger of abuse.

Assuming now that an arrest has been made, what are the rights and duties of the arresting officer? First and foremost he may and should search the arrested person for any concealed weapons; this will be dealt with in more detail below under the topic of search and seizure.[17] He is also under the duty to take the arrested person to a designated place of detention for arrested individuals. Normally that would be a police station house. In some states he is under the duty, if he can, to use as means of conveyance a vehicle that will not allow the public to see the face of the person arrested. That is why patrol wagons normally do not have a completely open structure. He is also under the obligation, within a reasonable time, to bring the arrested person

15. See sec. 12 of the Model Arrest Act, drafted under the auspices of the Interstate Commission on Crime.

16. Sec. 2.　　　　　　　　　　　　17. See chap. iv.

before a magistrate. If the arrest was on a warrant, he should bring the prisoner and the warrant before the magistrate who issued the warrant—a step called "returning the warrant"—or, if this is not possible, then before some other magistrate of the same court. This step must, as stated above, be taken within a reasonable time. If it is not, the further detention of the arrested party will be open to attack on writ of habeas corpus. What constitutes a reasonable time, of course, tends to vary. For simplicity's sake judges often tend to formalize it somewhat by designating a set number of hours—say, twenty-four or forty-eight—as being normally the measure of reasonableness, with either a longer or a shorter measure possible in exceptional cases.[18] It has also been suggested that we might advance the system of bail to a time earlier than that at which it now begins by giving a very limited authority to desk sergeants to release on bail for the time interval between arrest and the bringing before the magistrate. The thought, of course, is that, if the desk sergeant had such authority, that would be a factor to take into account in measuring reasonable time and might somewhat extend the measure of that time.

It is—or, if locally the law is not clear on this point, it should be—the right of the arrested person to have legal counsel admitted to him at once after arrest. As will appear below, this is the period of maximum danger of abuses of various sorts, abuses especially dangerous to the first offender and the innocent accused, where the services of counsel are therefore particularly needed.

At this point reference might be made to an extremely common but wholly improper police procedure—that of arresting an individual and then releasing him without bringing him before a magistrate (say, because the police have become convinced of his guiltlessness or because he has sobered up). Once an arrest has been made, it is no longer lawful for the police to exercise any discretion so far as the retention or release of that individual is concerned. The obligation has then crystallized to bring him before a magistrate before the lapse of more than a

18. For an attempt to make the measure more precise see the Model Arrest Act, sec. 11.

reasonable time, and there is no alternative. The exercise of the judicial power by the police in releasing the individual is wholly extralegal. It is sometimes made even more clearly illegal by the additional factor that the police will impose a self-determined and completely unlawful punishment of their own. For instance, they may informally adopt the procedure of not bringing a drunk before the magistrate but of simply keeping such a person locked up until many hours beyond the time when he has sobered up and then figuratively and physically kicking him out. Here, then, is the combination of two illegalities: the failure to bring the individual before the magistrate and the determination of guilt and of so-called punishment and imposition of it by the police themselves.

Up to now it has been our consistent assumption that there can be only one way of beginning a criminal proceeding against any person—that is, by means of an arrest. In other words, physically grasping hold of his body and bringing that body into court was the only way to initiate the criminal proceedings. Such a view was understandable at a time when criminal law was restricted to situations regarded as very serious and when practically everything criminal was treated in a drastic way so far as punishment was concerned. The means used to start the proceedings were no more drastic than the importance of the proceedings warranted. But this underlying assumption is no longer true. Today there are a great many offenses of a minor nature where an arrest is entirely out of line with the degree of the offense. Because of this it becomes necessary to consider the possibility of initiating criminal proceedings by some method other than arrest. This other method is known as a "summons." A summons is a communication—normally in writing—informing an accused person that he is to appear in a certain court at a specified time, under penalty of arrest if he fails to appear, to answer to a charge made against him. Such a binding appointment with the magistrate may conceivably be made by the magistrate himself or by a police officer as a substitute for making an arrest.[19] Summonses have long been used in our law

19. When the summons comes from a police officer, it is usually known by its slang name, a "ticket."

system for the purpose of getting corporations charged with crimes into court, since in the nature of things it is impossible here to proceed by arrest. But summonses can also be used to advantage against a natural person, where the violation charged is not a serious one, unless the violator is a known criminal or is, for some other reason, likely to present a particularly great escape risk.[20]

The many advantages of summonses as against arrests make a convincing case for their widespread use. With the growth of cities and the resultant congestion there has been a corresponding growth in the number and variety of minor offenses and ordinance violations. To an extent never previously possible any one of us may find that he is unwittingly, but definitely, breaking the law. In such an event it may be wholly disproportionate to the offense to subject the offender to a method of procedure that may be far worse for him than the maximum punishment that he can get even on conviction. Yet that is exactly what the arrest and lockup may mean. Furthermore, this punishment is imposed on him in advance of trial and while he is still presumed to be innocent. We first administer the major part of the punishment and then inquire whether he is guilty. The more innocent he is, the more painful is the ordeal for him. In addition, where there has been an arrest, the arrested person, whether guilty or not, can secure provisional liberty only by means of bail. This itself is costly and may be more so than the fine that may finally be im-

20. The summons is the normal way in which violators of city ordinances are brought into court, but it should be explained at this point that technically the violation of a city ordinance is not a crime, even of a minor sort. It is often mistakenly believed that violators of city ordinances have thereby become minor criminals. This is probably due to the fact that a violator of the city ordinance may be deprived of his liberty and may be locked up. Actually in the theory of the law the violator of a city ordinance is merely committing a civil wrong against the artificial person called the "municipality," and the only difference between committing a wrong against a fellow-citizen and committing a wrong against the city is that the city has much greater enforcement advantages. The private person can no longer (as he once could) keep his debtor locked up until the debt is paid, but the municipality can and does lock up both those whom it accuses of violations and those who do not pay the fine that they owe it and may keep the latter incarcerated until the debt is worked out. The wrong still remains a mere civil, and not a criminal, one, although often because of these additional facts it is referred to as a "quasi-criminal" action.

posed. So far as he is concerned it is no whit different from the punishment itself. The use of the summons completely eliminates all this, since there is no deprivation of liberty and hence no need to make any arrangements to secure release.

Finally, the use of the summons may be the only way in which as a practical matter a minor statute can be enforced. If only arrest is available, it means calling into play the cumbersome machinery of taking the prisoner to the nearest call box and standing with him until the patrol wagon comes with its driver and its other officer. Three public servants are now being tied up in the arrest process and in transporting him in this expensive equipment to the police station, where further space must be used to lock him up and where the services of a fourth functionary, the lockup keeper, must be called on. All this may easily add up to a tremendous drain on police manpower. It may make it almost the practical duty of a good police officer who sees a minor offense being committed in his presence hastily to turn his head and look the other way. He may be showing a great deal better judgment by refusing to see what is going on than by starting all this disproportionately complex and expensive machinery going. This is true not only in violations of city ordinances but also in many minor crimes.

The main argument against the summons is, of course, that the accused may readily take to flight. But this argument loses all its force where the maximum punishment that could be imposed upon him, even if found guilty, is infinitesimal compared to the disadvantages that he would suffer if he became a fugitive from justice. It is ridiculous to suppose that in such a case there is any danger of flight.

To what extent, tnen, is the summons used? In part this depends on, and is a reflection of, the efficiency of any given police force. If we have a hidebound inefficient force, we may expect it to use the method of arrest, because that at least is sure-fire: the police grab the fellow and hang on to him. It has the merit of simplicity. The summons calls for a greater degree of efficiency because it rests on the ability of the police department first to warn the offender that he is going to be called on and then to track him down if he does not appear. So police efficiency and the use of the summons might well be regarded as more or less roughly correlated to each other.

Recent statistics on the extent of the use of the summons are not available, but there is no reason to suppose that those of a few years ago are no longer accurate. In that year the police forces in England, where the summons is very widely used, had occasion to prosecute a total of well over 600,000 persons for all types of offenses, great and small. Of these 600,000 persons, over 500,000 or more—accurately 82 per cent—were proceeded against by summons. The English dominions and colonies do not have quite so high a percentage but still have a high one. In this country the summons is widely used for only one type of offense, the traffic violation. Excluding traffic cases, but including all other cases of summonses, a typical large American city at the same time showed that summonses were used not in 82 per cent of the cases or in 50 per cent or in 5 per cent but in four-tenths of 1 per cent of them. In other words, the use of the summons is so small as practically not to be in the picture at all. Perhaps our forces are not so efficient as some of the European ones, and perhaps it is easier to escape police discovery here than in Europe, but it can hardly be believed that the difference in efficiency and conditions is as great as that.

What, then, is to account for so slight a use of the summons? It is only partly inefficiency. Sheer inertia, the habit of doing things as they have all along been done, is an even bigger factor. But the biggest factor—and least to the discredit of the police—is a real uncertainty as to how far the local law permits substituting the summons for arrest. To this the answer ought to be that, if there is any uncertainty as to its legality, it is time that the matter be cleared up and that we make sure that this method of procedure is a proper one. It may be added that under the recently adopted Federal Rules of Criminal Procedure the summons may now be used in any case, however serious, if the district attorney is willing and asks that it be employed.[21] It is for him, as the representative of the public, to determine whether in any given case it is adequate and safe.

21. Rule 4(a).

IV

POLICE INVESTIGATION

THE problems raised by police investigation of a real or supposed crime are in the main of so specialized a nature as to be
outside the range of a general discussion of criminal-law enforcement. Only two broad topics fall within this range. One of these
deals with the questioning of suspects and abuses connected with
it, and the other with the search for and seizure of incriminating
evidence. In that order these topics constitute all that will be
dealt with in this chapter.

QUESTIONING BY POLICE

The common law takes off from the broad principle not only
that anyone may ask anyone else any question that he wishes but
that the one questioned may with equal freedom answer or refuse
to answer as his interest or whim decides.[1] Obstinate and unex-
plained silence may give rise to unfavorable and legitimate inferences,[2] but, if the person questioned chooses to suffer this disadvantage, he is free to do so. In this very broad sense, then, the
questioning of arrested persons by the police is not per se improper. But it is also obvious that the questioning here is under
special circumstances that may possibly, or even probably, lead
to pressure or abuses of one sort or another by the questioner
against the one questioned.[3] Such pressure is usually referred
to by its slang name—the "third degree."

1. Obviously a general statement such as this should not be understood as
applying to its full extent to questions asked in the course of official proceedings, such as trials, legislative investigations, etc. In such proceedings there is a
duty to co-operate by answering, unless the answer will tend to incriminate the
speaker.
2. Here, too, qualification will be necessary when we deal with a defendant
who at his trial elects not to take the witness stand in his own behalf.
3. The terms "pressure" and "abuse" should be understood in the broadest
sense, from the crudest of physical pain on down to much more subtle
methods. They may well include mere long-protracted questioning by relays of
police. In some aspects of our problem they may even extend to the granting of
undue favors in return for desired admissions.

The National Commission on Law Observance and Enforce-ment[4] concluded in 1931 that use of the third degree was wide-spread,[5] and there is no reason to suppose that conditions have signally changed since then. It is a problem that we tend to anes-thetize ourselves from by the name we give it. The term "third degree" does not sound anywhere near so nasty and unpleasant as does more realistic language (viz., the use of torture in law en-forcement). We likewise tend to deaden ourselves to considera-tion of it because we assume (often mistakenly) that "it doesn't happen to people like us." However revolting such an attitude may be to any right-minded person, there is no use in denying that this attitude exists and that it is a real factor when we try to meet the problem. Not only is such a position revolting; it is not even intelligently selfish. If the pressure to solve a crime is strong enough so that a police force which is in the habit of practicing the third degree feels that public opinion will stand for it, it will obviously see no reason not to practice it on your type and my type. It is only that they will want to be sure that they can get away with it (and with more prosperous victims this may not so often be the case). But in the very highly publicized crimes, which are for that reason regarded by the police as of great im-portance, it may well be that they will reach upward into areas that ordinarily would be immune from it, so that even this selfish attitude is at the best only correct to a limited degree. One is en-tirely warranted, then, in saying that both from the humanitarian and even from the selfish viewpoint it is a problem for all of us.

Before going on to consider what can be done to abolish the third degree, however, it will be necessary to describe in more detail why it is so seriously objectionable and even before that to point out that there is a so-called practical argument in its favor. It does often produce results, and, since its successes are more likely to be publicized than its failures, these successes are given a wholly unreal weight. Whether this "practical" argument is sound or not, it remains a factor and a big obstacle to overcome in our efforts to abolish this abuse. The arguments against torture

4. Popularly known as the Wickersham Commission.
5. *Report 11*, p. 4.

are not limited to the humanitarian one—conclusive though that alone should be. There are numerous "practical" ones as well.

One argument is that it tends to render the police less efficient as an over-all matter, because it is a reliance on easy and crude methods of work instead of on time-consuming efficient methods. In theory there is nothing to prevent a police force engaged in solving a particular crime from using simultaneously both the method of the third degree and scientific crime-detection methods. But actually one will never find, or only very rarely find, the two methods of approach being used side by side at the same time by the same police department. To quote from the National Commission's report: "As the New York prosecutor . . . said, 'It is a short cut and makes the police lazy and unenterprising.' Or, as another official . . . remarked: 'If you use your fists you are not so likely to use your wits.' "[6]

The department's thought-process and its normal pattern of behavior will take one course or the other; but, just as we cannot at one and the same time have a police captain typical of the modern policeman and also typical of the old-style "copper," so the headship—and, through the headship of the force, the man-power—will think in terms of one procedure or in terms of the other. It will not think in terms of both simultaneously. So a very real cost item is the promotion of inefficient methods of action at the sacrifice of modern and efficient methods. Akin and very closely allied to this is the argument that it brutalizes the police force and makes it into the merely repressive agency that too many people in any event believe it to be. Another objection is that, if practiced with sufficient viciousness, it may induce on the part of the victim not merely true admissions but false ones as well, in order to terminate the torture. Thus it renders all admissions and confessions more or less suspect, and at its worst we have the phenomenon (by no means a rare one) of jurors who, after their tour of duty, will freely admit that "they wouldn't believe a police officer under oath" or give credit to any admission made to police officers.

It is a pretty serious state of affairs when the police by their

6. *Ibid.*

own methods make their results completely suspect on the part of the public generally or, at any rate, on the part of the segment of the public that is serving as jurors. Yet that is a consequence of the belief that false as well as true admissions and confessions may be elicited. Incidentally, it is, of course, a wonderful means for the person who right after his arrest has made a true admission or confession to try to get away from it by playing on this general belief that the third degree is practiced, by the simple device of asserting that he was the victim of it. This alienation of the sympathy of the public is in the long run even more serious than just from the angle of the jurors' not believing confessions or admissions.

The alienation of public sympathy (or, to put it from the other side of the shield, the tendency of the public in many instances to sympathize with the offender, not only because we generally and normally sympathize with the underdog, but even more because some of us are hostile to the police) in and of itself is so serious for the police that one can hardly overestimate it. It is not generally realized on the part of the public how much of successful police work takes the very undramatic form of working on leads voluntarily supplied by the public. An anonymous letter gives a lead as to where a suspect may be found, or a citizen voluntarily comes in and supplies valuable information. True, that form of crime detection is not given widespread publicity because it is neither dramatic, on the one hand, nor particularly likely to feed the self-esteem of the police department, on the other; thus, we do not see many references to it and far less than its importance warrants. But it remains true that in crime detection the voluntary leads given by members of the community are perhaps the biggest of all the various sources of clues and information that the police may have. That source of information will progressively tend to dry up just as far as these members of the public are alienated from the police by third-degree practices. The citizen tends to think of the situation more and more in terms of asking himself why he should by his voluntary act make someone suffer the kind of things that people of that sort are likely to (or that he believes they are likely to) suffer. And so he keeps quiet and withholds his co-operation.

Contrast this with the situation in Great Britain, where the third degree, if not wholly unknown, is at any rate practiced much less often and less violently. It is not a mere unrelated accident that the British police receive a degree of public help and co-operation never dreamed of in the United States. This is probably the biggest single price that we must pay for the occasional successes of the third degree. Likewise not to be disregarded is its effect not only on the public generally but on the victim of such experiences. It is a major lesson in bad citizenship, featuring a mass of harmful material—discrimination against minority groups, distrust of the government, flagrant disregard of law, etc. And if we have a victim whose first and only contact with the law is along these lines, it is a lesson in civics in reverse that can hardly be overestimated in importance. One does not by any means have to be a sentimentalist wholly and heartily to disapprove of it, even while admitting that it does produce immediate results in individual cases.

What, then, can be done to eliminate, or at least to reduce, the third degree? Many reforms have been proposed, and it is far easier to criticize than to advance any cure-all of one's own. It has been suggested that it be expressly provided by law that any assault and battery committed for the purpose of eliciting a confession or an admission or other information shall be punished more severely than assault and battery cases generally are punished. For example, such conduct shall not be merely a misdemeanor with a jail sentence but shall be a felony. Where such statutes have been enacted, they have, however, proved the deadest of dead letters. No criminal prosecution is self-starting in the sense of not needing human beings to get it going. And here the human beings are just simply not going to start it. The prosecuting attorney does not propose to alienate those valuable co-operators of his, whose help he needs, by lightly initiating this kind of a proceeding. If it is initiated, the police are not going to be co-operative in this blow at their own structure. Police esprit de corps is a very highly developed thing. Add to this that there are very few, if any, witnesses,[7] and one can readily see why this particular method of coping with the third degree has proved entirely valueless.

Damage suits against the offending officers are somewhat more effective. But, very often, the police officer is judgment-proof, so that, as far as actual financial results are concerned, the victim has merely the satisfaction of having obtained an unenforceable judgment. Possibly the suit might include a malice count, under which the judgment-debtor may be locked up until he pays, thus adding considerably to the judgment's force. In short, the damage suit is a not wholly ineffective means of repression or a complete dead letter like the criminal action, but it remains far from being a full solution. There are other measures that likewise may be of some help. Making all confessions given to police officers automatically inadmissible in evidence would be very effective, but there are three serious objections to such a rule: (1) it might result in the inadmissibility even of a wholly voluntary confession; (2) it would mean that no one could question a suspect;[8] and (3) it incorrectly assumes that the sole purpose of the third degree is to elicit statements, by way of confession or admission, that can be used against the victim in court. This,

7. It is a common misconception that in a department addicted to the third degree practically every police officer will participate in it or, at the very least, will have firsthand knowledge of it. The contrary is much more likely to be the case, at least so far as the more serious instances are concerned. Even in such a force it is likely to be only the selected few who take care of this function. Thus a typical example would probably be along these lines: An individual is arrested and is suspected of participating in a serious crime which the police are under great pressure to clear up. He is asked a number of questions, and it soon appears that the questioning is getting nowhere. Then, informally, it is decided to let Officers Doe and Roe try their luck at questioning. It may even be that these two happen time and again to be the ones who are looked to at such a stage as this. They are left alone with the prisoner, and after an interval they report that he is now willing to talk or that he has signed a statement. Nobody asks any questions. "What you do not know won't hurt you." Then, if there is any investigation, who knows about this at first hand, and who is a potential witness? Only Officer Doe and Officer Roe and the interested party himself, the victim. So even in a force in which the third degree is said to be "widespread" it is by no means likely that every member of the personnel participates in it, but rather merely that it may, and frequently does, occur on the part of those who are charged with it. And this, of course, makes its suppression vastly more difficult.

8. It will be pointed out later that at the trial a defendant can, by refusing to take the witness stand, prevent any question from being asked of him.

however, is not the case. It may equally well be used to secure from the suspect (or from some third person not himself suspected but thought to have valuable information) leads for further investigations, by means of which wholly new evidence will be uncovered. In such a case there may be no plan or wish at all to use the statement directly in evidence, and hence making it inadmissible would be wholly irrelevant.

Again, it is often suggested that we should require more detailed records of all the events occurring between the arrest and the time when the individual is brought before the magistrate, because it is during that time that the major danger occurs. After he has been turned over to the sheriff at the county jail, the danger is comparatively small. But the obvious difficulty there is: Who will keep these records? The very people against whom the records are to be used are the ones who have the information that is to be incorporated in them; and, while they may keep detailed records of everything that occurs from the arrest until he is brought before the magistrate, a period of time of greater or shorter length may elapse between the time when he is in fact deprived of his liberty and the time when he is first formally booked in the records of the station. Who controls what happens during this interval of uncertain length? A wider use of the public-defender system may hold out some help, because it means that there is presumably somebody much more readily available who will concern himself with the rights of detained or arrested individuals. All these proposals would help. It is simply that they are not panaceas.

A more revolutionary suggestion that would go a much greater way toward solving the problem but that would be very difficult to apply under our usual constitutional provisions would consist in allowing some public functionary, be it the police or, according to continental European law systems, a subordinate member of the judicial hierarchy, lawfully to question and cross-examine arrested persons or in permitting that he be questioned at the trial. By permitting the lawful, controlled doing of that which the law now utterly excludes, it is contended that doing it extralegally will be made much less necessary and hence less prevalent. It is urged that, since the public demands that the police get results, it must give them the means to do so and that, if this seems drastic, it is nonetheless true that there is very often greater real protection in allowing greater privileges to law-enforcement officers and then controlling them than there is in imposing restrictions which prove nearly impossible to observe. The great difficulty here, however, is that this proposal calls for constitutional changes of so extreme a sort that, practically speaking, it would seem to be out of the question.

Perhaps the only real hope lies in the slow process of building up a more educated public opinion, so that public opinion itself may demand that it be abolished. In the long run, public opinion will solve a great many problems that cannot be solved any other way. But it is a painfully and discouragingly slow method, and one sometimes wonders whether any progress in educating public opinion is being made at all. At the risk of some repetition this may be made clearer. The advocate of the use of the third degree is always able to point out (and, unfortunately, correctly) that one more instance will not make any difference. Let the reform begin tomorrow but not today with today's pressing problem. And unhappily there is no convincing rejoinder to him. Almost certainly the evil will be with us for a long time, and it is only in the slow developing of a wiser public opinion, on the one hand, and the rise of younger police forces, more aware of the importance of efficient methods, on the other, that we can look for an ultimate solution.

SEARCH AND SEIZURE

The subject of search and seizures involves so many complexities, so many divergent views, and so many changes and developments that any really adequate analysis is impossible here. Even when confining one's self to generalities, it will probably prove impossible to avoid statements that are not, in some respect, doubtful or even erroneous somewhere. This word of caution should, therefore, be understood as applicable throughout this topic.

Our topic breaks up into two parts: (*a*) the criteria by which to decide whether a given search was or was not proper and (*b*) the consequences resulting from a decision that a given search was not proper. They will be taken up in that order.

The basic source of our law as to the propriety of any given search is the constitutional provision, be it state or federal constitution, that governs the officers, be they state or federal, who are making the search. Probably invariably it will be found that this constitutional provision is extremely general in its terms and merely provides that a search is proper if it is "reasonable" and improper if it is "unreasonable." It is left to the courts, with very little additional guidance, to determine what is reasonable and what is unreasonable. Thus it is at once converted into a question of policy. How has this policy question been handled?[9]

Prior to prohibition there were comparatively few cases in the highest courts that had to do with the allowable scope of searches. Under the view taken in many, if not most, states the evidence that had been obtained, whether the search was a reasonable one or not, could in any event be used against the person; therefore, there was on the whole little to be gained by successfully showing that the search in question was an unreasonable one, and accordingly the issue was not very often raised. The victim was remitted to his civil action against the person who had unreasonably searched him, but so far as the criminal law was concerned what came to their mill was grist. They made use of it in any event. Furthermore, on the whole, public opinion was not very radically or strongly concerned about this problem. The old abuses of a century and a half ago that had led the people of those days to a feeling of great anxiety about searches had been so effectively met by our constitutional safeguards that even memory of the abuses had very largely disappeared, and so, on the part of the generality of the citizens, there was no great concern about unreasonable, and therefore illegal, searches. So far as the wrongdoer was concerned, little sympathy was felt for the person who, on the basis of the search, was disclosed to be a criminal. As was mentioned above in the case of the third degree, when it is practiced on a palpably guilty person, it takes someone of fine balance and judgment not to be influenced by that fact. So it was, too, with the person who on a search was shown to be guilty

9. The treatment of this part of our topic is based very largely on an excellent article by J. B. Waite, "Reasonable Search and Seizure," in 86 U. of Penn. L. Rev. 623 (1938), where a much more detailed discussion can be found.

and to possess the incriminating items. As for the law-abiding citizen, he probably was not searched very often, and, if he was, normally he did not greatly object, or, if he did object, public opinion was that this was little enough to ask of him by way of co-operation. In either event there was comparatively little concern about illegal searches.

With the prohibition amendment, however, matters changed, and problems a:d implications were discovered that were never dreamed of when that amendment was advocated and put into effect. A great many people began to fear a search who had never feared one before, because they were involved in lawbreaking when they had previously never broken the law. Necessarily, that new-found concern about improper search in due time reached and influenced the courts, because public opinion inevitably in the long run gets itself reflected in the attitude of the courts, too. The public generally, and the courts in particular, attached a much greater importance to the question of the legality of a search than before. Cases grew much more numerous, and much more importance was attached to them. Whether a search was reasonable, and therefore legal, had a vastly increased significance.

Three fact patterns had already long ago been found "reasonable"—a search made with consent, a personal search of an arrested person, and a search made pursuant to a search warrant. All three will be considered in more detail below. There are, however, a great many other situations in which the law has by no means crystallized and become definite. Here the tendency on the part of most courts has been simply to announce that a particular search then under scrutiny by them was or was not a "reasonable" one. They have evolved their answer simply out of their inner consciousness, with apparently no particular analysis of the criteria to be applied in determining whether it was reasonable or unreasonable. The answer should in fact depend on whether, all things considered, including the interest not only of the individual but of society as a whole too, it is desirable to permit (and thereby to encourage) a given sort of search or whether the contrary is true. This necessarily involves the careful weighing of a mass of conflicting values (including, it may be noted, the difficulty or even impossibility of enforcing the law if the search is branded unreasonable) and is no simple task. But it is one that must be done if the determination of reasonableness is to be adequately arrived at. A snap judgment, based simply on personal emotion, will not do it. And here, also, too sharp a restriction on police activity, too much of a strait-jacket interpretation of the law when we are demanding of the police the achievement of results made impossible by our own strictness, is probably the surest way to promote the very abuses that we seek to prevent.[10]

There are, however, as was stated above, a number of fact patterns that have been recognized as constituting reasonable search. One of these is where the party who (or whose property) is to be searched has given his consent. It goes without saying that the consent, to be effective, must have been given with full knowledge of what was occurring and must be entirely voluntary.

Likewise it is always held reasonable to search the person of someone who has been lawfully arrested. Thereby there may be a timely discovery of a concealed weapon or a means of escape or of articles connected with the crime for which the arrest is being made. In some states when a person is arrested inside a house, it is also proper to search the room in which the arrest is being made. This undeniably constitutes a large extension, since the original, basic consideration of the safety of the arrester is almost wholly gone. Thus it is an extension that not all courts

---

10. The following, it is submitted, is an example of unrealistic approach: A proper search is being made (say, of an arrested man for a concealed weapon, or of a room specified in a search warrant for specified articles). In the making of this proper search, articles are come upon that do not fall into the above categories but that do tend to show involvement in some other crime (e.g., articles known to have been stolen). It has been held in some cases that the seizure of these unrelated articles would be unreasonable. Such a holding means entire forgetfulness of the whole reason for protection against unreasonable search. That reason is to guard ourselves against arbitrary action by governmental authorities. Obviously, that does not apply here, and to hold that there is unreasonableness here is to disclose how completely the sound public policy basis has been forgotten. A refreshing contrast, in its awareness of practical considerations, is the suggestion by the United States Supreme Court that the search of an automobile may call for more-than-ordinary liberality. The reason is obvious. The need for speedy action is much greater. The practical considerations are very different, and the area of what is "reasonable" becomes different too. Another extension—increasingly urged—of the area of what is "reasonable" is that the search of someone merely to see whether he is carrying a concealed weapon shall automatically and necessarily be shown to have been reasonable by the discovery of such a weapon.

have been willing to make. A few, on the other hand, have thrown out hints of even greater liberality—hints that there might be a proper search of other rooms than the one in which the arrest took place. All that, however, is more or less on the conjectural side.[11]

In the third place, a search is always reasonable when it is made in accordance with the terms of a valid search warrant. Such a warrant will specify the place or places to be searched and the articles that form the objective of the search. Ordinarily the search must be made in the daytime only. Finally, the search must be made within a reasonable time of the issuance of the warrant; the latter after such a time limit loses its force.

Let us assume now, that evidence was obtained by an improper (i.e., an unreasonable) search. What are the consequences of the impropriety? There is general agreement that the officer who is at fault may be sued for damages. This, however, may prove a barren remedy, partly because of the difficulty of showing monetary damages and partly because of the strong possibility that the officer will have little property available to satisfy such judgment as may be obtained against him.[12] The suit for damages may, therefore, prove only a partially effective mechanism to discourage improper searches. A much more effective one is to exclude, at a trial, any evidence obtained by means of an illegal search, no matter how valuable and convincing it might be, simply

11. Proponents of enlarging the area of allowable search have often sought to achieve their goal indirectly by attempting to increase the number of situations in which an arrest may properly be made (and hence, as a consequence of the arrest, the search of the arrested individual). Much less often have there been attempts directly to declare, by statute, that given searches were to be regarded as reasonable. Such statutes must, obviously, cross a difficult constitutional hurdle. A legislature cannot deprive one of a constitutional guaranty by the indirect device of declaring that to be reasonable which, in the court's view, is unreasonable and therefore forbidden. The constitutional problem is discussed by J. B. Waite, "Public Policy and the Arrest of Felons," in 31 U. of Mich. L. Rev. 749 (1933).

12. Making the government unit for whom the officer made the improper search also liable would meet this difficulty. Legislatures have, however, been very hesitant to impose on such units any liability for the improper conduct of their employees. Without such legislation the usual court reaction has been that, when he acts improperly, the employee automatically ceases to act *as an employee* and so ceases to represent his master.

because it had been improperly obtained.[13] This is the position taken by the federal courts and some of the states, though not by another group of states. Accordingly, the two views are referred to, somewhat misleadingly, as, respectively, the federal and the state rules.

The advocates of the federal view contend that the objective of the Constitution to discourage improper searches can only be effectively obtained by the exclusion of the evidence. If it may be used, then we are no longer giving the citizen the full value of the guaranty that has been extended to him, because the possibility of a damage suit against the officer who committed the search illegally is not enough of a deterrent to stop him from illegally searching. If we really want the guaranty to be effective, we must say that, when the improper action takes place, we will as nearly as possible wipe it off the slate; and that means the exclusion of any use of it as evidence in the courtroom. True, that incidentally provides a windfall for an undeserving citizen; it means that somebody who has no claim on our sympathy may go free. Undoubtedly, this is a high price to pay, but it is worth the price. In the same way, many of the safeguards that we have built up to prevent the conviction of innocent people may operate occasionally to protect from conviction a definitely guilty person. Furthermore, the law is placed in a most unfavorable light if it is willing to take the benefit of that which it declares was illegally obtained. By so doing, it in fact participates as a partner in the search. Confessions illegally obtained (say, by the third degree) are not admitted in evidence, and neither should this evidence be admitted.

Advocates of the state rule, on the other hand, argue that after all the constitutional provision merely forbids certain searches and says that such searches are trespasses. It does not speak of any consequence beyond that, and ordinarily the conse-

13. This view necessarily raises a further, and difficult, question, which will be only suggested here: How far down the line shall we go in rejecting evidence indirectly tainted by illegality? Let us assume that an illegal search discloses certain clues and leads for investigation which would not otherwise have been known to the police. These clues are then investigated in an entirely legal manner. Shall their results, too, be rejected? Where should the line be drawn? This difficult problem does not arise if even illegally obtained evidence is admitted. The problem is discussed in *People* v. *Martin*, 382 Ill. 192 (1942).

quence of a trespass is merely the possibility of suing the guilty individual for the damages sustained. Why should this trespass be given consequences of an entirely different and much greater sort? The argument that the law will be brought into disrepute by taking advantage of and using the illegal search is incorrect. The law is brought into much more disrepute when citizens see John Doe, who is discovered to have a house full of stolen goods, go free on the basis of what the general run of citizens will consider a mere technicality, for which they have no sympathy. As for the argument that the law is conniving in illegality, it is answered by the statement (more or less convincing) that, as soon as the officer begins to search illegally, he automatically makes himself a private citizen and that therefore the state is not a participant in, or involved in, his illegal search. Furthermore, says this view, it is not proper to exclude the evidence on the supposed analogy of our excluding confessions obtained by third-degree methods. Such confessions are excluded because the circumstances that make the confession an involuntary one are also circumstances that affect the reliability of the confession. We do not have confidence in the truth of the confession, but that is not the case in regard to illegally obtained tangible things; the illegality of our obtaining these things does not have the slightest effect on their persuasiveness as evidence against the offender.[14]

One concluding point needs to be made as to the choice between the federal and the state rules. The arguments made are all abstract, in the sense that they do not ask the most important question of all: How do the two rules work?[15] Does the federal rule, tying officers' hands as it certainly does, constitute an absolutely necessary restraint on the police? In states following the state rule is there far more unreasonable searching? The adoption of the federal rule certainly has meant that we have sacrificed a

14. The arguments pro and con are considered in detail in two articles, taking divergent viewpoints, by Albert J. Harno, "Evidence Obtained by Illegal Search and Seizure," in 19 Ill. L. Rev. 303 (1925), and by Thomas E. Atkinson, "Admissibility of Evidence Obtained through Unreasonable Searches and Seizures," in 25 Col. L. Rev. 11 (1925).

15. The failure to consider this primary, practical question reminds one strongly of the similar failure, discussed above, to give adequate attention to the same practical question in determining what is, and what is not, to be regarded as reasonable.

very definite and provable social advantage in regard to law enforcement. Is there in fact a corresponding gain? Perhaps, and perhaps not. But this is the kind of evaluation that must be made before we can jump to any conclusion one way or the other. And it is this, rather than abstractions, that should determine our answer.

One final word is necessary in order to restrict to its proper limits this comment on search and seizure. The constitutional provision is regarded not as sweepingly prohibiting all unreasonable searches but as a restriction applicable only on government officers. Thus where a private person improperly breaks into a home and carries on improper search, this is not within the scope of the guaranty. Therefore, even in a jurisdiction following the federal rule, evidence so obtained would be admissible.[16]

16. It has been argued that this constitutes one further argument against the logical soundness of the federal rule, because, it is said, as soon as the search is made illegally, then ipso facto the searching officer becomes a private person, and so the constitutional prohibition no longer applies to him. The courts taking the federal view have, however, refused to undo their own decisions by driving logic this far.

V

THE MAGISTRATE

Passing reference has already been made to roles played by judges in the proceedings up to the present stage.[1] Thus it is they who issue warrants of arrest and search warrants, and after an arrest has been made it is a judge before whom the arrested person must promptly be brought. There are a number of other functions which the judge must, or may have to, perform at this early stage in the case. These can be grouped under the headings "Summary Trial," "Preliminary Examination," and "Setting and Approving Bail." They will be taken up in that order.

These functions can be carried on by anyone in the judicial hierarchy, from top to bottom, but in fact they are almost invariably turned over entirely to those in the lowest rank—justices of the peace, judges of the local municipal court, etc. A judicial official engaged in one of these functions is normally referred to, not by his usual title (whatever that may be), but as a "magistrate." In many places, especially in large urban centers, there is so much work of this sort to be done that certain judicial officers devote their full time to it (viz., they function only as magistrates). With this we can proceed to the tasks that a magistrate may be called on to perform.

SUMMARY TRIAL

If the offense with which the arrested person is charged is a petty one,[2] it is the magistrate's duty to try the case and dispose of it, either by a conviction or by a discharge. Numerically these cases form a huge proportion of the total number of criminal

---

1. "Judge" as here used applies to all judicial officers, whatever their rank. It therefore includes justices of the peace.
2. Typical of this rather loose category are such offenses as drunkenness and disorderly conduct, soliciting to prostitution, petty gambling, minor traffic violations, etc.

charges, and from the standpoint of sociology they are unques
tionably of great importance—indeed, they are conceivably of
more social significance than the major crimes. They do not,
however, call for any further comment here as to the criminal
law and its administration.

PRELIMINARY EXAMINATION

If the charge is more than a petty one, it is automatically beyond the authority of the magistrate to try. Instead it is his duty
to conduct what is known as a preliminary examination.[3]

The purpose and present status of the preliminary examination
can be best understood by considering its history and the great
changes that it has undergone. Indeed, the very fact that its original purpose and its principal present one are so largely opposed
must be discerned in order to understand much of the present
confusion in it. Historically, unlike most of the stages in law enforcement that we shall consider, the preliminary examination
emerges from a definite statute. It is the creation of the legislature
(viz., parliament) and not of the common law. This statute is 1
and 2 Philip & Mary, chapter 13, section 4, and was enacted in
1554. The statute was the reflection of the fact that at that time
(and indeed for close to another three hundred years) there was
no organized governmental agency faced with the task of prosecuting criminals. There was no prosecuting attorney in England
at that time, and, from the standpoint of the preliminary examination even more significant, there was no police force. There
was literally no participation on the part of government in the
criminal proceedings at this stage. This necessarily operated very
largely to the benefit of undeserving persons, because it might be
possible to do away with incriminating evidence, or the gathering
of evidence might not begin until it was too late.

The situation in England was a great contrast to that prevailing
in the continental European countries. In those countries, then
as now, the government has as part of its structure a functionary
variously named in the various countries but most commonly
known here by his French name—"judge of instruction." He is a

---

3. The preliminary examination is often, but mistakenly, referred to as the
"arraignment." The latter term, however, when correctly used, refers only to a
wholly separate and much later stage in the proceedings (see chap. xii, below).

judge in name only. It is his function to examine the accused person soon after his arrest and through that examination to bring out the truth—to discover what the involvements, if any, of the accused person are with the crime and, if he is involved, what the evidence is against him. It is no doubt an examination for the benefit of the accused in one sense, but in one sense only; if he is not involved, then the effort to find out the involvement resolves itself into an effort to demonstrate his innocence. But it is an examination on the theory of "let the chips fall where they may." And since presumably the person was arrested only because there was some reason to suspect that he was involved, the examination is likely to proceed very much in fact along the lines of a cold-blooded inquisition into his guilt and to consist in efforts to question him so searchingly as to lead to the discovery of useful evidence against him. In that sense, then, it is really a part of the prosecuting machinery, if by prosecuting machinery we take the large-scale viewpoint that the prosecutor is desirous not only of prosecuting the guilty but of demonstrating the innocence of the innocent.[4]

The English law, prior to the above statute, never had any such device. This deep difference is due to the fact that there are two fundamentally different ways of looking at the judge's part in a criminal proceeding and, indeed, of looking at the proceeding itself. One way—that mainly prevailing on the Continent—is that the proceeding is one in which the government (including the judge) seeks to investigate a certain situation and to apply those measures that investigation discloses to be necessary. This may consist in turning the accused person loose if the investigation discloses that he is not involved. It may consist in exercising vengeance on him if it is disclosed that he is involved and the vengeance purpose of punishment prevails; or of punishing him for the deterrence of himself and others, or of applying reformative measures, if we are thinking in modern terms. But, in any event, it is the government's interest to investigate the situation and to do the needful as that term "needful" is then and there understood. The judge (both the magistrate and, later on, the

4. For those able to read French, Edmond Brieux's *La Robe rouge* will be an interesting demonstration of the abuses of which a judge of instruction might be guilty.

trial judge), being a participant in the government, is therefore a participant also in the resolving of this problem. This is usually called the "investigative doctrine" of criminal procedure. The investigative procedure, then, to sum it all up, visualizes the courtroom proceedings as basically consisting of two parties, and only two. The accused constitutes one party; the government, personified by the prosecuting attorney and the judge (and the jury, if there is one), constitute the other party. This other party is not interested in a partisan way but is interested in development of what actually occurred. There is no room, logically, for any third party.

In contrast to this is the "accusatory doctrine," which is the one typically followed by the English common law, which visualizes the proceedings as a three-party affair, just as a piece of civil litigation is a three-party affair. One party we call in civil cases the "plaintiff"; in criminal cases we call it the "prosecution" (or, to use the English term, the "crown"). The party against whom the lawsuit is brought, be it a civil suit or a criminal one, is of course called the "defendant." Here, then, are two adverse parties to litigation. Exactly along the same basic pattern as in civil cases these two parties are now before the judge (again including the jury), and the judge should feel himself a complete stranger equally to either party—as much to the prosecution as to the defendant. It is a three-party affair in the courtroom,[5] with one party accusing the other. At no stage of it has the judge any obligation, or even any right, to participate as a partisan. Thus under the common-law system the judge is an aloof figure—an umpire. He takes little or no part in the witness-questioning procedure[6] and in many states scarcely any more in the selection of the jury.

5. So completely was this view once taken for granted that a lawsuit could only be brought with the consent of both parties, just as today we feel that it takes the consent of both parties in order to have a dispute submitted to arbitration. The judge was merely an official arbitrator and inquirer. It need hardly be said that potent devices were invented to make sure that the defendant would be under no temptation to withhold his consent. These will be described in chap. xii, "The Arraignment."

6. His role here will be treated in more detail in chap. xiii. In the European systems the judge is the one who does normally all the questioning of witnesses, with the attorneys doing no questioning or very little, and that only with the judge's consent.

The Statute of Philip and Mary was a recognition by Parliament that there was some merit in the Continental viewpoint and that it might be desirable to have a limited degree of governmental participation here. Accordingly it created the device of the so-called "preliminary examination." Under it all arrested persons were to be brought before the magistrate and to be examined by him. He would then try to discover what evidence he could use against them and see to it that that evidence was not lost. If the evidence against the accused was so weak that, taken all in all, he found no probable cause to think that the accused *might* be guilty—not that he *was* guilty—it was the magistrate's duty to discharge him. But if he felt that the matter was, at the least, in genuine doubt, it was his duty to have the accused held for further proceedings.[7] Thus holding him came to be referred to colloquially as "binding him over"[8]—an expression used more often, however, in England than in this country.

As soon, however, as it was recognized that the magistrate could and should discharge an accused person who was clearly innocent of any offense, the preliminary examination took on a different or, at any rate, an additional role. It became no longer solely a prosecuting device but a protecting one at the same time. These partially inconsistent and conflicting purposes have, as was said above, been responsible for some of the confused and inconsistent thinking that characterizes this subject. In the ensuing centuries the protective aspect of the preliminary examination has come more and more to the fore. More and more, in the course of time, people have come to think of the preliminary examination, not as a prosecuting device, but as a device intended for the primary (or, so some people would believe, for the sole) purpose of separating the wheat from the chaff just as quickly as possible—a device to secure the freedom of the innocent as quickly as possible.

And so we find writers today saying quite properly what would have seemed utterly ridiculous to the lawyers of 1554, namely, that the accused may not be "deprived" of his "right"

7. These will be described in chap. vii, "The Grand Jury."
8. The preliminary examination is, therefore, sometimes called a "bind-over," and that term is often used to describe the magistrate's decision to have the accused held.

to a preliminary examination. The accused persons of 1554 would have been most willing to have been deprived of this stage as quickly and as thoroughly as possible! Thus we have an institution that, because of the vitality of the English legal philosophy and its accusatory analysis, has undergone an almost complete change in the course of the centuries. It might be difficult to find any more effective illustration of the way in which unrealized traditions and ways of thinking can make headway even against measures deliberately adopted to block such traditions and in the course of a century or two or three turn the modification completely around, so that in the end we discover that, as the French say, "the more things change, the more they are the same." (It should not be assumed from this, however, that the preliminary examination has wholly lost its prosecutory function. Even today it is in some small degree a prosecuting device, as will be indicated below.)

How, then, does this device function today? It commences, as we have seen, with the accused person being brought before the magistrate. Has he the right to testify in his own behalf, to bring in witnesses, to have counsel to advise him and speak for him? All these questions were, at the outset, when the device was first adopted, unhesitatingly answered with a "No." The judge might ask him questions if he wished. The magistrate might hear witnesses if he chose, but this was not in any sense a trial. The accused could not take any affirmative steps in his own behalf. He could not have anyone heard unless the magistrate was willing. And certainly he had no right to the aid and advice of counsel when the magistrate was merely determining whether the case should be dismissed or bound over. In the course of time, more or less completely, all this has changed, although it would be rash to assert that this has occurred everywhere in its entirety.[9] Thus, in practice and largely also in legal theory, most or all of these questions have been resolved in the defendant's favor, so that he is now regarded as entitled to tell his story, to call witnesses, to speak in his own behalf, and probably also to be repre-

9. For a much more detailed treatment of the legal problems involved here (and, indeed, throughout this book) the reader is referred to a clear and excellent treatise by Lester B. Orfield, *Criminal Procedure from Arrest to Appeal* (New York: New York University Press, 1947).

sented by counsel. It might be felt that this makes the preliminary examination scarcely more or less than a form of minor trial of the merits of the case. Superficially and in a certain sense this is true. However, the magistrate will constantly keep in mind that it is not necessary for him to be convinced beyond a reasonable doubt of the guilt of the accused person. He is under the duty to bind him over as soon as he is inclined on the whole to believe that there is probable cause to suppose that he may be guilty. That is enough to warrant further proceedings. This is not only in theory but in fact a very different thing from being convinced beyond a reasonable doubt.

Since he binds over if he feels that there is probable cause, he may become convinced that there is such probable cause long before all the possible witnesses, who will be heard later on at the trial, have been heard by him. Even if the defendant with his witnesses casts much doubt on the testimony of the prosecution witnesses, there may still be enough to constitute probable cause and to call upon the triers of the facts to determine which set of witnesses is telling the truth. So far as he is concerned, there would be no point in hearing further prosecution witnesses.

As was stated above, the preliminary examination still serves a prosecuting purpose. That purpose of course no longer consists in an inquisitorial examination of an accused who wishes to remain silent,[10] but there is another purpose of real importance. The case may be of such a nature that the prosecuting attorney realizes that he is dealing with witnesses who, while now willing to co-operate with him, are, from his experience in past cases of the same sort, very likely to be reachable—by threats, by money persuasion, etc.—by the defendant or the gang to which the latter belongs, so that they will not "stand up" when it comes to the trial (viz., tell the same story with the same degree of forcefulness). Naturally he desires as quickly as possible to get these witnesses on record, in order that, if later on they tell a different or much weaker story, he will be able to confront them on cross-examination with their earlier conflicting testimony. True, he

10. If of his own accord he chooses to take the witness stand, he can, of course, be searchingly questioned, in the hope of producing some damaging admission or information.

might also be able to show inconsistency with statements informally made to him or to police officers, but obviously this would be nowhere near so persuasive or damning a disagreement as would be the case if he can get them on record on oath in the open courtroom of the magistrate. And the mere fact that it is so easy to disclose any subsequent weakening will to that extent also lessen the likelihood of such weakening. Thus it would seem that an accused person should not be allowed to waive a preliminary examination without the prosecutor's consent. But we have moved so far from thinking of it as, in part, a prosecuting device that in many states the latter's consent is not required.[11]

From all the foregoing a few consequences can be developed. Since the examination is merely part of the process of the public making up its mind as to whether to bring a lawsuit of a criminal nature and is not itself a part of that suit (at least in the strictly theoretical sense), there is nothing to prevent a complaint from being dismissed, and then at a later date having a second complaint lodged against a person, with a second preliminary examination. This is not a case of double jeopardy, because, in so far as the law is concerned, there has not yet been any jeopardy, any more than it is a second suit for a private person first to decide that he will not sue somebody for damages and then later on to decide that after all he will. It is also possible, for the same reason, to amend or modify the proceedings in the preliminary examination, so as to bind over the person in question on a different charge from the one which the complaint originally contained. It may be that the preliminary examination will bring out that there is probable cause to suppose that he has committed a more serious crime or that the complaint is wholly erroneous in accusing him of a crime that he very definitely did not commit, even though some other one was probably committed by him. There

11. Rule 5(c) of the Federal Rules of Criminal Procedure does not require consent. It might be mentioned here that, wherever a federal rule is cited, the annotations to the Federal Rules and the accompanying comment supply a full citation of authorities, pro and con. These Rules were adopted by the United States Supreme Court and were in the main drafted by a committee of federal judges, working over a number of years and aided by the critical comment of experts in the field. Since in each case the Rules represent the crystallization of careful thought on the subject, the position taken in them must always be given serious consideration.

is no reason at all, then, why the bind-over should not be on such other or additional crime. Since this procedure is just a preliminary one, it also follows that there is, at this stage, no opportunity given to the accused person to enter any sort of a plea, either of guilty or of not guilty. Even if he were wholly willing to admit his guilt, matters have not yet reached the point where that is an appropriate step on his part.[12]

So much for the general description of the preliminary examination—what the theory back of it is and what it is supposed to accomplish. It is now necessary to look at the way in which it actually works in a typical American city[13] or village. There is probably a wider spread between the way in which ideally this procedure is carried out and the way in which it actually is in day-to-day life than is found in any other stage of our machinery of criminal-law enforcement. In theory the preliminary examination is an orderly proceeding conducted with a very definite end in view and advancing with decorum until that end is attained. In fact, the preliminary examination is probably the outstanding sore spot in the whole procedural sequence. The abuses and shortcomings are very different according as we look at the magistrate in a rural setting or in an urban one. In a rural setting in some respects the situation is not perhaps quite so bad. There the examination is carried on by a justice of the peace. Very often, since the justice is popularly elected, the holder of the office may be entirely unfit by past experience to perform this function. If so, it will probably be done very inefficiently and sloppily. But by no means all rural justices are of that sort, and many who start out most inadequately gradually, perhaps even rather rapidly, acquire sufficient experience for what is, after all, a fairly simple task.

The situation is at its worst in those big cities which have not established municipal courts, with some degree of professional skill normally to be found on the part of the magistrate. It will be bad even in those cities which do have municipal courts but in

12. It will be necessary later somewhat to qualify this statement under the Federal Rules.

13. Perhaps the best description available is one drawn nearly a generation ago by Raymond Moley, *Our Criminal Courts* (New York: Minton, Balch & Co., 1930), chap. ii. Too much of what is there stated remains true today.

which the tradition and personnel of the court and its methods of work are not up to adequate standards. If we are faced with that kind of court, it does not make much difference whether we call the functionary who is acting as a magistrate a judge or a justice of the peace; the result is the same. It is in the cities without real improvement that the magistrates courts are at their worst.[14] Everywhere people are milling around, with little or no order or decorum. The persons involved in the case then before the judge all crowd around the judge's seat. According to the kind of person that the latter is, he exercises more or less restraint upon them. He may or may not, according to his standards, indulge personally in direct wrangling, in argument back and forth, in most unseemly give-and-take.[15] The least interested person in the whole room is probably the assistant state's attorney. The noise, confusion, and disorder effectively hinder most of the purposes supposed to be achieved. It is a lesson in poor citizenship for many persons (and this is especially likely to include the foreign-born) whose first, and perhaps only, contact with our court system will be in surroundings like this and who are bound to come away from the scene with a most unfavorable impression of how our court dignity and efficiency are to be appraised.

Why, then, do we tolerate this sort of thing—almost without the demands for improvement that we frequently make in other areas (such as police efficiency)? In the first place (and mainly), it is because of an unfortunate and wholly mistaken tendency on the part of the average citizen to regard the preliminary examination as of little real importance—not of enough to warrant serious efforts toward improvement. There may, simultaneously, be real interest in efforts to improve the trial procedure. At that stage the intelligent citizen is profoundly concerned with the

14. A lively description of such a court can be found in Moley, *op. cit.* In fairness it should be noted that the scene described, in Chicago, predates the establishment of that city's municipal court. It was scenes like this that largely led to the creation of the court.

15. A recent newspaper item recounted that such a "judge"—what a degradation of the title!—after finding two men guilty of gambling by shooting craps, ordained that they should roll for it to determine which of them was to be punished and which one put on probation.

evils of courtroom fixing, courtroom inefficiency, etc.—all of them, of course, matters of high importance. But while it would be rash to say that there were never any cases of "fixing" a case in the criminal court itself, and, while any kind of abuse can be found anywhere if we look long enough, in the main, the stage where dishonest efforts to "fix" a case are most likely to be made, and having been made are most likely to be successful, is not the trial but the preliminary examination. That is the stage when the spotlight has not yet been turned on and when it is possible to operate with all the advantages of obscurity. That is the place, too, where the fixer needs to deal with only one person —the magistrate—not with thirteen—the judge and twelve jurors. That is the time when he is dealing also with people who are most closely connected with the political setup, at its lower and less attractive stages. The judge in the higher court is, by comparison with the magistrate, a figure of complete independence. The magistrate in his position, his ways of thinking, in everything, is infinitely closer to the "practical" political picture than is the judge. So what attorney who proposed to do the dishonest thing of fixing a case would be so utterly impractical and foolish as to neglect the opportunity to do so at this early stage? And one thing can be relied on: the persons who practice the fix, whatever else they may be, are very adequate practically. This is the stage when the maximum of crookedness can be, and is, practiced. And yet, with a misguided belief in our worldly wisdom, we regard the examination as too trifling to distract us from our concern over safeguards to be enforced at the trial stage. We insist on locking the barn only after the horse has been stolen.

In the second place, even when we are fully aware of the importance of the examination, it is not easy to blueprint what should be done to improve it. The volume of its work and the number of its cases are simply too great to introduce elaborate procedural improvements.[16] In the long run it will be as well, or

16. For a council of despair, listing the examination's shortcomings and advocating its abolition, see Vollmer, "Vestigial Organs," 7 *State Government* 91–94 (1934). Unfortunately so simple a solution is not possible. How are the examination's useful functions to be accomplished? If King Log is abolished, what will King Stork be like?

as ill, run as we, the voters, determine by the caliber of the men we select to run it for us. This is not a very satisfactory conclusion, because it does not offer any easy cure-all. Unfortunately it is probably realistic.[17]

SETTING AND APPROVING BAIL

We come now to the last of the magistrate's functions, his final contact with the criminal case—the setting of bail. In its nature this function presupposes that the case is not a petty one, where the magistrate, having summary jurisdiction, would finally dispose of it at once. It also presupposes that, the preliminary examination having been held, he has decided that there is sufficient (i.e., "probable") cause to bind the accused over to the grand jury. Here again it will be convenient to open the subject by a look at its history, and again, as in the instance of the preliminary examination, we shall find that we are dealing with a device that has undergone a surprising change in its long life, even more of a one than the examination, with its original purpose even more completely forgotten.

As we look back to the earliest days of English criminal law, we find that confinement behind bars played a much smaller part than it does now. This applies to both of the two purposes for which confinement is now used—that of punishment after conviction[18] and that of making sure that an accused person (and even, perhaps, an important witness) would be on hand and

17. An interesting, even if debatable, point is made by Arthur C. Train, creator of the famous fictional character "Mr. Tutt" and one-time district attorney in New York, in his book, *From the District Attorney's Office: A Popular Account of Criminal Justice* (New York: Charles Scribner's Sons, 1939). Train urges that would-be reformers are too much concerned with the political tieups of the magistrate. Certainly, he admits, they will produce favoritism, and that will produce bias; but in his opinion the insight into human nature and how people think that the practical politician must have if he is to succeed and that the magistrate, by having somewhat succeeded, necessarily does have is worth the price of some amount of political bias. This rough, crude, but fairly adequate understanding of human nature, with the ability to analyze who is telling the truth and who is not, is in his opinion worth the price of some political favoritism. Perhaps so.

18. In the early, formative days of the common law imprisonment as a punishment was very little used. In the long sweep of time it is a comparative newcomer. Death, branding, mutilation, and exile were the standard sanctions imposed.

available when the trial day came around. As a result there were few prisons, in our present-day sense of the term. On the other hand, there were comparatively a good many castles with dungeons or strong rooms—convenient places in which a noble powerful enough to venture it could incarcerate an enemy or, more likely, a recalcitrant serf. In short, though there may have been much imprisonment, it was imprisonment outside the criminal law and not a part of it. When an individual was arrested and charged with a crime,[19] it was therefore a very real problem as to what to do with him until trial day. He could not be safely turned loose, because he would disappear over the hill into the next valley and would never be seen again. He had to be physically restrained in some way. The magistrate would do the natural and obvious thing; he would call upon Sir Richard Roe, the owner of a strong castle near by, and would ask Sir Richard to confine the accused in one of his dungeons until the day of the trial. In other words, the law would have recourse to a private person who would act as jailer and custodian in its behalf. Each magistrate knew personally the individual to whom he intrusted this responsible task.

But a device that worked very well while the countryside was sparsely settled and the people who had the castles were all known to the magistrate began to break down, or at least to become more complex, as the population increased and as castles tended to disappear and to become more and more merely country homes. Magistrates began to find that they no longer knew the local people who might be utilized for such jailer purposes and, more and more, that they had to rely upon people unknown to them. The next step would be an equally obvious one. It would, of course, consist in an inquiry as to the background and financial responsibility of the person who was suggested as possibly a volunteer jailer or who offered himself as such. When we speak of his financial responsibility, we practically mean what real estate he had, as that was the only form of property of importance at that time. As it became increasingly probable that such an inquiry would be needed, magistrates by insensible de-

19. We are, of course, now dealing with a period far antedating the creation of the preliminary examination in 1554.

grees fell into the habit of requiring in advance that anybody who wished to be considered as a substitute jailer should save time by bringing along with him, when he came into court, a full statement of all his financial assets and a schedule of the property that he owned. The decision to accept him as jailer or not would be influenced by the conclusion as to whether this schedule showed that he was or was not a man of substance and responsibility. We have by now come a long way in converting the one-time friend of the magistrate into a stranger who must give an assurance that he is a safe person to receive the prisoner.

The next step was easy. To make doubly sure, the stranger was required to sign a bond whereby, in the event that he failed to live up to his obligation and produce John Doe in court on the day named, he would forfeit to the king a specified sum of money. In short, we have converted the situation into one of cash pressure on the jailer to make sure that he will do his task adequately. At the same time that these last developments were occurring, another was coming into the picture. More and more frequently the people who offered themselves as would-be jailers were friends of the accused person. It was for the jailer to determine how vigorously he would interpret his duties as jailer. It was up to him to determine whether to lock him in a dungeon and never let him out even for exercise, or to free him occasionally under supervision, or, perhaps, even to give him a good deal of freedom. Obviously the accused was deeply interested in having a friend of his picked for this task so that he could count on a high degree of freedom. Indeed, the freedom that his friend might accord him might be just about complete.

With that concept this whole procedure becomes entirely different from what it was in its origin. It is no longer a procedure of confinement but a procedure of more or less complete freedom under financial control. The old notion survives only in the name "bail"—a term which, like "bailment," suggests storing a thing (or, here, a person) with someone as warehouseman or bailor. And so today we think of bail solely in terms of the useful purpose that it now serves—the purpose of setting up an illogical, but workable, compromise between two social interests that cannot both be attained completely. There is, on the one hand, society's desire to have the law enforced, to make sure, that is, that the person who conceivably may be guilty is available for a trial and that whatever emerges from the trial can be carried out, and, preliminary thereto, to be sure that he will be on hand when his case comes up. That social objective would of course be best assured by keeping him under lock and key until the trial day. On the other hand, there is the other social objective that we express in the form of saying that everyone is presumed innocent until he is proved to be guilty—in other words, that it is socially desirable that no innocent person be deprived of his liberty and that the person whom we do not know to be guilty should be treated as innocent until we know him to be otherwise.

Not only do we not normally now think of the bondsman as a substitute jailer; the original state of affairs has been so thoroughly lost sight of that it seems to us a perfectly natural thing to accept, as perhaps the best kind of bail and the best kind of guaranty, the payment in open court, by the defendant himself, of a sum in cash. What could be a better guaranty of his dutifully appearing on the appointed day than that assets of a definite value are already handed over and come out of his own pocket? Yet historically cash bail was utterly inadmissible. How could these inanimate dollars or pounds, reposing in the strongbox of the court, act as a jailer? How could they lock him up, supervise him, and furnish him with food and drink to keep him alive? That was the very last thing that could be accepted for these purposes. It was no slight innovation when cash bail first was accepted.

Since bail is nowadays a procedure for the benefit of the defendant, a way of provisionally letting him go free, it is natural that in almost all our states there should be constitutional provisions which more or less completely guarantee to accused persons the right to release on bail.[20] These constitutional provisions are often even supplemented by a statute making it a criminal offense for a magistrate to refuse to set bail.

It is, however, often provided that where the charge is a capital

20. The statement must be made in this qualified manner because a very few states do not extend the guaranty, and, of those that do, most qualify it in the ways indicated in the text.

one (viz., where punishment is or may be the death sentence), and if in the opinion of the magistrate the evidence against the accused is strong, he may refuse to set bail. Much learning has been expended on the task of trying to describe how strong the evidence must be, but little has been added to the clarity of thought. About all that can be said is that there must be a "strong" case and that it is in the magistrate's discretion to pass on its strength.

Another qualification on the absolute right to have bail set may be mentioned here, although it involves a stage of the proceedings not yet before us. This is as to bail after conviction at trial and during review by a higher court after such conviction. According to the view generally held, the defendant no longer has any right to have bail set for him; he is in a radically different position from the accused person, whom we have been considering so far. The conviction removes the presumption of innocence, and on the contrary there is now a presumption of guilt. The trial court may in the exercise of its discretion allow even a convicted person to be free on bail pending an appeal, but it is no longer a right on his part. Furthermore, the incentive to escape is obviously a much greater one after conviction than before. Therefore, the danger involved in his being free is a greater one. Comparatively few cases are reversed on appeal. The majority, probably, are affirmed, and the appeal may be merely a frivolous one to gain additional time. He has every incentive to delay matters as long as possible by taking every step only at the last moment. That sort of an appeal certainly should be discouraged. The deterrent effect of punishment is seriously lessened if a convicted person is still free to walk the streets. If and when he is finally sent to confinement, his case has probably been very largely forgotten; therefore, in so far as we believe that deterrence is effective and successful, we should be unfavorably disposed toward release on bail after conviction.[21]

A final common limitation on the right to have bail set (and here we return to our proper time sequence, the proceedings before the magistrate) is in the case of persons who have been

21. This is substantially the view taken in Federal Rule 46(a)(2).

previously convicted of a crime of a specified degree of seriousness. In their case, in some states, the magistrate may in his discretion refuse to set bail at all.

Setting the amount of bail is a judicial task and can be performed only by a member of the judiciary; a statute purporting
to put this responsibility into the hands of an administrative official (e.g., a police captain) would be unconstitutional as an attempted deprivation of the power of one branch of the government in favor of another branch. Ideally the magistrate should
set bail at a figure which will be high enough to make sure that
the accused will appear, but no higher than that.[22] Determining
this figure is not an easy task. Obviously to be taken into account
is the seriousness of the offense. The nature and background of
the accused person are also highly important. He may be a
highly reputable citizen, whose great stake in the community
makes his taking to flight and disappearing very unlikely. Or
the complete opposite may be true. A complicating but inescapable factor, too, is his wealth. If he is a man of means, the
inhibition on him by the forfeiture of his bond will weigh
less heavily than if he is relatively poor. In that sense, then,
wealth may call for higher bond. Yet, as a further stake in
his present existence, it makes flight less attractive and so may call
for a lower one. All these factors must be taken into account.
In view of their complexity it is no wonder that in actual practice
magistrates tend to set up for themselves a minimum and maximum range for each of the more common offenses.[23]

Who may act as bondsman? In broad terms we can answer,
"Anybody who can make a contract." Today very commonly
even a corporation can—still another indication of how far we
have moved from the substitute-jailer notion. In some states

22. If the bail is intentionally set by the magistrate at a higher figure than
that, he will probably be just as truly violating the criminal law as would the
magistrate who outright refused to set bail at any figure whatsoever.

23. Apparently at variance with what has just been said is the common practice in large cities of allowing a police officer of higher than patrol rank to
handle the matter of bail in traffic cases and of having a fixed sum set for any
given violation. Actually there is no inconsistency. These are merely violations
of city ordinances. They are not crimes. Therefore, they do not fall within the
scope of our subject matter.

surety companies do in fact write only a small proportion of the bonds. In others[24] nearly half of the total is written by them. An important limitation is that attorneys may not sign bonds. The reason should be obvious—the almost certain conflict of interest that would arise. For example, an attorney's loyalty toward his client would call for efforts to minimize the charge and to secure adjudication of it as soon as possible. His interest as bondsman might be to make the case against his client seem as bad as possible, in order to increase the amount of the bond and therefore the fee for it, and to have the matter drawn out as long as possible, thereby also adding to his business. The simplest and best solution is to eliminate him from the possibilities.

The bail system has given rise to a great many abuses. Indeed, the disrepute into which the professional bondsman has popularly fallen is itself a proof of that. Hence it is occasionally urged that this profession should be forbidden—an utterly impractical "solution." Professional bondsmen serve a very useful social purpose. As things are now we cannot get along without them, and we should not even try. If someday our police develop such a degree of efficiency and such a change in their habits as to make arrests relatively rare and the use of summonses normal, the need for the professional bondsman will largely disappear. But so long as most criminal proceedings are initiated by means of an arrest, a deprivation of liberty, we certainly need also to provide means by which persons so arrested can secure provisional liberty. That means cannot be found, in many if not in most of the cases, in the unaided efforts either of the accused person himself or of himself plus his friends. He must have the services of a person engaged in this business, and, however unlikely the latter is to be elected to an exclusive club, he is performing a very useful social function. The abuses can be met not by killing off the scapegoat but only by analyzing what they are and seeking to correct them.

What is called for is control and regulation of the business, in order to do away with the evils that have been disclosed. These evils are in part directed against the person who has been arrested and in part against the state. So far as they represent different

24. Notably New York.

directions, they may call for different types of regulation. So far as accused persons are concerned, most frequently the evil that they suffer from is that the bondsman will charge inordinately high fees for his services. On hypothesis the accused may be, and is presumed to be, innocent. If he is innocent, certainly he is subjected to hardship enough without being forced to pay a large sum to secure the liberty that he should have had all along. Even if he is guilty, presumably the punishment, by way of confinement or a fine or both, is a measure of what he ought to be made to pay; and the payment to a bondsman is merely a surplus and additional penalty. Furthermore, the fee will be set as high as the bondsman feels he can make it. He will be limited only by the financial capacity of the accused person to pay, or to get his friends to help him pay, the fee and by the further limitation that may be imposed by the bondsman's competition with other bondsmen.[25] Furthermore, if a high fee is set, it may place the accused under great pressure to secure the cash needed to complete his payment. In the case of a guilty person (especially in a robbery case) the very height of the fee may operate as a compelling reason for him to go out and raise the money by the means best known to him; that is to say, by committing fresh crimes. In short, the excessive fee constitutes an evil both to the individual and to the community.[26]

Another, and even more serious, defect in the bail system has centered around the property scheduled by the bondsman and

25. This competition may be further cut down by the dishonest, but constantly recurring, expedient of splitting fees with lockup keepers to prevent the admittance of competitors. If such collusion can be proved, it will, of course, be punished; but it is not easy to prove.

26. Fees may work out in still another undesirable manner. The accused who is a first offender or is not an offender at all—in other words, the inexperienced person—is likely to have to pay a much higher fee than the veteran in crime not only because of his inexperience in dealing with bondsmen but also because as a business proposition he represents a greater risk than does the dependable veteran, who will be needing this sort of service again in the future. Incidentally, the veteran with his quantity business will expect wholesale rates; with the stranger it is a case of getting what the bondsman can, for the accused may never appear again. The ultimate in customer desirability (and so in low rates) is, of course, a well-organized gang. Thus it is apparent that the fee scale is likely to be highest for the most deserving cases and lowest for the least deserving.

its real value. Especially in the cities (and the abuses of the professional bondsman are primarily an urban problem) the courts either could not, or at any rate did not, exercise proper precautions to see that the bondsmen really had property that was adequate for the bonds they were signing. It is in the discretion of the court not only to set the amount of the bond but to determine whether the property scheduled comes up to an adequate guaranty that the bond really will be paid. In many cities this function was being performed so poorly that the collection of forfeited bonds amounted almost to nothing.[27] Practically the system had been reduced to release without security.

It has proved possible, however, to a degree not usually true to remove these abuses by regulatory legislation.[28] Such legislation applies only to the professional bondsman, as it is obvious that the abuses mentioned exist not at all or only to a very small extent where it is friends of the accused who sign the bond. The professional is defined as anyone who signs more than a specified number of bonds in a specified period of time.[29] The person who qualifies as a professional bondsman may operate as such only after securing a license and only so long as the license is in force. In order to secure and retain the license, he must deposit with the court a specified sum[30] in cash or its equivalent. There are careful provisions as to the scheduling of property, the relationship of its value to the total amount of bonds outstanding, and the creation of a lien on such property. The bondsman must also supply (under the penalty of possible punishment if he does not) full information as to the amount of the fee that

27. One survey showed that in a given year in one city the bonds forfeited (through the flight of the accused) amounted to $292,400. The amount actually collected on the forfeitures was about $1,500. In another city it was found in one case that the property scheduled was a triangle several hundred feet long and with a base of only six feet. There was no drainage, and it was constantly under water. It was independently appraised at a maximum value of $60. The bondsman, however, had "valued" it in his schedule at $10,000, and, through constant rescheduling, it was at one time the "security" for bonds totaling several hundred thousand dollars.

28. The Illinois Bail Bond Act of 1931, sponsored by the Chicago Crime Commission, is an excellent example.

29. Thus, for example, in Illinois three bonds in thirty days. These limits are hardly likely to reach the "amateur."

30. In the Illinois act $5,000.

he is charging and such information as he has regarding the sources of the fee on the accused's part. In addition, in order to render the above really effective, there is often set up a central bail-bond bureau as a clearing-house for information as to the real value of property scheduled and its conformity to legal requirements and the status of the bondsman and his cash deposit.[31] Such a bureau is vital to really intelligent decisions by the magistrate.

The bond having been approved and the accused released (if he can "make" the bond), the magistrate's share in the case has come to an end.

---

31. Such a bureau can also inform the judge whether this bondsman and accused had previously appeared before another judge and had tried to get his approval of this particular bond. Such "shopping around" for the most favorable terms to be found is a long-standing abuse.

VI

THE CORONER

WE HAVE seen that the proceedings before the magistrate will have terminated either in the discharge of the accused or in his being held for grand-jury action. In the normal sequence of events, therefore, we should now move on to the grand jury. It is necessary, however, to interrupt this sequence to consider the coroner, an official who functions in only a limited range of cases but who, if it is a case in which he does function, acts before the grand jury does. Here again it will be most convenient first to describe the origin of the institution, then to deal with the radical changes in it in the course of time, and finally to examine its present status.

The coroner has, probably, changed most of all the criminal-law agencies. When he first appeared on the scene, over seven hundred years ago, he was the direct representative, in the county, of the king.[1] He was needed because the king could not always be sure that the highest law-enforcement official in each county (viz., the sheriff) was fully living up to his obligations. After all, the sheriff was a local official who very possibly might feel more loyalty toward his local friends than he did toward the king. He would be a member of the local nobility and probably related more or less closely to many of its members and might very well be counted on by them to exercise considerable restraint and mercy when it came to collecting the taxes due to the king or seeing to it that all the obligations owed to the crown were performed. Not only were these obligations numerous; many were very much disliked. Hence the crown's need for a direct representative to see to their enforcement.

1. Hence the name from *corona*, or "crown." In some of the older writers he is referred to as the "crowner."

One very important source of royal revenue lay in the then prevailing practice of confiscating all the property belonging to a convicted felon. Thus, one of the coroner's duties as a supervisor of the enforcement of the tax laws consisted in watching over criminal prosecutions to see that these were initiated and carried to a successful conclusion. This, then, brought the coroner into contact with the criminal law. He was interested in all felony prosecutions. In the great majority of them there was little that he needed to do. Even though there was as yet no organized prosecuting machinery, the victim of the crime could usually be counted on to see that the law was enforced in all its rigor. But there was one type of crime in which this dependence on the victim's grudge broke down, or might very readily break down—those cases in which the victim was killed. The victim's family, if he left a family, might conceivably feel enough grudge to pursue the case; but this could not be absolutely counted on. It has always been easier to forgive the injuries suffered by others than those suffered by one's self.[2] Being able to feel more forgiving, it was more likely that they could be induced to drop prosecution in return for a property settlement. And so, quite naturally, the coroner developed a particular interest in those felony cases that involved the death of the victim.

In the course of time forfeiture of property on conviction of felony disappeared, and with it one might have expected that the coroner's interest, as primarily a fiscal officer, would also have disappeared. But by that time he had, through the centuries, so far established himself as the first-line prosecuting machinery in homicide cases (this was, it should be remembered, long before police departments existed and when he was the only effective prosecuting agency, except in so far as he was aided by the preliminary examination) that he was already more thought of as a homicide prosecutor than as a fiscal officer. And so, despite the elimination of confiscation, he continued to be active in these prosecutions. Indeed, in the course of time his

2. As La Rochefoucauld put it, we have all of us strength of character enough to endure the misfortunes of others.

other functions disappeared almost completely.[3] Consequently, today we think of him entirely as an official whose duty it is to inquire into all cases of deaths where there is any possibility of foul play or criminal fault. Thus, as a routine matter, he must always be notified in any case where a death occurred before a doctor was or could be summoned.

How, then, does the coroner conduct his investigation as to the possibility that a crime has been committed? He does so by means of what is called an "inquest." This inquest or inquiry is conducted with the aid of a six-man jury, which is brought together by him; and with it he proceeds to hear witnesses who may know something about what has occurred. These witnesses are practically free to testify or not as they choose; their testimony is heard, and they are asked questions which they may or may not choose to answer. In many respects there is a strong resemblance to trial procedure. After hearing all the witnesses who can be discovered and who are willing to testify and not claim that they may incriminate themselves by testifying, the coroner's jury and the coroner consider what they have heard, and the jury hands in its verdict. This verdict is not like the "guilty" or "not guilty" verdict of the trial jury (to be considered at the end of chap. xiii, "The Trial"), since nobody is on trial. This proceeding is at this stage directed against no individual specifically. There is no defendant; there is no accused person; there is simply an investigation into what occurred. The verdict of the coroner's jury, therefore, takes the form of a statement by the jury as to what, in the jurors' opinion, has occurred. Thus they may state that X came to his death by means of blows struck by a blunt instrument in the hands of a party or parties unknown, or perhaps that he came to his death by being struck by an automobile driven in a negligent manner by John Doe. If they do specify that, in their opinion, a crime was com-

3. Only one function of importance remains. If suit is brought against the sheriff, the latter cannot serve process on himself. It is the coroner who does so. A curious, though unimportant, survival of the coroner's fiscal duties is that in England, if hidden treasure is found, not only is it appropriated by the crown (viz., the government), but it is the coroner to whom possession must be handed.

mitted and then proceed to give the name of the person who they think was involved in the crime, then this person can be immediately arrested on a warrant issued by the coroner or by a magistrate. Such a verdict also means that the case is then and there ready for grand-jury action. Thus the coroner's office has become an alternative way by which homicide, but only homicide, cases can be presented to the grand jury. It entirely bypasses the magistrate and his preliminary examination.[4]

In this sharply restricted field how efficiently does the coroner work nowadays? The answer is easy. He is inherently and utterly unable to do his job well. If he is sincerely anxious to do good work, he can make his failure less extreme; but the basic reason that the coroner's system has broken down is because we are asking him to perform a job with means that render the efficient performance of that job utterly out of the question. Basically he is supposed to do a form of police work. He is supposed to conduct an investigation, to follow out clues, and to find out whether there was a crime and, if so, who the criminal was. How is he to carry on this police activity, not as an alternative to other methods that he may follow, but as the only method allowed to him? He must announce to the public that on such-and-such a day at such-and-such an hour he and six other persons will be at a specified place and will proceed to "investigate." That is, in the presence of any persons who choose to attend they will ask questions and hope to get answers.[5] This constitutes the entire range of method allowed to them. It need merely be asked how far a police department or, say, its detective bureau would get if it were limited to investigatory methods of that sort. It is obvious that it would get absolutely nowhere at all; and, however able the coroner is, he cannot

4. It should be repeated that the statement merely is that homicide cases *may* come to the grand jury via the coroner. It is entirely possible that, before the coroner can act or hold an inquest, the police will have already established definite enough information against an accused person so that they can secure a warrant for his arrest, he is arrested, is brought before the magistrate, is given his preliminary examination, and is bound over—all before the inquest can take place.

5. Obviously, the better their work and the keener their questions, the likelier they are to be refused an answer.

get any further. He is fatally handicapped by the procedural restrictions placed upon him.[6]

Furthermore, the coroner's jury is made up of laymen, so that even if there were the possibility of conducting a real investigation, free from restrictions, the jurors would suffer under all the handicaps that laymen suddenly called upon to do detective work would be under. But this work itself calls for training, experience, and special skills that the layman utterly lacks. Usually (and theoretically always) the jury is summoned from the general mass of the community, but in fact other methods of recruitment are sometimes followed. For instance, a coroner may wish to win favor with large voter groups like the American Legion, or the Knights of Columbus, or the Elks, or others, and may suggest that they send in the names of unemployed members. Then it is really that organization which selects the members of the jury. There is nothing objectionable about such a practice; those thus recruited probably will render just as good service as those selected otherwise. In any event, it will not amount to much. Still other coroners, especially in the big cities, adopt the rule that they will recruit their juries entirely from the full-time personnel of their office. A large-scale coroner's office has a large personnel of clerks, and the task of serving on a jury can be as much a normal part of the clerical work as any other part of it. There is a great deal to be said for this practice. The men are on a fixed salary, and the fees received as jurors can either be turned in or be

6. The public is frequently well aware of the poor work of the local coroner but is entirely unwilling to face the basic reasons for it. It is in this sort of atmosphere that we have the almost pointless demand (usually carefully fostered by a candidate for the office) of "a medical man for a medical job." It is not a medical job (except that in a rural county a "medical" coroner could perhaps save the county some money by performing his own autopsies); it is a police job and, in urban counties, an administrative one calling for supervision over large staffs. Even if a "medical" coroner had the leisure personally to engage in "medical" work, medicine is now so highly specialized, with so many branches of learning, that it is absurd to assume that the mere holding of an M.D. degree renders the holder much more able than the layman to carry on an autopsy or to give conclusions as to whether poison caused the death and, if so, what kind of poison or how far from the deceased the revolver was at its discharge. If we are going to pin our faith on specialists, our slogan had better be "a pathologist for a pathologist's job" or "a toxicologist for a toxicologist's job." The voters' response would be interesting to watch!

deducted from their salary. They may even develop a degree
of professional skill in acting as routine jurors.[7]

All the foregoing assumes a coroner anxious to do the best
work he possibly can. Not only is such an assumption not always
warranted for public officials; it is probably more often doubtful
in the case of the coroner than in that of any other official.
If by a lucky accident the coroner succeeds in bringing something important to light, it is not he who is the beneficiary
of this discovery, but the prosecuting attorney, who will afterward have to try the case. In many counties the prosecuting
attorney is the most important local political figure. He has
the greatest power, with the greatest amount of patronage to
dispense; he is the ranking political power in the county, or,
if he is not his own master, the political boss who controls him
is the great power. Immediately below him come the sheriff
and the coroner. Even if they belong to the same political party,
there is a great possibility of secret rivalry between the prosecuting attorney, on the one hand, and the coroner, on the other.
Each is struggling for the top position; each may, therefore, not
look with too much enthusiasm on the success of the other. Yet the
coroner, an independently elected official, not answerable to
the prosecuting attorney, is charged with contributing to the
success of the latter. At best this is an anomalous situation. It
will be aggravated many times over if the two officials belong
to different political parties.

All these factors have led a number of the states, notably
New York and Massachusetts, to the radical step of abolishing
the coroner's office entirely. In these states and in a number of
others the coroner no longer exists; he has disappeared. In his
place they have created by statute a new functionary called

7. The fundamental inadequacy of the coroner is best shown in a typical
newspaper item which every reader will surely have seen repeatedly. A murder
has been committed, let us assume, and it is strongly suspected that a person
meeting such-and-such a description is the guilty party. The newspaper item
reports, without comment or any indication of surprise, that "the inquest was
continued for two weeks in order to give the police an opportunity to conclude their investigation." What a revelation such a news item actually is! The
coroner's inquest that is ostensibly to help in clearing things up is postponed in
order to enable the police to function. In other words, the best help that
the coroner can give the police is to keep out until the police have had a
chance really to do a good job. His best co-operation is to do nothing.

the "medical examiner." The medical examiner differs fundamentally from the coroner both in his activity and in his status. He is merely an appointee of the prosecuting attorney, answerable to him and holding his post only so long as it is the pleasure of the prosecuting attorney. With that fact alone there are eliminated all possible rivalry and lack of co-operation. Like the coroner, he is charged with the duty of investigating all cases of deaths where criminality may be involved, but he investigates them entirely free from the formalism and the restrictions that the coroner was under, in whatever way seems best to him. There is no open hearing, no parade of witnesses. He is merely a specialized investigator, supplementing the efforts of the police by using skills which they (except in the large forces) do not have available.

VII

THE GRAND JURY

COMPARATIVELY early in the history of the criminal law it was established that a prosecution could be carried on only when it was initiated by a body known as the grand jury.[1] In other words, this body functioned as society's mind in making the decision whether or not to proceed with a criminal suit. How did this body come into existence, and what purposes did it originally serve? It probably arose in response to two different needs.

One of these—perhaps the earlier to be felt—arose from the wishes and desires of the judges who were to hear criminal cases. The organization of royal justice, when it was first emerging under the Norman and Plantagenet kings, consisted in judges who had their normal seat at the royal capital; that is to say, in the little town of Westminster, near London. That, then, was where they lived and spent most of the year. At fixed times, however, they were required to go on circuit, and, given the conditions surrounding traveling in those days, it does not take much imagination to realize that they probably did not look forward with keen pleasure to this periodic ordeal. It was something to get over with as speedily as, in good conscience, one could. The major task that each judge faced in each town consisted in hearing the criminal cases. A great many of them would turn out to be utterly baseless—mere matters of spite. But with no screening device as yet in existence they must have formed a time-consuming and annoying total. An obvious device to eliminate, or at any rate to reduce greatly, these baseless charges was to refuse to hear any charge unless it had been approved as worthy by the responsible local people. These, of course,

1. For complete accuracy this statement would have to be slightly qualified (see chap. ix, "The Information"). The qualifications, however, are not of present importance.

would consist of the men of local importance, substance, and dignity—incidentally, precisely the same persons who no doubt were originally the voluntary jailers described in the chapter on bail. These gentry would assemble a short time before the local assizes and would reserve for judicial consideration those cases that had some substance to them. The device was so useful that these groups acquired a recognized status and were required to take a "jurat," or oath, to do their work faithfully and well. Thereby as a body they became a "jury," and, in order to distinguish them from the small, or "petit," juries that functioned in the individual cases, they were known as the large, or in Norman French the "grand," jury. Naturally this grand jury varied greatly in size, and it is interesting that even today its size is a variable, ranging usually from a minimum of sixteen to a maximum of twenty-three.

At the same time that the grand jury was beginning to serve the purpose just described, it was rapidly serving another and, very soon, far more important one—one which the judges as representatives of the king were perhaps not so much in sympathy with but which they had no power to shut off. The grand jury began to assert that not only did the judge not need to hear cases unless it channeled them to him but that he actually had no right to hear any case unless it came from the grand jury. In this character the grand jury served as a hampering force on the judge. It acted as a means of restricting and preventing unbridled royal prosecutions carried on through the instrumentality of subservient royal judges and so became an instrumentality of local independence and local liberty. It is in this aspect that we find the grand jury, even so early as Magna Carta in 1215, already thought of as a means of popular safety and protection against arbitrary prosecution. And it is in this aspect that it has primarily come down to us today.

Today the grand jury has two unrelated functions assigned to it. One has no necessary connection with criminal-law enforcement and hence will here be mentioned only briefly. It is that of conducting periodic inspections of, and therefore to some extent investigations into, the public institutions of the area in its jurisdiction. It is, for instance, the duty of every grand jury to visit county institutions, such as the county hospital, the county jail, etc., during its term of office in order to determine how well they are being run and to look into conditions that may reflect upon the enforcement of the law or the management of the institutions. Thus it is within the competence, and therefore within the duty, of the grand jury to investigate into general states of affairs even when it is not directing its investigation at any person in particular and when the inquiry into alleged abuses in such-and-such a public or private field may or may not be expected to involve criminal conditions. It is in this capacity, too, that it inquires into the local prevalence of vice or gambling.

But the function of present concern and the one that occupies most of its time is the historic one of investigating criminal charges. Usually these charges have come to it on bind-overs from magistrates, together with a few referred to it by the coroner. It is entirely possible and proper, however, for the grand jury to be the first body to act in a given matter or against a given person,[2] thus by-passing preliminary examination and inquest alike. The possession of this power to initiate a proceeding, even if not often used, is of importance in at least three types of situations.

1. Hope for success in prosecution may depend on preserving complete secrecy in the initial stages of the investigation. It may be vital, therefore, to have nothing publicly known until, with grand-jury action, all the preliminary steps have been completed.

2. The prosecuting attorney, for political or other reasons, may have taken no action. It should not be in his power to stymie action by others.

3. A criminal situation, or the involvement of a given person in such a situation, may not previously have been suspected but have come to light incidentally through some other investigation.

2. Where the action is initiated by the grand jury as the first mover, it is called a "presentment." There is no difference of substance between a proceeding begun in the usual manner, by a bind-over, and one begun by the grand jury's own presentment. A warrant will then issue for the defendant's arrest. Such a warrant, not based on a complaint, is known as a "bench warrant," coming as it does directly from the court. It is also called a "capias."

It would be merely profitless circuity if the grand jury had to wait until the same matter reached it a second time through normal channels.

But, regardless of the source of the charge, in all of them the grand jury is acting as the mind of the community in deciding the question, "Shall there be a criminal suit brought against this particular person on this particular charge?" It follows from all this that in carrying on this responsibility it must be almost entirely its own master. Though there have been doubts expressed at times as to whether a grand jury could on its own responsibility investigate a matter not called to its attention by the judge under whom it is serving or by the prosecuting attorney, in general it is held that it may. Certainly, once it has entered upon an investigation, it is its own master and need not seek the permission of anyone to hear a given witness[3] or to follow a given lead.

The responsibility for selecting the membership of the grand jury is usually intrusted to the same official body (their name varies—"jury commissioners" is a common one) which makes up the lists for the petit juries.[4] As already stated, the number varies from sixteen to twenty-three. The tendency in the smaller counties with comparatively small budgets is to keep the grand jury at a minimum in order to cut down the expenses, as grand jurors are paid on a per diem basis. Furthermore, the time of service of a grand jury in a small county is usually sharply limited, simply because there is not much for it to do, and, therefore, it is not likely that, if only the minimum of sixteen jurors

3. This, like other sweeping statements hereafter, is not the law in every state. It is, however, out of the scope of this book to go beyond holdings generally agreed on.

4. An accused person whose case is to be considered by a given grand jury has certain sharply limited rights to raise objections to the makeup or membership of that jury. As they are restricted in scope, there is not space available to consider them here. See, for details, Lester B. Orfield, *Criminal Procedure from Arrest to Appeal* (New York: New York University Press, 1947), p. 151. It will suffice here to say that personal prejudice on the part of a grand juror is not usually a valid objection in this function of determining whether or not to bring a criminal action. The objection which has gained most publicity in recent years is that the jury was selected in such a manner as systematically to exclude members of a given race, thereby, it is claimed, depriving accused persons of that race of due process of law.

are called, one of those sixteen will drop out in the short time that it has to serve. In the big counties it is usually at the maximum strength, or somewhere near it, because, having so much more to do, it sits a longer time, there are more things that can happen to cut down manpower, and therefore it is wiser to have a substantial reserve. Under the common law the grand jury served for the term of the court that had convened it and ended its existence with the end of the term. Under the Federal Rules of Criminal Procedure,[5] as well as in an increasing number of state statutes, provision is made for the possibility of continuing it in existence for a longer time, if this is needed in order to finish an investigation then in progress.

In urban counties[6] there is sufficient work for the local grand jury so that one sits until its successor comes into existence. In rural ones, on the contrary, the work is quickly disposed of, and the jury may be very soon discharged, leaving new prosecutions to await the next jury. There is usually a provision that a grand jury must be convened at least once in every six months, but if the sitting lasts, let us say, fifteen days, there might well then be a period of inactivity of as much as five and a half months. If an accused person has been bound over near the beginning of such a period and if he is unable to make bail, he faces the serious hardship of an extended time in jail, merely waiting for a decision as to whether he will or will not have to stand trial. A method to correct this obvious injustice will be taken up later.[7]

We proceed now to the task confronting the grand jury and the manner in which that task is to be performed. Since its function is merely to determine whether proceedings shall be taken and is not to pass on disputed facts, only evidence for the prosecution will be heard, and only this will be considered in determining whether there is probable cause to believe the accused to be guilty. The accused does not even have any right to insist

5. Rule 6(g).
6. While, for brevity, the term "county" is used, it should be remembered that the important matter is the area included in the jurisdiction of the court which has convened the grand jury. This may, of course, cover several counties.
7. See chap. ix, "The Information."

that he himself shall be heard by it.[8] Since the accused has no right to present evidence, it may be asked whether he can complain that the indictment was based on insufficient evidence or on no evidence at all. A minority of states answer this question in the negative, both for the reason indicated above—that its decision is merely a preliminary one, in which it is socially desirable for it to have unfettered discretion—and because (as will be explained more fully below), since the grand-jury proceedings are secret, a decision should not hinge on disclosures by a juror as to matters which he has sworn not to disclose. In most states, however, the court in its discretion may examine whether any competent evidence at all was laid before the jury. If so, this is enough—the court will not inquire into sufficiency. The difficulty as to improper disclosure is overcome, in such states, by requiring the keeping of stenographic minutes of the proceedings.[9]

Another consequence of the grand jury's independence is that it is not limited to action on the exact charges on which the accused was bound over at the preliminary examination. It may add others, or it may drop the original ones entirely in favor of others. Indeed, there is nothing wrong either in theory or (in many states) in practice first to vote not to indict and later,

8. It is, of course, possible that the grand jury in the exercise of its own choice may call a witness against whom it later returns an indictment, but in such an event he comes before it by its, not his, choice. In such a case the problem of protection against self-incrimination arises. While there is no unanimity, the best view, it is submitted, is that, where the jury is in fact (whether nominally or not) directing its investigation against that witness, he should be warned that what he says may be used against him and that, if he is not warned, the indictment loses its validity. It is not, after all, asking too much, in such a case to ask the jury to warn the accused. But it is an entirely different matter if the jury is carrying on an investigation which apparently does not involve the witness at all. In such a case the failure to give warning is wholly natural and in no way suggests a desire to entrap him. It should, therefore, be for him to claim the privilege. Practically, however, the question is of no importance in many counties, owing to their routine practice of demanding that every witness, whoever he may be, must sign an immunity waiver before commencing to testify.

9. Formerly it was not the practice for a grand jury to keep minutes. Now, either by a change in practice or by statute, they are often required to be kept. This, then, raises the question as to the propriety of disclosing them to the defendant or other interested parties. While views vary widely in detail, the strong tendency is either to deny such disclosure or only to permit it under sharp limitations on the court's discretion.

for the same jury or a subsequent one, to reconsider and to vote an indictment. There has not yet been jeopardy, and the public is as entitled as a private person is to change its mind as to whether to sue or not. In some states, however, the danger of harassment of an accused by repeated grand-jury inquiries has been felt to be serious enough, so that reconsideration by a later jury is allowed only where there is new evidence and a court order calling for reconsideration.[10]

Incidental reference has already been made to the fact that the proceedings of the grand jury are not open to the public but on the contrary are strictly secret. Since all the other stages of the court proceedings are open to the public, secrecy at this point and the reasons for it call for comment. At the hearings the only persons normally present, besides the grand jurors themselves, are the particular witness who is then and there being heard and the prosecuting attorney. Today also, by statute or by common law, we usually permit the presence of a stenographer to take down the testimony and, in case of need, an interpreter. With these four individuals, we have exhausted the sum total of nonjurors who may be present in the grand-jury room during the hearings. When the process of hearing the witnesses has been concluded and the grand jury reaches the stage of deliberating as to whether or not to vote an indictment, the curtain is drawn still more closely. Nobody except the jurors may be present. Even the prosecuting attorney is not properly present, and, if he is, the defendant has as good grounds for raising an objection[11] as he would have for any other unauthorized presence. Before considering the reasons for this secrecy, it should be mentioned that at common law, most illogically, the witnesses were under no obligation to keep silent, thereby largely defeating the purpose of the rule. Today, however, either by statute or by a reconsideration of the common

10. A grand jury, in voting not to indict, is said to "ignore" the charge. This use of the word "ignore"—so different from its ordinary meaning—arose from the old-time practice of indorsing on the written charges a statement in Latin that "we [the jury] are ignorant of their truth." The opening word in this statement was "Ignoramus." Hence the charge was said to be "ignoramused," or ignored.

11. This, like all other objections based on the grand jury and its actions, will normally be raised at the arraignment (see chap. xii).

law, they are under substantially the same restrictions as are the jurors themselves.

Various purposes are served or supposed to be served by this secrecy, and they vary not only in their force but also in the duration of time that the secrecy is called for.

1. The reputation of a person against whom groundless charges have been brought is protected from the damage that it would suffer if it were known that he had been under scrutiny. This purpose would call for permanent secrecy but is one of very limited scope. It applies only to those cases in which the grand jury is the first body to act. It cannot extend to those more numerous cases which are before the jury as the result of a bind-over.

2. To accomplish its purpose, a grand jury must have complete freedom of action, as has already been said. Such freedom would in fact be very much cut down if its hearings were open to the public or if information could be supplied to the public as to exactly what occurred. Witnesses are more likely to talk freely and openly, without restraint, and to tell all that they know if there is no attendant publicity. This very convincing reason partially, but only partially, loses its force after indictment. On the one hand, the witness will then in any event have to tell his story in open court. On the other hand, the knowledge that, though this is so, his testimony will remain unknown if no indictment is voted will tend to freer disclosures by a witness who is influenced by such considerations.

3. Secrecy, it is said, is necessary in order to prevent the flight of the defendant before he can be arrested. Not only is this reason sharply limited in time; it is usually greatly overrrated in importance. It cannot apply to the accused who has been bound over, as he is already aware that proceedings are in progress against him, and, if he proposes to flee, he will scarcely need the grand jury's action to start him. Thus it only applies to cases initiated by jury action. Even in these its force is limited. The person with a guilty conscience will be keeping close enough tab on the people who know about his guilt so that he will be well aware of it if there is a steady procession of them to the grand jury. He will smell a rat very quickly indeed, and the

indictment will not come to him as a surprise either. Thus the only one against whom the secrecy will be really effective and who will be surprised by the action will probably be an innocent defendant. And he is, of all defendants, the one who, in any event, is least likely to flee.

4. Lastly, and most important, secrecy is imposed so that an unscrupulous defendant may not be exactly informed as to the evidence available to the prosecution and thereby be put in a position to build up a perjured defense.[12] Obviously this reason is a temporary one.

With such diverse reasons for secrecy and such difference in their time extent, there is, as might be expected, great variance as to the extent to which secrecy will continue to be imposed after the proceedings have moved to a later stage. But it is safe to say that at no time will a juror be heard as to what influenced him to vote as he did. There is authority even for the view that he may not speak as to what occurred in the jury room. An obvious disadvantage of such a position is that it would make practically impossible any inquiry into irregularities and abuses that may have occurred during the deliberations.[13] It would seem that a juror should be allowed, therefore, to testify as to objective facts of an objectionable nature, even though not as to subjective matters, such as what influenced his vote. An additional or separate safeguard might be to permit disclosure only when the court, in its discretion, considers it advisable.[14] While this would to some extent raise the danger that a disgruntled and untruthful juror could sabotage his body's work, it would

12. It could be argued that this danger could be met at least partially by the prosecution's not bringing in before the grand jury all its witnesses. But the difficulty here is that the trial court may not permit (or only permit under restrictions) the bringing-in of witnesses who did not appear before the grand jury (see Orfield, *op. cit.*, p. 256). Furthermore, even if there were no such limitations, it is obviously undesirable to put the prosecution in a position where it must hold back all its case except the bare minimum needed to secure an indictment. It should feel perfectly free to have the whole story told to the grand jury.

13. Such, e.g., as the intoxication of a juror or, in a controversial case, threats of personal violence.

14. This is the view taken in the Model Code of Criminal Procedure (§ 145). As it is fully annotated, any reference to it constitutes simultaneously a reference to all pertinent decisions up to its date.

not be an undue risk but one well worth taking for the resultant gain.

One more question remains to be considered in regard to the grand jury's work. Is there any time limit within which it must act? On the minimum side there is none; a grand jury may act as speedily as it chooses. On the maximum side there is a statute of limitations, just as there is for civil actions. While the statutory periods vary, typically a few crimes of the most serious nature may have no limit, those of less import a specified number of years, and minor ones only some months.[15] If an indictment has been found within the appropriate time limit and has later been held defective, it may nonetheless serve to stop the running of the clock, so far as a later one, free from the defect, is concerned. It should be noted that these comments have nothing to do with the wholly separate question of how soon, under the guaranty of speedy trial after the indictment has been found, the trial must be held. This will be considered later.

Having voted, or refused to vote, an indictment, the grand jury's part in the case comes to an end. In the latter event the accused is discharged. In the former he is held for trial. Before moving on to that stage, it will be necessary, however, to consider somewhat more closely the nature of an indictment and also an alternative to grand-jury action—the "information."

15. Thus in Illinois there is no limitation in time at all for the four crimes of murder, manslaughter, arson, and forgery. (It is easy to see why no time limit is put on the first two, and a forgery may not come to light until many years have passed; but it is difficult to see why arson should not have any limitation put upon it when robbery, kidnaping, and treason are limited.) As to other felonies, the limitation period is three years. For misdemeanors it is eighteen months, except for a specified list of very small misdemeanors that we have met with under the heading of summary jurisdiction, where the limitation period is thirty days and where, in any case, there is no grand-jury action called for.

VIII

THE INDICTMENT

INCIDENTAL reference has been made in the preceding chapter to the indictment[1] but without describing it or analyzing its purpose. The indictment consists of a statement of the facts charged against the defendant and constituting the asserted offense and a designation of the offense which they constitute. Before considering further what the foregoing sentence implies, it is necessary to list the purposes served by an indictment and to describe its origin and authorship. The indictment serves three purposes that are so basic that it is no wonder that it has a history as long as that of the grand jury itself. These purposes are so inherently necessary that they will continue to be with us as long as it is possible to foresee. Therefore in that sense an indictment or a document performing the same function is bound to be with us indefinitely.

One of these purposes of the indictment is to inform the accused person of the charge that will be brought against him at the trial, so that, being aware of this charge, he may prepare his defense accordingly. True, if he has been bound over by the magistrate, he already has a fairly definite idea of what the charge is, but even here it is more or less necessary to him because the bind-over may not particularize minutely and even more because the grand jury may have chosen to indict him on some other charge than that named in the bind-over. Where he has not been bound over and the grand-jury action is the first, it is of course particularly obvious that he needs this information. To that end it is necessary for the indictment to contain a statement of the factual situation that the prosecution will try to prove at the trial. In addition to informing the de-

1. Except where the context indicates the contrary, the term "indictment" is used in this chapter to include a presentment (see chap. vii, n. 2).

125

fendant, another purpose served by the indictment is to inform the trial judge what the case involves, so that, as he presides and is called upon to make rulings of all sorts, he may be able to do so intelligently. The third purpose of the indictment is to serve as a record for all time of what it was that this defendant was charged with on this particular occasion, so that, if in the future he is again charged, he will be able to point out in a definite unanswerable way that this is a charge that has already been disposed of and that he therefore cannot be called upon to answer to a second time, or, conversely, if he falsely sets up the assertion that this is a matter that has already been disposed of, so that there may be a means of showing that this charge is a different one from the one that was previously disposed of.

It would seem obvious that these three purposes of an indictment are so fundamental and so practically necessary that the indictment or an analogous document will be with us for a long time to come.[2] From them, also, it is evident that at the trial the prosecution will be limited to proof of the charges contained in the indictment. Facts not in support of the indictment cannot be shown, even though incidentally they may reveal the defendant as guilty of some other offense. For such other offense there must be (and may be) its own indictment.

The actual drafting of the proposed indictment is done by the prosecutor. In the earlier English law, before the creation of a public prosecutor, this meant the private party—usually the victim—who was the moving influence in the case. Today, of course, it means the prosecuting attorney.[3] This instrument is

2. Since the purposes just indicated are by no means solely for the benefit of the defendant, it follows that he cannot waive an indictment by the grand jury. Statements to the contrary usually turn out to mean merely that he can acquiesce in the substitution, for grand-jury indictment, of another form of procedure—the information—which will be considered in the next chapter. Apart from this qualification, the indictment is a jurisdictional fact which alone gives the court the jurisdiction to hear the case, and a so-called "conviction" without this jurisdictional basis would be a mere nullity. This being so, it would follow that the defendant had not been in jeopardy and that, if he is afterward brought to trial on a valid indictment, it will be jeopardy for the first time.

3. The drafting of an objection-proof indictment calls for such skill and specialization that in the large urban counties some particular assistant state's attorney will emerge as the indictment expert and may spend his entire time drafting them.

laid before the grand jury at the time when it hears the evidence against the accused. After the evidence has been heard, the jury deliberates as to whether "probable cause" has been shown—whether enough of a showing has been made to warrant trying the accused on the charges contained in the indictment. If twelve jurors[4] so vote, it is enough, and the instrument has become an indictment.[5] If less than twelve so vote, the charges are ignored, and the accused is discharged.

It now becomes necessary to consider the actual wording of the indictment—what statements it must contain and what tests it must meet. We shall soon find that these were, and to some extent still are, extremely exacting. This is due to a historical cause which has had a deep influence throughout the criminal law, substantive as well as procedural, with its influence on the structure of the indictment merely one of many. From the first emergence of criminal law until roughly the end of the eighteenth century it not only was a simple system characterized by terrible severity of punishment; it was heartily supported in this extreme severity by public opinion. Some two hundred crimes could be, and were, punished by public hanging, and exile, mutilation, and branding were commonplace. Convictions were simply and easily obtained, and this too met with public approval. Then, almost imperceptibly, a slow change occurred in the mental climate. There was growing horror at what came to be thought of as the savagery of the past. Acquittals, rather than convictions, met with favor. It is, of course, trite to point out that any strong enough and deep enough change in public opinion will sooner or later make itself felt in the law and be reflected in judicial decisions. So judicial activity insensibly came to be directed toward securing immunity and freedom

4. Curiously enough the number twelve is always the one required, although obviously it constitutes a very different proportion of the jury as that varies from its minimum of sixteen to its maximum of twenty-three. There has been much speculation, mostly unconvincing, as to the reason for the number twelve (also the total membership of the trial, or petit, jury). One guess is that it is somehow connected with the twelve apostles.

5. It was at one time the custom, when an indictment had been voted, for the foreman to indorse on it the words, "This is a true bill." Hence the alternative, but now nearly obsolete, name for an indictment was a "true bill."

for accused persons rather than convictions and punishment for them.[6]

Under the common-law structure of adherence to established precedents any such goal would be sought not by a frank and admitted change in the accepted legal rules but rather by interpreting more and more strictly the requirements that the law had long recognized. Nowhere was there a more promising field for this sort of development than in scrutinizing the adequacy of indictments. Extreme strictness at this point could also be a convenient, though indirect, means of meeting the fact that, at the beginning of that period, there was practically no possibility of appellate review for an unfairly convicted defendant. The "discovery" that the indictment was inadequate could supply an extremely convenient escape from injustice.

It had always been necessary to charge the offense and in so doing to allege all the elements necessary to constitute that offense. There came, gradually, to be an almost incredible strictness in judging whether the allegations were sufficiently precise to give the defendant adequate information. Nothing, it was said, could be left to inference.[7] Everything must be expressed, in order to give him his due. The almost ridiculous result was a detail of statement and a complexity of language that soon made an indictment no longer intelligible to any but a trained reader, thus exactly defeating the court's pretended goal but admirably fitting in with the real one of multiplying the requirements to be met. The strangeness—to the layman, at least—of the documents that finally began to emerge was heightened by another factor—one which might well be called "the survival of the unfittest." Where an indictment was clearly, and obviously, good, phrased in all the necessary details and lacking none of the various requirements, defense counsel, anxious to appeal the defendant's conviction, saw that it was hopeless to criticize it. What then would be the fate of this well-drawn document? It would be known to the prosecuting attorney who drew it and perhaps to some of his successors in that office

6. Nowhere is there a better illustration of the points here being made than in the law of larceny.

7. In the language of the courts nothing could be "intended." This obviously unusual meaning for the word "intend" is probably directly derived from the French *entendre*, "to understand," "to infer."

if they chose to rummage through old files and dig it out. It would be known to the defense counsel in that particular case. But, as far as all the rest of the world was concerned, it would soon be forgotten, if it were ever known at all.

We may compare to this the fate of a less skilfully drawn one. Numerous defects and points of criticism might, it was hoped, be urged successfully against it. The reviewing court, however, let us assume, after considering each objection, concludes that it is barely sufficient. Every point has been considered with care, and its language set out in detail. At once it is enshrined in the court reports as a model that has been tried and found not wanting. It becomes the pattern for future draftsmen to look to. In other words, the chance for immortality of an indictment is best if it is so full of possible defects as to have engaged the long-time attention of the reviewing court but is barely good enough to have come out safely from that review.[8] Its near unfitness has insured its survival.

In recent decades the trend has reversed. With punishments reduced in severity and with efforts, rudimentary perhaps, to reform offenders, there is once again a tendency to press for convictions, and with it, too, the courts display a tendency to relax ultrastrict requirements. How far this has gone was shown by a recent survey which disclosed that over the United States as a whole less than 1 per cent of the criminal cases brought up for review were reversed because of faults in the indictment. This has been achieved not solely by the more liberal interpretation of the indictment's language but also by the increased use of relaxing devices. Before considering these latter, however, it will be necessary to give some attention to the principal requirements which indictments had (and, in relaxed strictness, still have) to meet.

The first and foremost requirement—full and precise allegation (viz., statement) of every necessary fact—has already been referred to. How far this requirement ought to carry us may be open to debate (and will be referred to again, below, in considering the so-called "short form" of indictment), but the argu-

8. See, for more detail, Arthur C. Train, *From the District Attorney's Office: A Popular Account of Criminal Justice* (New York: Charles Scribner's Sons, 1939), pp. 63 ff.

ments for this requirement are obvious and sound. To be criticized was the ridiculous extreme to which it was at one time carried. A few examples, picked at random, may be cited. To establish, for legal purposes, a cause-and-effect relationship between a blow and a death, the latter must follow the former by not more than a year and a day. An allegation that a blow caused "instant" death was held not enough, since it was not expressly stated that it was within a year and a day. Again, an allegation that the defendant murdered "Viola Hughes" was objectionable because it left to inference the fact that Viola Hughes was a human being and not a dog or a cat, the killing of which would not, of course, be murder. In another case the event in question was stated to have occurred on the "15th day of July, 1855." The court refused to infer that this was A.D. 1855. In still another it was stated that the victim languished a specified number of days and "then die." This, it was held, made no sense at all. Had it said "then died" or "then did die," it would have been intelligible. But "then die" called for inference and interpretation and was fatally inadequate. Fortunately, absurdities like these are now largely things of the past. But a full statement of the facts is still usually called for, and, as this is a requirement founded on sound sense, it will no doubt long continue.

Growing out of the need to allege all the facts is the rule that it will not be enough to set up mere conclusions instead of the facts from which these conclusions are derived. Thus, for instance, it will not suffice to say that the defendant "attempted to commit arson." When we say of someone that he attempted to do something, we shall find on closer examination that we are not thereby stating a fact but rather a conclusion arrived at from such facts as that he piled up combustible materials, that he lighted a match and set fire to the pile, etc. When the indictment merely sets forth the conclusion, the grand jury is simply inviting us to accept its inference without telling us on what it is based.[9] But here, too, the rigidity with which the

9. A weakness in this proposition which apparently was never fully realized lies in the real impossibility of distinguishing between "facts" and "conclusions." On closer scrutiny what has appeared to be a fact turns out to be only a conclusion resting on remoter "facts," which are open to the same criticism themselves. This problem, however, is beyond the scope of this book. But here, too, the line was drawn at a point governed not by the problems of a particular case but by the time in history when that case came before the court.

requirement is interpreted has varied from slight, to severe, to fairly slight again. For instance, a defendant is charged with receiving stolen goods. The indictment must state that the goods were "stolen." Most of our courts will probably say that that requirement is satisfied by merely pinning the label "stolen" to the goods and that there is no need to set up the facts on which the conclusion that they were in fact stolen will rest—to say that they were stolen goods is to allege a fact of them, not a conclusion. Why, then, are the courts so ready to accept "stolen" as an allegation of fact and not as a conclusion? For the very simple reason that they had had to pass upon many indictments in which the words "stolen goods" were used long before the days of microscopic analysis of indictments. They had long before committed themselves to the view that "stolen" was an adequate statement, and they did not choose to reopen that question. Thus the actual and effective scope of this whole requirement calls equally for logical analysis and an examination of the positions to which the court has locally committed itself.

Allied to the matter just dealt with is the question whether the indictment must allege the intent with which the wrongful act was done and, if so, in how much detail. The argument for requiring full allegation of intent is obvious and clear. To constitute a crime, there must be both a criminal act and a criminal intent. Since both of these elements are necessary to constitute a complete crime, and since the indictment must allege all the facts necessary to constitute a crime, it inescapably follows that the defendant's intent must be fully alleged. The logic of this position is complete. Yet a contrary position can also be maintained. It can be argued that, while intent is a fact, it is a fact of a peculiar sort, in that it cannot be known directly but can only be inferred from other facts which are known to us. In other words, a statement that a certain intent was present represents merely an inference and a conclusion from the known facts. While it is true that the indictment should allege all the facts, it is also true that it should not set forth conclusions, which add nothing to the picture and which the jury is itself capable of drawing. These are the two extreme positions. Mostly the courts have taken a position somewhere between them. They have tended to hold that if the crime is one which is satisfied, not with any general wrongful purpose or intent but only with one specific kind of wrongful purpose, such as, for instance, assault and battery with intent to kill, which is not satisfied with the general wrongful intent adequate for an ordinary battery, then the existence of this specific intent must be specifically alleged. If, on the other hand, the crime is one that does not require a single specific kind of intent but is satisfied with any one of two or three or four or more different antisocial purposes (as, for instance, murder is satisfied with the intent to kill or the intent to commit a very serious crime that normally does not involve killing or any one of several other kinds of wrongful frames of mind), then there is no need to set up in precise form what the intent was, as the court will be willing to let it be inferred from the external facts that are alleged. Some courts have added to this last view the illogical requirement that in such cases, however, there must be in the indictment some adverb that expresses disapproval. For instance, that the defendant "feloniously" did so-and-so or that he "maliciously" did so. It is submitted that this is pointless and needless. It clearly is only a conclusion, on the one hand, and unenlightening, on the other.

This seems to be brought out especially clearly in burglary indictments. Burglary is a crime satisfied with any one of a number of wrongful purposes, of which the purpose of stealing is merely the commonest but by no means the only one. Therefore it has been held quite rightly that there is no need to allege in detail what the intent was. But then it has also been said that the indictment must state that the acts were done "burglariously." It is difficult to see what this word adds. It does not aid the defendant in preparing his defense, the judge in making his rulings, or future searchers in determining what transaction was disposed of in the particular case. It is merely useless formalism, reminding one of a book on etiquette.

Another area in which there is considerable disagreement as to the extent of the necessary allegations consists in the meeting and denying of defenses that the defendant might make. Manifestly it is not part of the "statement of an offense" to meet and deny all the range of possible defenses. Thus, for example, in a murder indictment which describes, let us say, a woman's killing of her husband in the course of a drunken brawl in a tavern, it is not necessary for the indictment to deny that she was then and there a soldier in the United States Army, that this was wartime, and that her husband was a soldier in an enemy army. Nor do we require any allegation to the effect that she was not the county sheriff and her husband was then and there under sentence of death and that she was lawfully executing him. To use a less fanciful illustration, insane persons are not capable of committing crimes, yet it is not required that the indictment allege the sanity of the defendant at the time of the asserted crime. All these are matters that the defendant may (if he can) raise at the trial, but they may be disregarded by the prosecution until then. This is so, we are told, because they are not part of the "gist" of the offense—part of its sum and substance. But what is and what is not part of the gist? It is simplest—and most accurate—to state at once that no clear line of cleavage has been worked out and that for each offense recourse must be had to the local decisions, if any.[10] At one time there was a tendency to adopt a rule which would at least have been definite but for which little else could be claimed. Under this view, where an offense was created by statute, we should regard as part and parcel of the gist of the offense everything contained in that section of the statute which set up and described the offense, while anything found in other sections should be regarded merely as a defense, and, therefore, for the defendant to raise, and that the indictment need not negative. Superficially this seems an easy and convenient solution, so long as we are dealing with offenses created by statute. But the trouble lies in the fact that there is no necessary correspondence between what constitutes the gist of the offense, on the one hand, and the division into sections, on the other. Fashions in statutory drafting differ almost as definitely over a period of

10. A good illustration of the difficulty of reaching an answer simply by logical processes is found in the crime of rape. The act in this crime consists in forcible intercourse without the woman's consent. Is the fact that she was not the defendant's wife part of the gist, so that it is necessary expressly to allege that she is not, or may the indictment be silent on this matter? Probably most persons would, offhand, suppose the latter to be correct. If so, they would be in error.

time as fashions in clothes. The expert in statutory drafting very probably could look at a statute on a subject that he was wholly unfamiliar with and make a good guess as to the approximate date when that statute was enacted. A generation or two ago it was the fashion to draft statutes with long sections and long sentences. These would normally conclude with numerous provisos that qualified the sweeping language with which the long sentence began. All this would be contained in one section. Today, for better or for worse, it is the fashion to use brief sentences and brief sections. The first section sets forth an offense, and each of the various qualifying situations appears in a separate subsequent section. The fashion in drafting has changed, and we have a different view as to what constitutes the clearest and easiest way to say what is to be said. Yet this does not denote any difference in purpose or plan. Thus to make the drafting of the indictment hinge in part on the division of material into sections makes this new type of statute-drafting signify something very different from what would be signified under the old form, whereas probably there was no intention to have any such distinction at all. Such unintended consequences should, obviously, be avoided.[11]

Where persons' names appear in the indictment (viz., the defendant's or the victim's), mere initials will not suffice. The first name must be given, or, if it is not known, that fact must be stated in explanation of the apparent inadequacy.[12] Or it may be necessary to give a description of an article. All that the law says is that the article should be described in an adequate way; what is adequate will depend upon the circumstances. Is a description of the thing that was stolen which merely reads "125 pounds of brass" an adequate description? Purely as a description it would seem so. We can visualize 125 pounds of brass as a definite thing or things—a lump of metal or pieces of

11. The authorities on this matter are gathered in the annotations to sec. 175 of the Model Code.
12. It may occasionally happen that parents not favored with even moderate common sense choose to name a child by a one-letter name. For example, the variation in the name "Jay" which spells it simply "J." This, of course, thereby ceases to be merely an initial. It should be mentioned, however, that the Model Code, sec. 157, would greatly relax the name requirements.

metal totaling a weight of 125 pounds that consist of the metal mixture we call brass. The allegation would be sufficient, and it would be supported by proof of the larceny of just that sort of an object—125 pounds of unworked metal of the mixture called brass. It would not, however, be supported by proof that what the defendant had taken was seventy-five candlesticks, each weighing a pound and two-thirds, and each constructed of brass. They would more naturally be described in terms of what they are rather than in terms of their raw material. In short, we do not so much face here a problem of adequacy of description as of correspondence between indictment and proof.

The draftsman of an indictment is, however, not merely faced with the problem of alleging enough. He may also find himself in trouble if he alleges too much or in too much detail. If, for instance, in a larceny charge a more than adequate description of the goods stolen is given and unnecessary details are included, the proof at the trial will have to bear out all the details so given. That "a black horse" was stolen might suffice, but if there is the added (unnecessary) statement that it was "a black horse with docked tail," the charge will not be supported if the tail was not docked. Thus all unnecessary language is potentially dangerous. The draftsman should not count on being saved by an occasional generous court's calling the added words mere "surplusage" and hence to be disregarded.[13] The indictment may also say too much by simultaneously charging the defendant with more than one offense or with divergent versions of how the offense was committed.[14] In either of these events the courts said this was ambiguous and uncertain; it was a double charge and called upon the defendant simultaneously to prepare himself against two or more different versions. He would not know which version would be the one relied on. It was not fair to put a defendant in such a predicament. This sort of defect was referred to as "duplicity." Sympathetic courts of some decades

13. An example of surplusage would be that in which a murder indictment asserted that the killing was committed not only "with malice aforethought" (which is a requisite part of murder) but also "without having the fear of God before him" (which is not a requisite part). The latter statement would be merely disregarded.

14. But see below on the device of multiple "counts."

ago displayed considerable skill in discovering a duplicity;[15] today there is an appreciable chance that the two factual versions will be regarded as identical, with the second merely amplifying the first.[16] It would be dangerous, however, to count on it.

A more generous treatment has been given to two other necessary allegations—venue and time. Every indictment must contain both: it must state where the offense was committed (i.e., its "venue") and when it was committed. Otherwise than what one might expect in the light of what has just been said, it is not necessary that the proof at the trial correspond exactly to the time and place alleged. It is enough if the proof shows that the offense occurred in a place over which that court has jurisdiction. In short, the venue allegation is not so much for the purpose of giving information as to the facts of the offense as it is to establish the fact that the court has jurisdiction.[17] In exactly the same way the allegation as to the time when the crime was committed is merely a jurisdictional one to show that the statute of limitations has not barred prosecution. The proof does not have to correspond to the time alleged.[18] It is enough if it appears that it was committed within the period of limitation,

15. E.g., an indictment charged the defendant with violating the liquor laws in that he sold spirituous or intoxicating liquor. This, the court said, was duplicitous, because two different things were charged. While there were many intoxicating liquors, not all of them necessarily were spirituous; some of them were merely fermented. Spirituous signified distilled, so that the two words could not be connected with each other as being merely alternative ways of stating the same thing. The indictment therefore, it was held, charged him with two different things, against both of which he might have to defend himself.

16. E.g., where minors were not allowed to play billiards without parental consent, a billiard-hall proprietor was charged with thus allowing a minor to "play or roll billiards." This, he contended, was duplicitous, as "playing" was one thing and "rolling" was another. Here, however, it was held that these were merely two different ways of describing the same thing, as though they had been joined by "to-wit."

17. In some instances the offense as part of its nature requires that it be committed in a specified type of place. Thus at common law the crime of burglary required breaking into a *dwelling*. Obviously the statement that the place alleged need not be proved does not apply when the place is a constituent element in the crime.

18. Here again there is a qualification paralleling that in the preceding note. Time may be a part of the offense itself. Thus burglary requires that the breaking-in be during the *night*. This thus becomes an element in the crime and must be proved.

viz., within the maximum time limit allowed. Obviously this much slighter strictness may confront a defendant with a real uncertainty as to what he will really have to defend himself against at the trial. If so, his remedy lies in asking for more precise and binding statements from the prosecution. They will be dealt with shortly, when considering a bill of particulars. It needs only to be added that the proposed Model Code[19] would do away with requiring any allegation at all regarding venue and time. It would be presumed that the offense was within the court's jurisdiction in both respects, unless the matter was raised by a showing that it was not.

In the face of all these strict requirements the common law and, more recently, statutes have developed certain relaxing devices. Some of these have already been indicated. Several very important ones must now be described. First and foremost is the device of multiple counts. The grand jury may not, at the time of finding the indictment, be certain as to which factual statement out of a number of possible ones represents the one that at the trial will emerge as the true one and therefore as the only one on which a conviction can be based. Yet, as has been indicated, only that factual version may be proved at the trial which is charged. Thus, in order to obviate this difficulty, a grand jury may vote not one but two or three or any number of indictments, each differing from its fellows only in a slight variation in the factual statement, so that, no matter which one of them will emerge as true, there will be one of the indictments that will fit it and will justify that proof. More simply than that, all these versions of a single transaction may now be incorporated in one indictment, each version being referred to as a "count" in the indictment. Thus each count is a complete statement of an offense—an inadequate or incomplete count may not be supplemented and aided by language found in another count—and proof as to any of them is germane and proper. The usefulness of multiple counts is particularly evident in charges of larceny, embezzlement, and obtaining property under false pretenses, where very slight factual differences may determine which crime has been committed. If only one count

19. Secs. 158 and 159.

were allowed, not only would it be necessary to commence all over again; it might even be impossible to secure a conviction at all, as the second jury might conceivably view the facts in a different light and believe that the first charge, and not the second one, was the one proved true.

Another device has greatly eased the problems of the draftsman of an indictment without changing the form or the wording of the latter. Defects in indictments are classed as either "substantial" or merely "formal." As will appear later,[20] merely formal defects must be raised at an early stage in the subsequent proceedings. If they are not then raised, they are waived and cannot later be raised for the first time. Substantial defects may, however, be raised, even for the first time, at any stage during the trial or even later. Obviously this means a huge difference in the practical value of the defect to the defendant. If it must be raised at once, there is a great likelihood that the matter can immediately be taken up again by the grand jury, and a new indictment voted by it, free from the defect. Thus the defect has merely gained a few days' delay. But, if it is of substance, the need to begin over again with a new indictment involves much greater inconvenience to the prosecution. In the meanwhile a new grand jury may have come in; the witnesses will all have to be called in again, their co-operation may be reduced and their memories dimmed, public interest has grown less, and hopes that the whole thing will be allowed to blow over have mounted. In short, many different advantages may come with delay. But whether a defect shall be characterized as substantial or formal may be a close question. In recent years there has been a marked tendency toward the latter, and many a defect that would once have certainly been held substantial is now pronounced formal only. By relaxing the consequences of error, the strictness is in effect itself relaxed.

Another device which, likewise by indirect action, has relaxed the strict requirements of indictments without expressly changing them is the bill of particulars. By a bill of particulars is meant a supplementary document supplying more precise and particular details than, at the outset, seemed needed and hence

20. See chap. xii.

more than, at the outset, were supplied. In strict logic the bill of particulars should be, and in the older cases it was, regarded as wholly inappropriate so far as indictments were concerned. The indictment, it was said, was either adequate, and hence good, or it was not adequate, and hence bad. If it was good, the defendant was furnished all that he needed and all that he was entitled to. If it was bad, objection could be made at a suitable time, and the indictment would be quashed. Thus in neither event was it appropriate for him to ask for a bill of particulars, and such an application should be denied. However logical this may sound, in fact it is a most unrealistic position. There are numerous instances in which an instrument (and the indictment is no exception) appears, when only it is looked at, to be fully adequate and detailed but where for special reasons, easily made apparent, this turns out not to be the case and where, therefore, further details are needed. For example, if the defendant is charged with a continuing offense, such as maintaining a common nuisance in that he blocked a public way with his truck, it may be highly important for him to know what occasions will be brought up against him, as his defense may be a very different one for different occasions.

It should, therefore, be recognized that in criminal proceedings, too, there is a legitimate place for the bill of particulars. The sharply logical approach is, however, correct to the extent that we should never slip into the error of believing that an indictment which, judged by the rules previously worked out, is inadequate and bad can be made adequate and valid by supplementing it with a bill of particulars.[21] It is the defendant's right to insist that the charge against him rest on grand-jury action and only on grand-jury action.[22] This right would be circumvented and partly lost if an incomplete indictment could be supplemented and in effect made complete by a bill of particulars created by the prosecuting attorney. Whether the defendant should have this absolute right is another question; but, so long as we do accord it to him, it

21. In this connection see also the discussion below of the "short form" of indictment.
22. This sweeping statement will have to be qualified (cf. chap. ix, "Information").

should not be indirectly denied.[23] In view of the foregoing it may be wondered how the bill of particulars can then be regarded as a relaxing device against strictness in drafting indictments. This it is nonetheless, because the very fact that a bill of particulars is in reserve for a defendant's use will have, perhaps unconsciously, an effect on a court. If it is necessary to determine, in a situation without binding local precedents, whether certain border-line averments should or should not be required in an indictment, and whether in their absence the defendant was or was not given adequate information, the knowledge that a decision against their necessity will not leave the defendant helpless but that the door is still open to him to get really needed information will consciously or unconsciously make for greater readiness to uphold the indictment. In that sense, and in that sense only, the possibility of a bill of particulars can be properly regarded as a factor in reducing the strictness of indictments. Its existence tends to make courts a little more ready and willing to regard an indictment as not defective, which, were it not for this possibility, they would probably wisely call inadequate and defective.

Akin to the matter just discussed is the question whether an incomplete, or defectively worded, indictment can be cured by amendment. If the amending is done by the grand jury which first found the indictment (or perhaps, too, by a subsequent grand jury), there can be no doubt of its propriety; the agency that has the power to create has the power to modify and complete. But this is not the way in which our problem will be raised.[24] It will be squarely raised only where the "amending" is by the prosecuting attorney. Obviously, in the strict sense of the term this is not an "amendment" at all, since it is not ac-

23. For an excellent discussion of this point see Lester B. Orfield, *Criminal Procedure from Arrest to Appeal* (New York: New York University Press, 1947), pp. 238 ff. Orfield points out that, where the indictment is inadequate, not only would prosecution be based in part on charges outside the indictment but there would even be the constant risk that the facts and transaction which led the grand jury to act were not the same ones which the prosecuting attorney later set up in the bill of particulars. There would then be a complete denial of whatever right the defendant had to grand-jury action.

24. In fact, indictments are never amended by grand juries. It is simpler and safer to replace the defective instrument by an entirely new one.

complished by the creator of the instrument. That term is generally used, however, and hence will be employed here. If such
amending is permitted, it must be obvious that we have opened
up a very wide and important door of escape from the rigidity
of indictments. Under the older decisions a sweeping position
was taken: indictments could not be amended. In more recent
years, however, there has been a tendency to differentiate between amending in matters of substance and amending in matters of form. The former, it is still held, is improper and bad.
It is an attempt to substitute for the work of the grand jury the
work of another. Amending in matters of form, on the other
hand, is conceived of (in some states) as in no way a change in
authorship; it leaves the indictment the creation of the grand
jury, despite the polishing of details by the prosecuting attorney.
Undoubtedly there are weighty arguments of convenience in
favor of this view; a minor slip, an inadequacy of small consequence, can be corrected at little or no inconvenience. Logically,
on the other hand, it is more than difficult to justify, however
inconsequential the change. It is still a change coming from an
outside source. Logically the court might well refuse to recognize the change as having any effect or validity whatsoever and
proceed to treat the indictment as though no attempt to modify
its terms had been made at all. If the deadline for raising formal
objections has not yet been passed, the objection should be sustained, despite the amendment. If it has been passed and the
defendant now raises it for the first time, then it should be overruled, not because of the meaningless attempt at correction but
because correction is no longer needed. In the list of devices for
getting away from strictness in indictment drafting the method
of amending would seem to rank very low.

In the main the relaxing devices so far described all accomplish
their purpose by indirection—multiple counts make possible the
choice of various forms of expression; "formal," rather than
"substantial," defects reduce the consequences of error; a bill
of particulars or an amendment may, in part at least, give a
chance to correct a slip. In a few situations statutes[25] have di-

25. The common law has, in the matter now under discussion, shown little
or no initiative.

rectly authorized simplified factual statements. Thus reference has already been made[26] to the simplification that the Model Code would authorize in allegations of time and venue. There are a few others, the most important, perhaps, being in regard to allegations involving description of money. Thus in larceny of money, at the time when strictness of interpretation was in high favor, almost insurmountable requirements of precision as to exactly what numbers of what denominations of coins had been stolen could be, and were, imposed. Anything less than this, it was solemnly pronounced, would unfairly handicap the defendant in preparing his defense. To state the mere total taken would not be enough. Fortunately the absurdity of this was so apparent that it soon gave rise to statutes providing that it should be sufficient to allege the total sum of the money without necessarily specifying exactly what the makeup of that sum was. There have been a few other similar direct simplifications.

By far the most extreme example of simplification of this sort, however, is represented by the so-called "short-form" statutes. Typically such a statute will set forth certain forms for various crimes, declaring them to be adequate. Thus in a murder charge the indictment form may merely state that on a specified day at a specified place the defendant murdered a specified person. All factual details are left for specification in a bill of particulars.[27] This, of course, constitutes the ultimate in simplification. It is a safe statement that the short-form innovation has not proved a success and has been little used even in those states where there are such statutes. Their constitutionality is at least doubtful on the twin grounds that they do not supply the defendant with the facts charged against him and that so abbreviated a document no longer constitutes an "indictment" by a grand jury. There are also serious practical disadvantages.[28] Thus one very obvious danger is that it makes the drafting of an indictment so simple a process, and so easy a one, that it may lead to the slipshod procedure of a prosecuting attorney's asking a subservient grand

26. Text at n. 19 above.
27. Not all short-form statutes necessarily go as far as this.
28. Some of these may apply also to the devices already considered, but to a much smaller extent.

jury to vote an indictment first and carrying on his investigation later. Plainly, this is a real and serious danger, since the mere fact that an indictment has been found against a person is likely to do almost as much harm to his reputation as a conviction. To require at least some formulation of specific facts not only lessens this danger; it jacks up the efficiency of the prosecutor's office before, rather than after, it is too late.

While the short form's convenience to the prosecutor is obvious, it is usually not popular even with this official. Why this should be so can easily be understood by putting one's self in his place. If he is conscientious, he will do his best to secure a conviction which will not be reversed. If he is ambitious, he will have the same goal. His office files are full of forms used by him and his predecessors—forms tried and not found wanting, with not a single detail and adornment left out. What inducement is there for him to experiment with this innovation, merely to determine its constitutionality for the benefit of his colleagues and successors? It is no wonder that in many states short forms have been on the statute books for years but have not yet undergone the constitutional test by being used and being carried to the supreme court.

As a concluding remark on the general matter of the language of the indictment, it should be mentioned that the difficulties and their importance can easily be overemphasized. Actually, today (as has already been said), very few cases are reversed because of defective indictments. Not only are courts unsympathetic to such contentions; the accumulation of forms which have proved adequate and, in the larger offices, the development of specialists in indictment drafting have likewise contributed largely toward fully meeting this problem.

IX

THE INFORMATION

UP TO now our assumption has been that every criminal trial (except for the very minor charges, over which, as has been stated, the magistrate has summary jurisdiction)[1] must be preceded by, and rest on, an indictment by a grand jury. Yet it is obvious that this constitutes an extremely cumbersome procedure, involving the services of at least sixteen citizens, and possibly as many as twenty-three, to carry on a screening process already begun by the magistrate at the preliminary examination and possibly, too, by the prosecuting attorney in the exercise of his authority to drop prosecutions. It will not be a matter of surprise that there has been pressure for the development of a simpler and more direct procedure. In fact, such a simpler procedure, parallel to the grand-jury indictment, has long been in existence in England. In some minor offenses, never beyond the misdemeanor category, the king's attorney was permitted directly and on his own initiative to commence a criminal action, basing it on a statement drawn up by him and setting forth the pertinent facts with the same detail in every way as would be called for in an indictment. This document was, however, not called an indictment but an "information."

The only respect in which the remarks made in the preceding chapter relative to the rigid requirements of an indictment do not apply here is as to the logical appropriateness of amendments. There is no such inappropriateness, since here it is in fact the creator of the instrument who is changing it. If the defendant's interests are guarded by the court against sudden change without warning, even amendment as to substance, and not mere form, would seem to be wholly proper.

Informations, however, were never widely used. This was

1. See p. 87.

due to two reasons. One lay in the centuries-old view, already described, that fairness normally demanded that a grand jury give its approval to the initiation of proceedings. The other one arose from the fact—a very peculiar one to our present way of thinking—that until comparatively recently there was no public official in England corresponding to our American prosecuting attorney—a fact which, as has already been seen, has affected the law's development in numerous ways. In the first instance the criminal case was started only by the zeal and energy of the victim or the victim's family.[2] Thus the only functionary who could file an information was the attorney-general. But he, in turn, would normally be fully occupied by matters far more important than the minor cases to which informations alone extended.

In this country the extent to which informations are used ranges all the way from not at all to almost entirely. Thus in some states there is express constitutional provision that all criminal proceedings shall be upon, and only upon, indictment found by a grand jury.[3] At the other end of the scale are provisions that criminal prosecutions may be based either on indictment by a grand jury or on information, with no qualifying or restricting language, thus making the two methods exactly equivalent to each other as alternatives, regardless of the nature and seriousness of the crime charged.[4] Between these extremes there is a mass of states which neither wholly allow nor wholly

2. Even deep into the days of Queen Victoria the prosecuting attorney in a great many, if not most, of the more important criminal cases was specially employed by the crown for that specific case in exactly the same way as the defendant would specially employ a barrister to defend him. Perhaps one of the reasons why criminal-law practice has been on a higher standard of repute in England than in this country has been that the successful criminal-law practitioner in England would at times find himself on the prosecution side rather than on the defense side—to the great advantage of a more objective viewpoint. The point emerges forcefully in the career of Sir Edward Marshall Hall, the leading criminal lawyer of his day. His biography by Marjoribanks can be recommended as both informative and interesting.

3. This sweeping statement is subject to two qualifications. One is that the guaranty usually does not extend to proceedings under martial law. The other qualification (which may not be expressly mentioned in the constitution but is always read into it) is that the guaranty of grand-jury indictment is not applicable to those minor offenses over which a magistrate has summary jurisdiction.

4. So in England the grand jury has, practically speaking, disappeared as a prosecuting mechanism in favor of the information.

forbid the use of an information, but permit it under various combinations of circumstances. Generalization here becomes impossible because various circumstances and factors may be taken into account, with some emphasizing one factor and others another, while combining them in various patterns.

Thus we may find that an information is permitted as an alternative method in all misdemeanors but is excluded as a possible method in all felonies; or, similarly, the line may be drawn depending upon the seriousness of the punishment, with informations permitted in all misdemeanors and all felonies not punishable by death but not in capital felonies. Again the line may be drawn by requiring that, before an information can be filed, the accused be entitled to have a preliminary examination by a magistrate. (It will be remembered that a grand jury can be the first to act, thereby depriving a person of his preliminary examination.) Or this guaranty of a preliminary examination may extend only to more serious charges. Or, lastly, securing leave of a court of record may be a prerequisite to an information.[5]

Obviously all sorts of combinations are possible between these types of screening devices, emphasizing the degree and seriousness of the offense, the presence or absence of a preliminary examination, and the presence or absence of court permission.[6] It should be added, at this point, that if a state chooses to commit itself, in part or even in whole, to the use

5. Where the permission of a court is necessary, the proceedings conducted by the judge to determine whether or not to grant permission constitute what newspapers often refer to as a "one-man grand jury."

6. The language of the Illinois constitution is peculiar. After specifying that prosecution shall be by indictment, it goes on to state that the grand jury may "in all cases" be abolished. Does this mean that the legislature has only the choice between wholly retaining and wholly abolishing the grand jury? Or does it mean that the legislature is entirely free to determine whether, and, if so, to what extent, to substitute information for indictment? The legislature has assumed that the latter is the meaning, since it has provided in the act setting up the Municipal Court of Chicago that that court shall have jurisdiction to try misdemeanors committed inside the city limits and that these proceedings may be upon information, without at the same time in any way modifying the requirement of grand-jury action for cases brought in the Criminal Court of Cook County (in which Chicago is situated). An incidental result of this has been that the Municipal Court has acquired a practical monopoly of the local misdemeanor cases because of the greater simplicity and convenience of proceeding by information.

of informations, this will not constitute so radical a modification of historical precedent as to deprive an accused person of the "due process" which is guaranteed him under the federal Constitution. It is entirely permissible for a state to follow its own wishes in the matter.[7]

In view of this freedom of choice it is necessary to consider the respective advantages and disadvantages of the two methods of procedure. Neither has an entire monopoly of either. The great merit always claimed for grand-jury action is that it is a protection for the individual citizen against arbitrary and unjustified criminal prosecution launched solely by one possibly biased official. It means, it is urged, that only where there is a basis for the prosecution will a prosecution be launched and that that decision will be made in the democratic way which has come more and more to characterize Anglo-Saxon legal procedures.

At one time this danger was in fact a great one, as prosecutions were often little more than semilegalized examples of royal tyranny, and such a safeguard as this was very definitely needed. It does not follow, however, that the need remains unchanged today. The prosecuting attorney has himself become part of the democratic structure and is normally an elected officer. Whatever may be true in isolated cases, normally he is not acting as the tool of an autocratic master. Furthermore, even if in some slight degree the danger still exists, it may be asked to what extent the modern grand jury serves as a protection. Granted that at one time the grand jury was a powerful restraint upon prosecutions, and that action was taken by it only on the basis of careful and independent decisions of its own, is

7. It should be pointed out that Congress has no power thus to modify the procedure for serious federal offenses, since the Constitution clearly forbids it. If, then, an accused has been bound over by a federal commissioner (in the federal system the term "commissioner" is used where we have used the word "magistrate"), he is entitled to insist on an indictment as the basis for any further proceedings. May he, however, waive this guaranty if he chooses and permit the federal district attorney to file an information; that is, is this a waivable right? There are, after all, many constitutional guaranties that may be waived and others that may not, so that the mere statement that there is a constitutional guaranty does not supply the answer. Under Federal Rule 7(b) it is provided that in a noncapital case he may so waive. What the possible inducements are for him to do so will be considered later.

that still true today? No doubt in the great majority of cases
the grand jury not only hears the evidence but after hearing
it makes up its own mind whether to vote the indictment or not.
But what is here involved is not the great majority of cases,
where there is nothing wrong, but only the exceptional case in
which the prosecuting attorney might be a vindictive prosecutor.
It is only then that the question really arises. In such a case it
is more likely than not that the grand jury will be largely guided
by and, therefore, influenced by the attitude and the views of
the prosecuting attorney, and its decision whether to vote an
indictment or not may be little more than a rubber-stamp reflection of his attitude, as shown by his arguments and the
energy with which he presents his witnesses. Indeed, there is even
room seriously to argue that the citizen's protection may be
actually lessened by the grand-jury action, because in any situation whatsoever protection is really cut down, if we do not
centralize and spotlight responsibility on the person who in fact
carries the responsibility. The pliant grand jury may serve as
a convenient shield to hide behind.

There are, however, other arguments in favor of retention
of the grand jury that are not so often raised but that carry
much more force. Thus the possibility of grand-jury action
has a very real importance and, therefore, advantage in those
crimes that in one way or another involve problems of official
corruption or crimes that have religious aspects to them (viz.,
where minority religious groups are the victims of the criminal
conduct). The same is true in crimes that in one way or another
have a racial aspect to them and in conspiracies that have to do
with these various matters. Plainly it is then desirable to bring
into play or keep in play a weeding-out body that will represent
a cross-section of the community where, because of this special
aspect, there would be too great a danger were the entire decision intrusted to one person, the prosecuting attorney. He himself might be involved in sympathy or in direct contact with
the group whose prosecution was in contemplation. This constitutes so strong an argument that it would be folly to abandon
the use of the grand jury entirely and to abolish it as an institution. The utmost length to which we should go is to replace it
for the usual prosecution, while holding it in reserve for any

situation where for one reason or another there is fear of a biased or inadequate action by the prosecuting attorney. It should always be possible in such a state of affairs for the court to empanel a grand jury.

Another argument in favor of the grand jury that has considerable force is that it may enable the prosecuting attorney to get his witnesses on record. There may be much more danger of their changing their story where they have merely been interviewed in the privacy of his office. Furthermore, their appearance before the grand jury can be compelled by means of a subpoena. His personal interview does not enjoy this advantage. The grand jury, moreover, is also useful in the very fact of its being made up of representative citizens. It may be convenient through their help to determine at an early stage whether the case should be prosecuted or not. In many instances this must be decided on extralegal considerations. An example would be found in a so-called "mercy killing." If the community attitude is such that a trial jury will not in any event convict, then, the sooner the community attitude becomes effective, the better. The grand jury is a means to obtain the community reaction at the earliest possible date.

Finally, apart from its directly criminal activity, the grand jury must in any event be kept in existence as a body charged with the responsibility of supervising the jails and various other county institutions and seeing to their cleanliness, adequacy, and safety. If it exists for this purpose, there is correspondingly more argument for making suitable use of it in its criminal function as well.

All this, however, is not enough to warrant a refusal to allow informations as alternative ways to proceed. In the great majority of cases, in which these considerations do not arise, the method of information may, and does, hold out great conveniences and advantages. This is disclosed by the fact that, in the states which permit the wide-scale use of informations as an alternative to indictments, we find that the information is actually employed in 95 per cent of the cases.[8] These advantages

8. Reference has already been made (n. 6 above) to the fact that in Chicago the Municipal Court has obtained practically a monopoly of the local misdemeanor cases.

are felt both by the prosecution and by the defense. Most important is the greater speed of informations. It is only in counties with a very large population—probably with an urban center—that a grand jury will be in continuous session. In rural areas it will quickly terminate its work and may then be discharged. In that event nearly six months may elapse before the next grand jury comes into existence. During all this time the accused, despite the presumption of innocence, is either waiting in jail or is out only on bail. The information can, on the contrary, be filed at once. Nor do witnesses disappear or lose the vividness of their memory. The only person who would normally benefit from delay and who would, therefore, welcome it would be the guilty accused. He alone stands to gain by any growing forgetfulness of the witnesses or any developing haze in the clarity of their memory. And, of all those whose interests we may consider, he is obviously the least appealing![9] But even the guilty person may in many instances wish for speed. He may know that an indictment is inevitable and that the case against him is so strong that he will plead guilty. The sooner he begins to serve his sentence, the better, since time spent waiting in jail does not count for him.

Furthermore, a grand jury is an expensive piece of machinery. It involves not only jury fees but also those of witnesses as well as salaries for bailiffs. It makes heavy demands on the time of a substantial group of citizens who serve on it and on witnesses who in any event have probably already told their story at a preliminary examination[10] and, if the case is at all important, in an interview with the prosecuting attorney. Not only is all

9. It should go without saying that urging the desirability of speed does not mean favoring such rush action as to involve the danger of injustice by providing no time to prepare a defense. In a case where a crime was committed in the morning, the accused was at once arrested, an information was filed at noon, a plea of guilty was entered in the afternoon, and the convicted person was in the state penitentiary by evening, the United States Supreme Court very properly held that there was necessarily a denial of due process.

10. In an urban center this loss of time by witnesses can be, and is, greatly reduced by having the magistrate hold his examination in the same building where the grand jury sits and by having the grand-jury hearing immediately after the bind-over. But such time economy is not always possible. The two steps may well constitute two wholly separate annoying calls on the time of a witness.

this a disadvantage to the witness; it is such also to the state, because the state is confronted with steadily decreasing cooperation and with the highly probable unwillingness on the citizen's part to become a witness in the first place, where this can be avoided by not coming forward voluntarily with useful information. Considering the importance to police and prosecutors of information voluntarily supplied, this must be an important consideration and may be a significant factor in the efficiency of the information (a matter which will be discussed shortly).

With so many weighty arguments pro and con there seems to be only one conclusion that is free from doubt—the inadvisability of adopting either of the two extreme positions: wholly abolishing the grand jury in favor of the information, on the one hand, or, on the other, completely rejecting the information as a possible method of procedure. Which of the various compromise positions should be taken is a more difficult question. Drawing a rigid line, based on the seriousness of the punishment, seems undesirable, although requiring leave of court in more serious cases may not be unwise. Probably best would be a sweeping permission to use informations but preserving the possibility of summoning a grand jury as a stand-by method where needed. But it can be said with considerable confidence that, wherever the line is to be drawn, it should not hinge on whether there has or has not been a preliminary examination. The efficiency of our typical magistrates (as has already been pointed out) is not such as to make it wise to assign this screening function to them.

Turning now to the efficiency and convenience of the information as a selector of what cases should be prosecuted, the experience of those states which use it seems to be highly favorable. Nowhere, where it has been tried, has it been abandoned or rejected. On the contrary, where it is available, it has practically completely supplanted grand-jury indictment. Furthermore, comparison on the basis of the percentage of convictions in total prosecutions shows a higher figure for informations than for indictments, indicating at least the possibility of more discriminating selection. Nor is this surprising. Where indictment is used, the prosecuting attorney can always blame the failure to obtain a conviction on the grand jury—they should never, he will assert, have indicted in the first place. But if he himself is the one who is responsible for the prosecution, it is his fault, and he will show a much greater care in selecting the cases beforehand. At the same time, any argument based on percentage of convictions should be used with great care, as the percentage figure can so easily be meaningless or even deceiving.[11] The figure may be kept high because prosecutions are initiated only where the case is so strong that a conviction is a practical certainty.[12] Nor is this the only device by which to keep convictions high. As will be discussed later in more detail, it is possible for a prosecuting attorney, on an indictment or information charging a person with a felony, to waive the felony and ask merely for a trial on a misdemeanor that is comprised in the felony.[13] There is little to prevent a prosecuting attorney unduly anxious to secure a high proportion of convictions, and thereby a high average, from making a deal with the defendant whereby he (the prosecuting attorney) will waive the felony, with a possibility of penitentiary confinement, in return for the defendant's co-operating to the extent of pleading guilty to the misdemeanor. If it is a case where probation is permissible, the deal may be even further sweetened by his agreeing to recommend that probation be granted by the judge. Everyone emerges well content. The prosecutor has his conviction, instead of the hazards and uncertainties of a trial, and the defendant his freedom or, at worst, a short jail term. If he has a record of prior convictions, there is not even the factor of loss of good reputa-

11. Voters might, very often, bear this in mind when asked to re-elect a prosecuting attorney because of his success in obtaining convictions.

12. There is a complete and obvious analogy here to baseball fielding averages. A poor fielder may well have a high average by never going after the hard ones. When they are not tried for, they are not missed. The percentage of convictions can also be kept delusively high by listing, not the number of defendants convicted, but the number of charges on which there were convictions. If there are numerous charges against one person, he may be as ready to plead guilty to all of them as to one if his sentences are concurrent.

13. For instance, it is a felony to steal an automobile; it is merely a misdemeanor to tamper with one. If X has been indicted on the charge of stealing an automobile, it is possible to find him guilty, on that charge, not of larceny of the automobile but merely of tampering with it, because the smaller is comprised in the greater (see chap. xiii).

tion to alloy his satisfaction. Even the innocent accused (and here the "deal" is at its worst) may prefer a light though undeserved punishment to the risk of worse. But even with all these qualifications it is not wholly without significance that the conviction percentage is higher in informations, especially as studies have disclosed that there was not, accompanying it, any higher percentage of waivers of felony or of probations. In other words, two of the negative factors that might have reduced or eliminated the value of the rate of convictions were both investigated and found not to be present. In its actual and practical working the information seems to have confirmed the theoretical case for it.

X

JURISDICTION AND VENUE

THE indictment having been found (or the information filed), the case now goes to the trial court for trial. Before commencing on this proceeding, however, it will be necessary to consider what particular court has jurisdiction to try a given criminal case.[1] It is not planned to deal here with true jurisdictional questions,[2] as these involve substantive, rather than procedural, law. Suffice it to say that any sovereignty may, if it has the power, direct its courts to act in reference to any matter, anywhere. Ordinarily, however, nations act only in situations falling into one or the other of two types: (1) the personal and (2) the geographical.

1. The personal type is that in which one (or both) of the parties to the dispute is a citizen or subject of the nation in question. Instances of this are the only recently abolished consular courts maintained in some oriental countries by various Western countries. Until a few centuries ago this basis of jurisdiction was one widely relied on. If two citizens of France were to engage in a fight in Rome, it was for the king of France to deal with them (if he could lay hold of them—a matter which was his problem). It was none of the concern of the Roman authorities. This basis of jurisdiction is now, practically speaking, obsolete.[3]

---

1. Logically the points made in this chapter should precede the chapter on the grand jury, since a grand jury convened by a given court has no wider jurisdiction itself than has the court which convened it. For reasons of convenience, because the issue of jurisdiction will only be raised when the case is before the trial court, it has been postponed to this place.

2. Viz., where an act that is undoubtedly criminal involves more than one sovereignty, which of these should be regarded as the one where (or against which) the crime has been committed.

3. For this reason nothing will be said regarding the many practical difficulties raised by it. There was not only the problem of getting the parties into court (unless a local court was maintained, as, for instance, a consular court)

2. The geographical type is that in which the nation within whose boundaries the crime is committed is the one to feel itself offended. Under this viewpoint the nationalities of the doer and of the victim are irrelevant. This is the basis on which universally jurisdiction is based today.[4] Here, too, however, special problems may arise. Mostly these deal with the problem of exactly locating a crime involving several countries. If X, standing in Country A, fires a bullet which strikes Y in Country B, and Y crawls into Country C and dies there, where has the murder been committed? Which is the country that is offended? In slander by radio is the crime committed where the speaker is, or the broadcasting station, or the hearer? These are all questions of substantive law and, as already stated, fall out of our scope.

It is within our scope, however, to examine which particular court within a given sovereignty is to carry the responsibility of conducting a given criminal trial. Here, too, the common law has rigidly adopted the geographical test, giving jurisdiction[5] to that court, and that court only, which functions in the area in which the offense occurred[6] and to which the handling of criminal matters is intrusted.[7] This limitation of competence to

---

but also the question of which sovereign had jurisdiction when two foreigners of different nationalities were involved. The recent Fascist attempt to revive this doctrine has, happily, come to a deserved end.

4. Special provision must, of course, be made for crimes committed on the high seas.

5. In the present problem of which court in a given sovereignty is to deal with a case the word usually used is not "jurisdiction" but "venue."

6. It is, of course, obvious that, in determining "where" a crime was committed for the purpose of determining venue, exactly the same problems will be encountered as were mentioned just above in connection with jurisdiction. Indeed, so rigidly logical were some of the early writers that they expressed serious doubt whether the venue for a murder charge could properly be laid in either county, where a blow was struck in one county and the victim thereafter died in another! Such uncertainties as to the correct venue are nowadays usually disposed of by statute.

7. The statement is made in this restricted manner because, of course, courts are not differentiated merely on the basis of rank—lower and higher—but also on that of function. Thus a probate court or a court of claims or a tax court obviously has nothing to do with criminal matters—no "criminal jurisdiction." There is hardly ever any difficulty in determining which local court has criminal jurisdiction, as the instrument that creates the court—be it a written constitution or a statute—will speak adequately as to the kind of matters that it is to deal with. One, and normally only one, court receives as part of its share the criminal work. (There are occasional partial exceptions. Thus in Chicago mis-

the local court only has in the United States been even raised, in most or all of the states, to the status of a constitutional guaranty of local trial.[8]

---

demeanor cases may be heard in either the Municipal Court or the Criminal Court of Cook County.)

An apparent, and to some extent real, clash may, however, arise where there is locally a juvenile court and the charges are against a juvenile. Which court is to deal with the matter? In theory the juvenile court has no concern in a crime as such. It exists simply to implement our doctrine that the citizen who is below a certain number of years is a ward of the state. The state owes to this citizen a degree of attention, care, supervision, and helpful guidance that it does not owe to the adult citizen. In order to implement this obligation, the state has set up a special court for those wards who are under a specified age. This court is to shield the juvenile from a bad start in life by taking such protective steps as may be needed. This need will usually be indicated by one or the other of two situations. It may be shown because the juvenile is a homeless orphan or because his parents are unable or unfit to carry out their responsibility. In short, the ward's need for care may be shown by his being what is technically called a dependent child. Or the need for state supervision may (perhaps even more frequently) be shown through his engaging in conduct that points definitely to future lawbreaking. He is then referred to as a "delinquent child." The manner in which the delinquency has shown itself may or may not be (but very probably is) in conduct which, were it to be committed by an adult person, would unquestionably be regarded as a crime. Assuming that the child is not so very young as to be outside the criminal law (seven years of age, at common law), which court is to exercise jurisdiction? The juvenile court, as presenting a delinquency, or the criminal court, as presenting a crime? The issue may be avoided through one or the other court's yielding—for example, if it finds that the other has already taken the matter up—or it may be avoided by the arresting police officer's exercising discretion as to the direction in which to channel the case, thus making it likely that the other court will never even hear of the case.

[Footnote 7 continued on p. 157]

8. This view is not necessarily that of other law systems too. For instance, in Germany it is entirely possible to have the trial elsewhere than where the crime was committed. Our doctrine is rather an outgrowth of the jury system as it was in its origin, when the jury was made up of a group of persons who had personal knowledge of the crime. Persons that we should today describe as the witnesses got together and decided what they knew to be the facts and what, as a consequence, the guilt or innocence of the accused person was. Obviously it was logical that the trial should be held where the witnesses clustered in greatest numbers, that is to say, in the immediate neighborhood in which the crime was committed. We adhere to that view even though today our notion of the jury has become an entirely different one.

But in England since 1925 there has been an abandonment of the old principle of local trial as necessarily the only one; it is now possible by statute to hold the trial (as in continental European law) where the accused person is apprehended. It is only one more example of how often English law has broken more radically from the past than American law has. Another example mentioned in the preceding chapter is the practical disappearance in that country of the grand jury as a prosecuting mechanism and its replacement by the information.

The law having thus committed itself to the local basis of venue, are there any direct or indirect exceptions? The answer is, "Yes, a number of them." Even the common law created one, although in its best tradition there was an avoidance of a frank admission that it was an exception. A larceny charge might be brought in any county into which the thief removed the stolen property and not merely in the one where he actually took it. True, it was pretended that this was no exception by asserting that every moment of possession constituted "a fresh taking"—a position which, had it been logically followed out, would have meant that there were as many larcenies as there were counties involved, and so, presumably, there might be an equal number of convictions! Actually it was merely a recognition at an early date that larceny is a peculiarly mobile crime. The typical thief in the days when this doctrine of "continuing trespass" took

----

[Footnote 7 continued from p. 156]

But a real competition may, and occasionally does, arise. In that event three solutions are possible, and all have support: (1) the first court to take jurisdiction may insist on retaining it; (2) the juvenile court may claim jurisdiction; or (3) the criminal court may claim it. Enthusiastic advocates of the juvenile court were greatly disappointed when the Illinois Supreme Court, in *People* v. *Lattimore*, 362 Ill. 206 (1935), took the last view. It is submitted, however, that this disappointment was somewhat unrealistic. The issue is almost sure to arise only in instances of particularly atrocious or serious crimes, involving juveniles of far more than minor concern. It may be granted that the criminal court is unequipped to deal constructively with them and that what little chance of their redemption remains will probably be lost. It does not follow that, in the larger view, society's interest is served by forcing them on the juvenile court. The danger constantly overhanging every juvenile court is that it will insensibly and gradually take on the psychology and attitudes of a criminal court and that the public will tend so to regard it. Such a change seriously undermines and lessens the efficiency of the court in dealing with the great majority of its cases. And it is a change sure to be speeded by its handling serious cases of young criminals. It seems more than doubtful that the slender chance of saving these latter is worth the inevitable cost to the vastly larger number of dependents and lesser delinquents.

Not to be confused with juvenile courts (which, as has just been said, are not criminal courts) are the increasing numbers of "youth courts." These are criminal courts which devote their entire time to criminal cases involving accused persons in the fairly young age brackets (brackets that are of great and steadily growing importance). Such youth courts are usually given a wider range of punitive and rehabilitative measures than can be used for older offenders. These courts need not be described in detail here, since they are part of the criminal-court machinery and are merely specialized in regard to the defendants dealt with. As to the punitive and rehabilitative measures available to them see chap. xv.

shape was a cattle thief, just as in every primitive community. That was the kind of property that could be run away with. It was a highly mobile situation. Since he moved rapidly with his plunder, other areas might quickly become involved. And the enforcing of the law was in the hands of people who owned the cattle and who were just as bitterly resentful of the cattle thief as our own western frontier was; and they proceeded to formulate the law the way in which they would secure the maximum protection against this public enemy. An efficient means to this end was to allow the proceedings to be held wherever it was simplest and most convenient. By statute the doctrine has in some states been extended to kidnaping and to receiving stolen goods.[9] The doctrine is always phrased as a matter of substantive law (which logically it is not) and will not be further dealt with here.

Another and less drastic departure from local proceedings has been created by an innovation in the Federal Rules. Rule 20 would permit defendants apprehended in a federal district other than the one where their alleged crime was committed to plead guilty in the district where apprehended provided the United States district attorney in the district where the trial would otherwise have taken place consents. Thus, to have the situation arise, two elements are needed: the defendant's wish to plead guilty and the district attorney's willingness to allow such a plea in this other district. Because it is restricted to a plea of guilty, the problem of inconvenience to witnesses is automatically excluded, since there will be no taking of testimony. At this writing the constitutionality of the rule has not yet been finally determined.[10]

9. Another extension, which cannot be dealt with here, is to apply the doctrine even across the lines of separate sovereignties (viz., across state lines). Here a doctrine that at least began as a practical one quickly loses that character. What is the effect of a trial and acquittal in State B on a second trial in State A? In the event of a conviction what measure of punishment shall be used, State A's or State B's? What of a pardon in State B? What if the rules of law differ? It would be far simpler and more convenient instead to force the accused's return to State A by the methods to be described in the next chapter.

10. The argument against it is that the court of the district where the arrest was made does not have jurisdiction and that jurisdiction is not a thing that can be conferred by the process of waiving a right; viz., while certain rights can

Another and older qualification on the strict local-jurisdiction rule has been formulated to meet the problem created by offenses committed very close to the county line,[11] and where, therefore, it may be difficult or impossible, in advance of trial, to know where trial should take place. To meet this situation so-called "county-line statutes" have been passed in some states, providing that the jurisdiction of each criminal court should extend, not merely to the county line, but to a specified number of feet (600 is a fairly common figure) beyond it. Thus there is created a border belt that is equally within the jurisdiction of two courts. The constitutional fate of such statutes has not been uniform. Some courts have struck them down, as perhaps depriving a defendant of that trial by a local jury—a "jury of the vicinage"— that is his right. Others have upheld them on the argument that the term "vicinage" is one of more or less uncertain meaning and that it is not an unreasonable thing for the legislature to interpret the constitutional provision, guaranty of a trial by a jury of the vicinage, as meaning something that had a larger area than county so that it could still be the "vicinage" even where it comprised the slightly larger area that these border-belt statutes substitute for the county area.[12]

Similar difficulties in determining just where an offense was committed may arise if it occurred in a moving vehicle, such as a train or an airplane, which, perhaps, was in several counties within a short period of time. Here, too, in similar fashion statutes have been enacted providing that the trial might take place in any of the various counties through which the moving vehicle

be waived by a person who is before a court that is entitled to hear and receive a waiver, it is impossible to create a competent court, vested with jurisdiction, by any so-called "waiver process." As the innovation is an interesting and perhaps promising one, it is to be hoped that these arguments will not prevail.

11. The jurisdictional limits may be other than county lines, of course, but they frequently conform to county lines; hence this term will be used for the sake of convenience.

12. In Illinois the guaranty in the constitution is of trial by a jury "of the county or district." Under it a statute of this kind was held unconstitutional in *Buckrice* v. *People*, 110 Ill. 29 (1884). "District," it was said, had the same meaning as "county" and so did not enlarge the allowable area. True, the word is not used elsewhere in the criminal law, and hence there is no direct clue as to its meaning. But presumably it was put in for some purpose. If it is merely synonymous with "county," what can that purpose be?

passed during its journey. Their constitutional fate, too, has been varied.[13]

While the foregoing are ways in which the possibility of non-local trial may present itself, it is far more likely to arise as a result of the contention by the defendant that he cannot locally obtain a fair trial.[14] Since local trial is, today at least, looked on as principally a protection for the accused, and only secondarily as a convenience for the witnesses and the prosecution, he may ask for and obtain a change of venue to another county, provided he can show reasonable grounds to believe that because of local conditions and prejudice a fair determination of his guilt is locally impossible.[15] It is necessary, in order to obtain such a change of venue, that he convince the judge to whom he makes his application not that there will be the impossibility of a fair trial but merely that there is a strong probability of it. In that event the trial will then be held in such other county as the judge may designate. Obviously it is for the judge to exercise considerable discretion as to whether a sufficiently convincing showing has been made.

Another possibility is that the defendant may contend that the judge who is to preside in his case is himself prejudiced

13. Such a statute, too, was enacted by Illinois. Strangely enough it was upheld in *Watt* v. *People*, 126 Ill. 9 (1888). Though only a four-year span separated the two Illinois decisions and the personnel of the court was largely the same, there was no attempt to distinguish the earlier case—indeed, it was not even referred to. It is difficult to believe that this was due to forgetfulness of so recent a decision. Was it because the court already felt doubtful of its earlier wisdom and found silence the best way out?

14. Whether the prosecution may make such a contention will be considered after dealing with the defendant's rights.

15. There is disagreement as to when the change of venue should be asked for. Under one view it should be asked for at the earliest opportunity, before the trial procedure is entered upon, so as to involve the minimum of inconvenience to all concerned. Only by so doing will the accused have acted with the requisite diligence. On the other hand, the other view holds that he should not raise this point until there has been an effort to get together a fair and impartial jury and to have them hear the case in an unbiased way free from pressure. If he asks for a change of venue before then, he is complaining of an injustice that may never arise. He may, however, under either of these views, be required, prior to asking for the change, to give notice to the prosecuting attorney that he proposes to ask for it, so that the former may marshal his evidence in opposition if he wishes to do so.

against him.[16] May he have his case transferred to another judge? At one time the answer was "No"; the law acted on the rigid (and obviously unfair) assumption that all judges were always unbiased. But under the modern view, either by statute or by change of common law, not only may a change of judge be asked for but we have swung to the opposite swing of the pendulum by holding that the change must automatically be granted. To hold otherwise would be to ask an allegedly prejudiced judge to pass on his own prejudice. The defendant may, however, be required in some states, by rule of court, to furnish certain supporting papers indicating a basis for the asserted prejudice, even though their truth cannot then be passed on by the judge.[17]

The final question is, "To what extent, if at all, does the prosecution have a corresponding right to ask for a change of venue or of judge?" So far as the latter is concerned, it should have rights identical to those of the defendant. There is no consitutional guaranty to the defendant entitling him to insist that the trial shall be conducted by the first judge to whom it is assigned. But a different question is raised where the prosecution asks for a change of place of trial, say, because the defendant belongs to a powerful faction or family or because for some other reason he will be given special favor locally. Constitutional guaranties are not conferred with the restriction that they are not to apply if it is inconvenient or inadvisable. So to limit them would in fact deprive them of all meaning. Accordingly, there is no corresponding right for prosecution change of venue.[18]

16. This, too, is referred to as a "change of venue," thus producing an unfortunate ambiguity. It will here be called a "change of judge."

17. Normally there is no requirement, as there may be when asking for a change in the place of trial, that he notify the prosecuting attorney of his plan to ask for a change of judge. The reason for this is of course obvious; this is not a matter for the discretion of the judge and the hearing of arguments pro and con. Since no evidence will be gone into, there is no need for the notice.

18. A few courts have held otherwise but without successfully meeting the argument contra.

XI

EXTRADITION AND RENDITION

HAVING seen, in the previous chapter, that courts will deal only with those cases which, according to the tests applied by them, fall within their jurisdiction, what sort of a situation is created if an accused person flees the country and is found to be in another country? Trial of him in the latter (usually called the "asylum country") is impossible. Trial of him in the country of origin is, under our practice, likewise impossible, since (as will be described in more detail later) a trial can take place only if the accused is present. At first this dilemma meant that the fugitive was in fact free from any danger, so long as he remained away, since there was no mechanism whatsoever for the surrendering-up of a person who had fled across national lines.

For a long time now, however, nations have operated under treaties with one another whereby, under the circumstances laid down in the treaties, they would co-operate by arresting and turning over to the authorities of the demanding nation certain specified persons. Typically, in these treaties, it was required that the demanding nation show to the asylum nation the fact that bona fide criminal proceedings had been begun against the accused, and in the normal treaty it was very carefully specified what kinds of crime alone were to be considered under these treaties.[1] This procedure is known as "extradition." Since the separate states in the United States are, for criminal-law purposes, separate sovereignties, basically the same problem and the same solution of it apply among them. Where, however, it is an interstate matter, the term usually used is not extradition but "rendition." As in extradition, the demanding state need merely

1. The reason for thus restricting them to specified crimes was that no nation which was the asylum of some fugitive proposed to be put in the position of being bound in honor to give up someone who was merely the victim of governmental persecution.

162

show that criminal proceedings have been in fact launched against the individual in question. To that end, the governor of the demanding state will transmit to the governor of the asylum state a certified copy of the indictment (or information) containing the charges. The governor of the asylum state will then issue his own warrant for the arrest of the individual and for turning him over to authorities from the demanding state when they arrive and, meanwhile, for his retention in the custody of the authorities of the asylum state.

Plainly these proceedings may take some time, with several days elapsing between the time the certified copy of the indictment is sent to the governor of the demanding state as the first step and the arrest as the final one. To prevent the flight of the accused during this interval, it is usually provided that, where the authorities in the demanding state announce, even by telegraph, to the authorities in the asylum state the fact that rendition proceedings are about to be begun, a magistrate in the asylum state may issue a fugitive warrant, ordering the immediate arrest of the accused and his detention, pending the arrival of the complete papers.

An increasing number of states is also providing by statute for the rendition, under specified circumstances, of witnesses who are needed at the trial and who by leaving the state have made themselves unavailable. This type of legislation is usually based on a model act prepared by the Commission on Uniform State Laws.

XII

THE ARRAIGNMENT

THE steps (or so many of them as may be involved) described in the preceding chapters having been completed, the defendant will be brought before the court which will ultimately try him.[1] This first appearance is, however, merely preliminary. It is known as the "arraignment." At it he is informed of the charges against him,[2] either by reading the indictment to him or by informing him of its substance. He is then asked what his answer to them is. At one time he had a fairly wide range of choice as to methods by which his guilt or innocence could be determined.[3] Today, if he denies his guilt, only one method of determining the truth is still in use—that of trial.[4] Thus his choice

1. Under the early law the arraignment could take place immediately after the finding of the indictment. Today a "reasonable" interval—a few days, usually—is allowed to elapse. More important, usually, is the question of how long the prosecution may defer this, as well as the other steps in a trial. State constitutions generally guarantee a "speedy trial," but there is no agreement as to exactly what constitutes "speedy." There may, too, be differentiation between the rights of defendants who are free on bail and those who are awaiting trial in confinement. Finally, there may be difference of view as to the consequences resulting from a denial of speedy trial. Under one view a defendant is then entitled to immediate trial, with no further delay accorded to the state. Under another he has been irrevocably deprived of the kind of trial that he was entitled to and, hence, must be discharged.

2. Today, in contrast to the earlier rule, he may usually ask for, and obtain, a copy of the indictment prior to the arraignment. He may or may not, according to local practice, also be entitled at this time to a list of the witnesses that the state expects to call to testify. If under the local view he is entitled to such a list, witnesses not listed may, nonetheless, be called by the state, but only with the consent of the court. Such consent will be given only where the state can show a good reason for not listing them, and the defendant will probably be further protected against surprise by being granted a continuance if necessary.

3. By ordeal by fire or water, by battle, by compurgation, or by trial.

4. The word "trial" is not related to the verb "to try" in the sense of "to endeavor." It and its accompanying verb stem from the French word *trier*, "to sort out." The Old English expression for choosing a jury trial was "putting one's self on the country"—the country being the residents thereof, who were to determine the question of guilt, instead of leaving it to divine determination, as did the other methods.

of answer is limited: he can plead guilty or not guilty, or he may, before choosing either of these pleas, make one or more of several other answers, each of which will be described before taking up the guilty and not-guilty pleas.

Before considering these various answers, it should be pointed out, however, that there is always the possibility that a defendant may refuse to answer at all. At one time this course of action by him completely stalled the legal machine—no further steps could be taken.[5] This, however, did not mean an easy road to immunity for defendants—far from it. Pressure could be, and literally was, put on him to answer by laying him on his back and placing heavier and heavier weights on his chest[6] until an answer was squeezed out of him.[7] Less dramatically today a refusal to answer —a "standing mute" in legal terminology—is considered as the equivalent of pleading not guilty.

Thus the arraignment was at one time a proceeding of great importance and significance, with very much hinging on it as to whether the case could go on, and which channel, out of a wide variety of channels, it would take. In each of these aspects it has lost standing and stature. It has grown steadily less significant, though it still preserves certain purposes. As has already been stated, the defendant may still make a variety of answers. Indeed, as will be shown, there are certain points and objections that either must be brought up at this time or be lost. But its loss of stature is clearly demonstrated by the fact not only that complete arraignment with all its formal steps may be waived but it will be assumed that it was waived from the mere fact that a defendant proceeded to plead without asking that the complete formalities be observed. By so doing, he has shown that the substance of his rights was given him, even though in an informal manner, and he

5. This is a logical result of the view, already described in chap. v, that the court in a criminal proceeding is a third party, utterly disinterested in the litigation and merely supervising its course, like a sort of arbitrator. The consent of both parties was necessary to give the arbitrator any standing. The refusal to plead prevented the court from gaining capacity to hear the case.

6. Hence the common phrase, "to press someone for an answer."

7. A brave and obstinate defendant might allow himself to be pressed to death. Since, as a result, he would not be convicted, his property would not be forfeited to the crown and his family thus left destitute.

cannot later on complain that a full and formal arraignment did not take place.

What, then, are the various choices open to a defendant and the various steps that he may take? They fall into three broad groups, and a defendant may avail himself of as many of them as the facts of his case permit. The only restriction on him is that, generally speaking, the contentions falling in Group I must be raised before those in Group II and Group III, and those in Group II before those in Group III. If not, they will be lost to the defendant.[8]

The first group is made up of contentions that go not to the root of the matter (viz., the merits and truth of the charges against him) but merely to the procedural steps thus far taken (viz., their adequacy and correctness). Upholding such contentions would presumably merely delay matters until proceedings could be taken that were free from such inadequacy or error. They are merely dilatory contentions. Thus (solely as examples), the defendant may assert that he was deprived of a preliminary examination though he had not waived it, that the grand jury was improperly constituted or had functioned in an improper manner, or that the indictment (or information) was defective or incomplete in its statement of the charges against him.[9] Since these matters are, in the main, capable of being corrected and the proceedings recommenced, it is obviously practical wisdom to insist that, if they are to be raised at all, it be done at the earliest opportunity, when there will be the minimum inconvenience in starting afresh.

A glance back at the examples just given of procedural defects

8. Some qualification, it will appear, will be needed to this sweeping statement (see n. 9).

9. If the asserted inadequacies involved merely formal defects in the wording (i.e., matters of no moment or substance), the comment in the text stands correct. If, however, the inadequacies involved matters of substance and importance, for example, the indictment alleged nothing that, even if true, would constitute an offense or (similarly) alleged only some, but not all, of the sum total of facts necessary to constitute an offense, this objection, being of a substantial nature, may be raised, even for the first time, throughout the trial. Silence at the present stage does not waive them (see also in chap. xiv the discussion of the motion in arrest of judgment). Obviously, then, the classification of objections as being merely formal or substantial is highly important. As has already been pointed out (chap. viii), the shift in classifying from the latter to the former has served the courts as a convenient relaxing device against the consequences of strictness in indictment-drafting.

will show that they all fall into one or the other of two kinds. Either the defect is one whose reality or nonreality can be determined simply by examining the written records available to the court (allegedly defective indictments would be the best example) or the defect is one whose existence or nonexistence can be determined only by an inquiry into the facts of the situation—for example, that the grand jury permitted unauthorized persons to be present during its sessions. Plainly these two kinds require different methods of action in determining the validity of the objection.

The former kind, raising as it does only questions of law, could be and is dealt with, alone and unaided, by the judge presiding over the arraignment. Such defects are raised in what is known as a "motion to quash." According as the judge finds the defect valid or not, he will sustain or overrule the motion. The other kind of objection, whose validity depends on the determination of a matter of fact, necessitates the hearing of testimony by witnesses and therefore a jury to decide what the truth is. It is raised by what is known as a "dilatory plea." If a defendant relies on numerous defects, it is entirely probable that it may be necessary for him to raise some by motion to quash and others by a plea, and of course he may then do both, assigning each of the various defects to the procedural method proper for it.

Under the earlier common law it was the duty of the trial court to impanel a jury for the sole purpose of hearing these factual issues and of disposing of the plea accordingly. Today the court is often given the privilege of postponing the decision of this issue of fact and submitting it, along with the principal issues, to the jury that will actually try the case on the merits. Under the more advanced codes, including the Federal Rules,[10] simplification has gone even further, and motion and plea are combined into one procedure—often given the intentionally new (and hence unincumbered by precedents) name of a "motion to dismiss."[11]

10. Rule 12.
11. What may be raised, and for how long, in a motion to dismiss is discussed by Lester B. Orfield, *Criminal Procedure from Arrest to Appeal* (New York: New York University Press, 1947), pp. 284 ff. The federal rule also provides that, if the motion to dismiss is sustained, the court may order the defendant held in custody pending the initiating of new proceedings, free from the procedural defect that caused the sustaining of the motion.

The simplification thus effected goes deeper than appears at first glance. The impression probably given by the statement just made in the text was that it would always be easy to determine whether the objections that the defendant raises would fall into the area assigned to the motion to quash or into the area assigned to a plea. Actually it would be found, however, that there are many border-line situations where the decision into which group the objection falls is anything but easy. Yet the two differ from each other not only in the form of procedure but also in several other respects of importance. The degree of reviewability of the court's decision on motion and on plea may be different. It is also possible that the motion to quash that contained other than formal defects may be made at a later time than the arraignment, according to the procedure of many states. Thus much more than a mere matter of form is involved, and the penalty for making a wrong guess may conceivably be a severe one, besides the obvious inconvenience of having to make a choice, even if the choice were an easy one. It is, therefore, not surprising that procedural reform has often taken the shape of breaking down the distinction between motion and plea.

Let us assume, now, that the defendant has no procedural objections, of either kind, to make or that, having made them, they have been overruled.[12] We then come to the second group of defense matters that he may raise (although, as will appear from a description of them, it is comparatively rarely that they arise in a case). This group, like the first group, does not go into the merits of the case in the sense of determining whether he is a guilty or an innocent man; but, unlike the first group, success here terminates the proceedings without hope for the prosecution to recommence them. Hence the pleading raising this group is called a "special plea in bar."[13] The plea may set up the fact that the defendant has already been tried on this charge and has been acquitted; that, having been tried, he was convicted and has served his punishment; or that he has been

12. If he wishes a higher court to pass on the correctness of the ruling, it will not be brought to such court at this time, but only later, at the end of the trial, when and if he carries the case up for review.
13. In Illinois all special pleas in bar are abolished, and the matters that they raise are included in the plea of not guilty.

pardoned for his offense.[14] All three call for an inquiry to determine whether his claim is in fact true. If so, the proceeding terminates. If not, we pass on to the last group of choices open to the defendant.

This group deals with the real merits of the charge against the defendant, and he may make one or the other of two mutually exclusive pleas—guilty or not guilty.[15] The former will be considered first.

The plea of guilty admits the entire charge against the defendant. It admits totally and severally, item by item, all the elements of the crime that the indictment charges. While there has been some doubt as to whether, on a plea of guilty in an offense that has various degrees, it admits the most serious degree that the indictment refers to, it will probably be held to do this too. In other words, it is a sweeping expression of his failure to contest anything that the state has brought up against him

14. Former jeopardy (also called "double jeopardy")—proceedings begun but terminated before reaching either an acquittal or a conviction—may also in some states have to be pleaded specially. It is a fundamental assumption with us that an accused person shall not be called upon more than once on the same charge. If he has once been "in jeopardy" of conviction, he cannot again be brought to trial, unless he himself waives the claim (e.g., by asking for a new trial or by appealing his case to a higher court). This then raises the question, "How far must the earlier proceedings have gone in order to become jeopardy?" It is impossible to answer this question in terms of a definite point, up to which it is not yet jeopardy and after which it is. It depends not only on the point reached but also on the reason why the proceedings are terminated. As soon as a trial jury has been selected, jeopardy has attached, in the sense that the prosecuting attorney cannot thereafter terminate the case and then later recommence it. For better or for worse, from then on, so far as he is concerned, he must go through with it, or it is ended. On the other hand, the trial may terminate with the defendant's consent or because of his fault; in such case he cannot complain if fresh proceedings are begun later, and jeopardy will be said not yet to have attached. Finally, the trial may have ended because of some circumstance making its continuance and the reaching of a valid verdict impossible, but for which neither the defendant nor the prosecuting attorney was responsible. Examples would be illness of a juror, the efforts of someone to tamper with a juror, or any event that made it impossible to continue the case with confidence that a fair result would be reached. Here, too, no jeopardy has attached.

15. Contrary to popular impression (based on newspaper reports, in which, naturally, only the hard-fought cases are likely to be described), pleas either of guilty or of not guilty are the only ones in the overwhelming majority of cases. Orfied states (op. cit., p. 283) that in a federal survey of 34,240 cases, this was true in all but 1,857. And those pleading guilty far outnumber those pleading not guilty. In some states 95 per cent of all the convictions are on pleas of guilty. The national average is said to be 85 per cent.

and puts the case at once into the same stage that, on a not-guilty plea, would be reached only after the trial had taken place and a verdict of guilty had been brought in by the jury. Thus it constitutes a most serious step for the defendant to take, and, as a result, a court may accept this plea only after setting up certain important safeguards. A court confronted with a defendant who announces that he wishes to plead guilty should carefully explain the consequences of the plea to him. Indeed, in many states the record must show affirmatively that the court so explained it and that despite this explanation he persisted in his determination to plead guilty.[16] In a few states the plea is not even allowed in capital cases. In others the defendant is protected against ill-advised action by permitting the court in any case to refuse to accept a plea of guilty.[17] Finally, where such a plea has been entered and it later appears to the court that despite the explanation it was done without a true understanding, the court may, and should, permit a withdrawal of the plea if so requested.

There is, however, a difference of view as to the effect of such a withdrawal. Under the minority view it is held that it still stands against him as an admission of guilt and, hence, at a subsequent trial may be used as evidence against him. Obviously it could, and probably would, be looked on by the jury as almost conclusive against him, but why, say the proponents of this view, should this admission, solemnly made in open court, be given less significance than one made much more thoughtlessly elsewhere? The logic of this position can hardly be denied. The majority of courts, however, hold that, if the plea has been withdrawn, it should be treated as though it had never been made. In their opinion the minority rule really makes a nullity of the withdrawal. If, they say, for reasons of social policy he is to be permitted to withdraw the plea, then, logic or no logic, he should get the substance, and not the mere shadow, of this privilege.

It has, of course, been assumed in the foregoing comments

16. It is frequently charged that courts, desirous of setting a high record of convictions, have been less than careful to live up to this obligation. See hereon 79 Penn. L. Rev. 484 (1931).

17. Federal Rule 11 so provides. The original common-law view was to the contrary; if the defendant persisted, the court had to accept the plea.

that the defendant's plea of guilty was to the full offense charged
against him. It is possible for him, however, with the consent of
the court and the prosecution, to plead guilty to a smaller offense
comprised within the larger (more serious) one charged, the
more serious charge being waived by the prosecution.[18] The
limitations in the foregoing statement must, however, be carefully noted: It only applies where the offense to which he pleads
guilty is comprised within, and is a part of, the offense charged,
and it can only be done with the consent of court and prosecutor.[19] To permit this procedure has certain practical advantages
so great that it can hardly be forbidden. There has been such a
considerable increase in crime and hence in the burden placed
on the prosecutor's office and on the community as a whole that
any proper time-saving device should be used. Mitigating circumstances may by it be given due weight and may well be
treated more wisely than they would be by a jury. Finally, the
prosecutor, though convinced of the defendant's guilt, may be
doubtful of his ability to secure a conviction on the full charge.

These considerations are of such force that the power to take
lesser pleas should continue to be given to court and prosecutor.
At the same time it is a dangerous authority and one that can
very well be abused. For an ambitious and not too scrupulous
prosecuting attorney, anxious to build up a record of convictions, it offers an easy and sure method of getting them far preferable to fighting to establish the offense that has really been
committed. With this in view the indictment may even have
been drafted to contain charges not supportable in court but
nonetheless highly useful for bargaining purposes of this sort.
At its worst this power may even be used to coerce a plea of
guilty to a small offense out of a defendant conscious of his
innocence but still afraid of the possibility of an unjust conviction on the larger charge. The way to meet these possible abuses,

---

18. E.g.: charge of assault with intent to kill and plea of simple assault;
charge of murder and plea of manslaughter; charge of larceny of an automobile and plea of "tampering with an automobile."

19. As the offense charged (and waived) is so often a felony, and the
offense admitted merely a misdemeanor, the whole procedure here described
is usually referred to as "waiving a felony." It is also known as "taking a
bargain plea."

however, is not to eliminate this useful power but to guard against its abuse.[20]

The plea of not guilty is almost as sweeping and broad as its converse, the plea of guilty. It is a denial of the truth of each and every part of the charge against the defendant and puts every allegation in issue.[21] This inclusiveness arose from the fact that at one time a defendant did not have a right to be defended by counsel. Since he lacked expert advice, it was necessary to make the pleading procedure as simple as possible. He could not be expected to single out certain defenses for special pleading. It was held, therefore, that his simple plea of not guilty would cover everything.[22] Now, with the defendant having the right to counsel, the reason for the rule is greatly weakened, and at the same time we have. come to realize the great, and perhaps unfair, advantage given by it to the defendant. The preliminary examination has probably already indicated the nature, and many of the details, of the prosecution's case against him. The precise language of the indictment has completed his information. He, on the other hand, can hold back any hint of his defense until the last minute, thereby making it difficult or impossible for the prosecution, in the limited time available to it, to show its weakness or even falsity.

As a consequence, in an increasing number of states there are two defenses which (either by statute or by court order) must be plead specially or (much the same thing, practically) must be indicated by advance notice. These are insanity and alibi. Insanity is included both because the preparation of testimony on it takes considerable time and hence is not feasible on

20. In the federal system and in a few states there is a plea similar in most respects to a plea of guilty, called a plea of "nolo contendere." Under it the defendant in effect says that, though he will not admit his guilt, he chooses not to contest the matter. Where it is allowed, its effect, so far as the criminal prosecution is concerned, is the same as in a guilty plea. Its only difference is that in any civil litigation which may involve the same issues it cannot be used against the defendant as an admission. It is little used even in the few courts which recognize it.

21. Thus, it will be noted, it is much broader in scope than the same plea in civil litigation. This is the plea which is often (and incorrectly) called in the newspapers a "plea of innocent."

22. Even the statute of limitations and (as indicated above) in many states previous acquittal, previous conviction, and pardon would thus fall within it.

a moment's notice and because we can hardly ask the prosecution in every case to be prepared to meet it should it be raised. Alibi is included because, of all defenses, it is the easiest to build up on perjured testimony and one of the hardest to disprove without time for careful investigation.[23]

After the defendant has pleaded not guilty, there is in many states statutory provision as to the minimum number of days to be accorded to him before the trial is to begin. Such a period may be specified as one day or may range as high as five days. More frequently, perhaps, it is merely specified that he is to have a reasonable time.

23. In those states requiring notice of alibi defense there is much diversity as to how much time is then to be accorded the prosecution to meet it and, more important, how much information the notice must contain. The requirements may range all the way from a bare notice of an intention to claim an alibi to listing of the names of the witnesses whom the defendant plans to call, with none permitted to testify who is not so listed.

XIII

THE TRIAL

BEFORE commencing with the trial a comment must be made which is applicable to substantially all the rest of this book. Up to now the discussion, though uniformly brief, has been inclusive, in the sense that there has been an effort to give some notice to all the most important phases of each subject. This will no longer be the case. Those highly important aspects in which the criminal trial (as well as subsequent proceedings) is like the civil one will be passed over without comment, on the assumption that the reader is, or will become, acquainted with them elsewhere.[1] Only matters in which the criminal proceedings are different or which present special problems will here be noted. The necessity for brevity will, it is hoped, excuse the resultant lack of continuity and completeness.

THE JURY AND ITS SELECTION

Historically, if a trial takes place,[2] a jury is the sole instrumentality for determining the facts.[3] Even the possibility of providing any other mechanism is generally excluded by specific provisions in the state constitutions (as well as the federal Constitution) guaranteeing the right to trial by jury. As the language of these provisions varies somewhat, the scope and extent of the guaranty do also, but in the main there is no wide divergence of views. It is generally agreed that the guaranty does not apply to or include those minor offenses over which the magistrate

1. Only a few of many possible examples are such matters as the qualifications necessary for eligibility for jury service, challenges of jurors, the desirability of jury trial as a social institution, rules of evidence, expert witnesses, note-taking by jurors, impeachment of his verdict by a juror, the right to refuse to testify on grounds of self-incrimination, etc.
2. I.e., there was no election of trial by ordeal or by battle, while these were still possible, and no plea of guilty.
3. The extent to which today a jury may be waived and the facts determined by the judge will be taken up below.

174

has summary jurisdiction.[4] Jury trial never was part of the machinery in these minor cases, and it was held that, when the guaranty of jury trial was imbedded in the constitution, it should be regarded merely as imbedding it to the extent to which it was already applied and not as a constitutional innovation extending it to areas to which it did not previously apply.[5] Another limitation which has in some states been placed on the scope of the guaranty, even in serious crimes, is that it applies only to those crimes that were such when the constitution was adopted. New crimes, first created at a later date, would not come under it[6] and might be tried without a jury. There are at least two serious objections to such a view. One lies in the difficulty of determining what constitutes a "new" crime.[7] The other and more serious objection is that, if we believe in the desirability of jury trial (and, so long as the guaranty is there, it must be assumed that we do), we would seem to be committed to the same view of its value and social utility whether we happened to be applying it in the determination of the facts of a new or of an old crime.

4. See chap. v.

5. There are a few states which refuse thus to narrow the guaranty or which have one so phrased as necessarily to make it applicable also to summary jurisdiction cases. Thus in Massachusetts the defendant had a right to a jury trial even in these cases. To lessen the resultant cumbersome procedure, the Massachusetts legislature enacted a statute providing that in the first instance the trial should be by a magistrate without jury, unless the defendant immediately asked otherwise. If he was then acquitted, that terminated the case. If he was convicted, he could then have a jury trial. Two shortcomings to such a statute are obvious. For one thing, since such a second proceeding will frequently be asked for, the hoped-for saving in time will be largely lost, since in many instances two trials will be held instead of one. In the second place, it may be doubted whether such a statute really preserves the full guaranty. Juries will soon realize that the very fact that a minor case is before them is an indication that the magistrate thought the defendant guilty. They will, therefore, themselves presume him guilty. The substance of the guaranty would then be largely gone.

6. This view may well be taken where the wording of the guaranty speaks of "jury trial as heretofore enjoyed." An example is Pennsylvania.

7. Is it a new crime if the name of the crime is merely changed? Is it a new crime if the punishment is greatly increased? Is it a new crime if the later statute in part covers old ground and in part innovates? If the "old" crime and the "new" one cover the same ground in part, the prosecuting attorney could determine whether or not to allow the guaranty to apply by his choice of which statute to proceed under. It is a weak "guaranty" that depends on the will of the opposite party!

A problem more frequently encountered in this area than the extent of the guaranty is as to whether an innovation or change is to be regarded as merely altering the details of a basically unchanged legal institution or, on the contrary, as so deeply modifying it as in effect to create a new institution, thereby taking away jury trial. For example, does a statute which reduces the size of the jury from the time-honored one of twelve to nine or even to six violate the constitutional guaranty? As might be expected, there is here a great deal of disagreement. Some courts hold that the essence of jury trial is that persons not otherwise connected with the court machinery (viz., laymen) are called upon to perform part of the functions of the court (viz., the deciding of where the truth lies in the disputed facts). And that is still true whether the jury is of twelve or of nine or of six. Thus the reality is still there. Others, on the contrary, maintain that the jury trial that is guaranteed is by an unchanged organization and group that has crystallized into the shape of twelve laymen. If this pattern could be modified, it would be possible by successive steps to reduce it to six or to five or to three or even to one, thus eliminating the cross-section of lay view represented by twelve. The point at which to draw the line, they maintain, is at the beginning.[8]

In recent years there have been increasing numbers of cases presenting increasingly complex facts. As a result trials may extend over a much longer time than was formerly the case. There is, therefore, greater danger that a juror may during the course of the trial become ill or otherwise incapacitated. Accordingly, we find statutes or rules of court[9] giving the court (i.e., the judge) the authority to impanel one, two, or even four alternate jurors who will participate fully with the regular jurors in hearing the testimony but will share in arriving at the verdict only if needed to fill a vacancy.[10] Even this has been, rather

8. All this, of course, concerns only what is guaranteed to a defendant as a matter of right, and that he may not be deprived of. It does not deal with such changes in the size of the jury as may be made with his consent.

9. E.g., Federal Rule 24(c).

10. If there were a vacancy and there were no alternate, the trial would, of course, have to begin all over again with a new jury unless, under local law, the defendant could, and was willing to, consent to go on with less than twelve.

unconvincingly, asserted to be a partial denial of jury trial because, if an alternate is called on to serve as a regular juror, the verdict will in part reflect the view of one who during the hearing of the evidence did not expect to participate in the deliberations and who, therefore, may not have given the same amount of attention to the witnesses that he would have, had he known that his views would play a part. Thus it means (says this view) that the defendant is being tried by eleven regular jurors and one half-interested, half-informed juror with a full vote, and to that extent he is deprived of a jury trial. Perhaps the major impression left by such an argument is that of the extreme ingenuity that counsel is capable of in finding reasons to attack the constitutionality of statutes that prove to be inconvenient!

Even if we are in a situation where concededly the defendant has a right to insist on a jury trial, is this a right which he may, if he so chooses, surrender and waive, or is it a right of such great social importance that even he, the beneficiary of it, will not be allowed to surrender it?[11] There has been relatively little difficulty in arriving at the conclusion that he may consent to go on with a jury of reduced size, either from the beginning or from the time one of its members becomes incapacitated.[12] But may he entirely waive a jury and place on the judge the responsibility not only of ruling on the law governing the case but of determining the facts of it? Until 1930 the overwhelming view was that he could not. Indeed, there was only one state, Maryland, which completely opened the door to waiver.[13] In that year the United States Supreme Court gave a qualified approval to waiver,[14] and in the same year Illinois, which had not

11. A plea of guilty, though it eliminates the jury, is not, correctly considered, a "waiver" of the jury as the means of arriving at the facts. By admitting them in full it eliminates the need for a jury. The guaranty does not insist that there must be a trial.

12. Even here, however, there is no unanimity. There are holdings that, though he may entirely surrender a jury, his choice must be one way or the other. He cannot equivocate and partially retain, partially surrender, it.

13. This was the Maryland position since Colonial days. It became so ingrained that an attempt to pass a statute excluding the power to waive was assailed on the very ground that this would deprive the defendant of the "right" to be tried by the court.

14. In *Patton v. United States*, 281 U.S. 276 (1930).

permitted it, gave unqualified approval.[15] Both decisions were unexpected and furnished great impetus to the movement for permitting waiver. Today it is partially or entirely permitted in over half the states. Those which restrict it do so on one or the other, or both, of two qualifications. It may be restricted on the basis of the possible punishment to be imposed (e.g., capital punishment)[16] or, similarly, on whether it involves a felony or merely a misdemeanor. It may be restricted by permitting waiver only with the consent of the court and of the prosecutor.[17] If, as will be argued shortly, there are situations in which fairness to the defendant requires permitting him to waive, it is extremely difficult to understand requiring him to get the prosecution's consent so to do. It has also been urged, but without success,[18] that a defendant who had waived his right to be represented by counsel could not likewise waive a jury.

What, then, are the principal factors that in the overwhelming majority of cases have led to the waiver of a jury in instances where it is permitted?[19] Some of these advantages inure only, or mainly, to the public and hence may have had little influence on the defendant's choice; others represent direct benefits to him. As for the public, waiver has the advantage of much greater cheapness and speed. It is a more economical way of dealing with cases. The possibility of adequately disposing of cases is enormously increased without hurrying them. The time-consuming slow process of jury selection is eliminated, and the often long-drawn-out questioning and cross-examining that are necessary properly to get a case before a jury are eliminated. In

15. *People* v. *Fisher*, 340 Ill. 250 (1930).

16. The argument for this restriction rests not only on the argument that the waiver means too much to the defendant but also on the terrific and unfair responsibility it places on the judge.

17. This is the federal view (cf. Rule 23[a]). It was also the Illinois one (*People* v. *Scornavache*, 347 Ill. 403 [1931]) until by statute, in 1941, the choice was left solely to the defendant.

18. *Adams* v. *United States*, 317 U.S. 269 (1942).

19. A Maryland survey (Frank, "Trying Cases without Juries in Maryland," 17 Va. L. Rev. 253 [1931]) showed that in Baltimore 10 per cent of the accused pled guilty (a very low proportion of the cases), 4 per cent elected to have a jury trial, and 86 per cent chose a bench trial. In the rural areas the disparity was not quite so great, but even in these areas there was a heavy balance in favor of jury waivers. In Illinois likewise the proportion of cases in which there is a waiver is much greater than of those in which a jury is demanded.

addition, it is a much simpler procedure because it does away
with the need to rely on complex rules of evidence to a large
extent. While it is perhaps erroneous to say that these rules took
their origin in the fact that we have jury trial, it would certainly
seem to be true that they are largely retained because we have
such trials. With the elimination of the jury, the obtaining of
the information is much simplified. This simplification means not
only greater speed but also less chance that errors will be made,
calling for later reversal by a higher court. From the defendant's
standpoint, he, too, if he is innocent, will favor speed. He will
have no wish to have the witnesses' recollection grow dim. Nor
will he be counting, for his protection, on the reversal of a
conviction.

Regardless, however, of his guilt or innocence, the possibility
of waiving the jury and casting himself on the mercy of the
court is very welcome to any defendant who is suffering from,
or fears that he may suffer from, one form or another of local
prejudice. If the defendant belongs to a minority racial group
or religion, he may seriously fear the effects of prejudice in the
jury. That fear may not be so definitely capable of being established as to entitle him to a change of venue, where he has to
show some ground for his fear, but the fear may be a perfectly
sincere one nonetheless and may even be a justified one for all
his inability to put his finger on the proof of it. He will perhaps
very much welcome getting his case away from a cross-section
of the community and into the hands of a judge in whose balance
he has much greater confidence. Another type of case in which
prejudice may appear is one involving a high degree of emotional content where the community's feelings have been greatly
stirred up. This would be particularly obvious when the case
has received much newspaper publicity, with some papers even
actively maintaining his guilt. Finally, the defendant who knows
that, fairly or unfairly, he would make a very poor witness on
his own behalf is saved from the difficult choice of running
this risk or the equally great one of remaining silent. The court,
he may hope, will be more objective.[20]

20. At the same time there is a danger here for counsel without experience
in the particular court involved. Before a jury he and the prosecuting attorney

Assuming, now, that there is to be a jury trial, the basic problems of getting a jury selected are much the same in criminal cases as in civil ones and, therefore, for the reasons already given, will not be treated here. Only a few matters, of particular importance in criminal law, need comment. One of these is the length of time through which the selecting of a jury may drag, as compared to its speed in England (and, to a considerable extent, in Canada).[21] In England the taking of more than half a day to secure twelve satisfactory jurors is a matter for comment, with the first twelve examined often being chosen as a unit. In this country, on the other hand, the selecting may run into weeks, with the first selectees cooling their heels waiting until the last of the twelve may be picked. Various reasons combine to produce the difference, and it is important that we should understand them in the hope that by such understanding we may go a little way in cutting our time, so far as these reasons are susceptible of correction.

In part the difference is due to the fact that in the United States criminal cases receive a degree of pretrial publicity that is utterly unheard of in England, and not only is the quantity of publicity vastly greater in this country but so also is the freedom of expression by the newspapers of opinions (either by innuendo or by direct statement). As a consequence our prospective jurors are likely to have a degree of information about the case and a possible bias that is unknown in England. It is difficult to see what can be done about this difference, because the obvious remedy of cutting down on newspaper publicity would run dangerously near abridging the freedom of the press, with a worse state of affairs at the end than in the beginning.

---

are on an equality with each other at least in the sense that both are before twelve strangers, neither of them at the outset knowing anything about their individual quirks and the kinds of arguments that will or will not impress them. On the other hand, putting himself before the judge may give the prosecutor some real advantages. The latter has, perhaps, had many cases before this judge. He knows just what type of argument and approach is most advisable.

21. The situation is not so bad as the cursory reading of newspapers would indicate. Delay will be at its maximum in the highly publicized cases, where there is the greatest likelihood that prospective jurors have already formed opinions. Nothing is said about the much greater number of unspectacular cases in which everything proceeds with dispatch.

Another cause for greater American delay is the smaller amount of judicial control that our trial judges have over the jury-selecting process. They are less willing to reject the challenge of a juror's fitness on perhaps fanciful grounds. By sustaining a challenge, they thus make it necessary to commence the examining process afresh with the next venireman.[22] This unwillingness is in turn due to two main reasons. One is that, being often politically elected, they do not care to antagonize counsel and thereby make enemies for themselves, as they certainly would do by forcing a juror on someone who did not want him. But a more important and also a more creditable reason for their hesitancy lies in the failure of reviewing courts consistently to back up and sustain trial judges in the rejection of fanciful objections. In the face of this prospect the wise judge may feel that it is far preferable to sacrifice the time spent in examining this venireman rather than, by forcing his retention, to risk a later reversal, thus forcing a complete new trial. The British judges, on the other hand, are not elected, and they are usually strongly backed up in their discretionary rulings by their reviewing courts.

Still another important but not widely realized reason for the difference between the two countries lies in the fact that in England the population is much more homogeneous, whereas here it is highly heterogeneous. The more homogenous the population—which is simply another way of saying the more like one another the people are—the less significance there may be in whether the jury is made up of a group of Richard Roes or of one of John Does. After all, John Doe and Richard Roe are very much the same, and so, all things considered, there is a strong likelihood that, no matter who is finally chosen, they will not be very different from any other group of twelve who might have been picked.

This certainly is not true in this country. There are not only tremendous economic differences here (which of course is true only to a less extent in England) but also tremendous differences both in the cultural level and in the kind of cultural background that may be represented. While there are high differences of cultural level in England, too, the background is a more uniform

22. I.e., prospective juror.

one. For that reason, even if there is not complete homogeneity between all Englishmen, there is a less sweeping difference than is possible here, where the background may range all the way from the stolid northern European to the volatile southern one. And not only can there be more variation here but the chances are much greater in the United States that the racial background, and hence the cultural makeup, of the person may be hidden by name changes, because name changes are far more common here than they are in England. Thus, both from the greater variability of the human material and from the greater difficulty in determining what particular variety of human being one is, there is a much greater need to search into the constituent elements that may form the jury.[23]

Furthermore, the examination into the potential jurors is made more important (and hence is longer drawn out) in the United States because our jurors are believed (probably correctly) to be on the whole less obedient to instructions from the judge (and therefore knowing whom one has on the jury is more important) than English jurors are. We are still fairly close to the heritage of Jacksonian democracy, when everybody was as good as everybody else. Our jurors may remember very well that last year His Honor was merely a practicing attorney, and they know that, when his term is over, he may very probably be one again. It is a far cry from the highly respectful attitude that the English juror shows. To some extent we may find the contrast even in this country, where probably on the whole the instructions given by federal judges are listened to with much more urgent concern than are those of their state counterparts.

Finally, in most states (as will appear below) the judge is sharply limited in his right to question witnesses or to comment to the jury on the meaning and significance of the evidence which it has heard. Leaving the jury thus unguided necessarily enhances its independence and hence increases the importance of care in selecting its members.

From the foregoing it is plain that we shall not soon equal the British in speed of jury selection. The differences lie too deep.

23. The existence of property qualifications for jury service in England, as compared to their absence here, still further produces, respectively, homogeneity and heterogeneity.

But it is also evident that some improvements are within our grasp. One, not so far mentioned, would consist in the much greater participation by the judge in the task of questioning veniremen. Under the Federal Rules[24] it is in the judge's discretion to take over the task himself, although in that event he must permit counsel to ask such further questions as may be proper. But it is he, too, who determines what is proper!

Historically, once the jury was selected, the jurors were not allowed to separate and mingle with outsiders until, at the end of the case, they were discharged. Such a rule was workable so long as cases normally were very brief, probably beginning in the morning and ending by afternoon. But, with cases growing increasingly long, the enforced separation became a more serious matter, and jurors increasingly resented this enforced segregation from the rest of the community. It became a potent factor in increasing the unwillingness of citizens to render jury service. As a consequence the early doctrine of no separation has been replaced by the newer one that it is within the discretion of the trial judge whether to keep the jury together or to permit its dispersal between court sessions.[25] Ordinarily the judge will exercise his discretion in favor of permitting a separation, except in capital cases. In these cases the issue is of such significance and importance, and the possibility of pressure on jurors when they are out of sight of the court and of the bailiff is so great, that here the presumption is on the other side. But even in this instance it will probably be left to the judge's discretion. However, after a jury has retired to consider its verdict, no separation is normally permitted, and it will be kept together until it is discharged, regardless of the nature or seriousness of the charges.

DEFENSE COUNSEL

The defendant's right to be represented by counsel is a matter of such significance that it should be treated in a seminar devoted

24. Rule 24(a).
25. The exercise of the discretion should never depend in any part on the consent or nonconsent of the defendant. If such were the case, juries would soon become aware of it and, if not allowed to disperse, would tend to put the blame on the defendant for their unwelcome confinement. The prejudice to him would be obvious.

to it alone. The extremely brief treatment given it here is based on the assumption that such a seminar is available.

The single topic—the right to counsel—in reality comprises three different questions. They are: (1) May a defendant insist on having his spokesman in court beside him? (2) If he has no spokesman, what steps must the court take to inform him that he has the right to have one and perhaps even to insist that he have one? (3) If he is indigent and cannot provide himself with counsel, what method should be used to furnish him one? These questions will be considered in that order.

1. In misdemeanor cases it has always been the defendant's right to have counsel speak for him. He did not, however, at first have the same right in felony cases. This rule, exactly reversing what we might expect, was unconvincingly rationalized by the assertion that, where the charge was of a felony, the consequence of a finding of guilty was so severe to the defendant that the court out of sympathy to him would constitute itself the defendant's spokesman and the representative of his interests. Thus he was not entitled to have counsel because he did not need any. A more realistic explanation might find significance in the fact that conviction on a felony charge at that time carried with it the confiscation of all the felon's property—a consequence not true in misdemeanor cases. There is room for the suspicion that a more ardent desire was therefore felt for felony convictions and a wish that they be not jeopardized by aid from too-efficient counsel. In any event, a defendant can today insist, in any charge, that he be allowed to have his spokesman by his side.[26]

Furthermore, he has a right also to implement this by having such opportunities as are necessary for private secret conference with his counsel, so as to discuss the case with him and give him all the requisite information. If counsel is appointed for him, time must be allowed for the former to prepare himself. The right to have a spokesman is, however, waivable, and, if the court is satisfied that the defendant is fully aware of what he is doing, it can permit the case to go to trial without defense counsel.

2. Considerably more difficulty arises in the second question.

26. Today this right will probably begin as early as the preliminary examination. It will be recalled, however, that the law is in a state of flux as to the extent of his rights at this stage of the proceedings (see chap. v).

How far must the court go in informing the defendant that he may ask for counsel, and what are the consequences of not fully so informing him? The federal courts, under the Supreme Court's interpretation of the Sixth Amendment, must in all felony prosecutions see to it not only that the defendant is fully informed of his right but also that counsel is provided, unless it can be shown that, knowing his rights, he nonetheless did not wish to have counsel (i.e., waived it). In the famous Scottsboro cases[27] the Supreme Court also held that under the due-process clause the states were required to go equally far in all capital cases. In later decisions it was held, however, that in less than capital cases the states need not guarantee counsel to a defendant, and some states have availed themselves of this freedom.

This, it is submitted, is a backward step, in both its aspects. Not only should counsel be made available to a defendant who asks for it, but also those arguments of public policy and fairness that lead us to the feeling that he must be provided with counsel ought also to lead us to the feeling that he must be told that he has this right. The urge of public policy is at least as strong in regard to the silent defendant. Since he does not ask for that which he may receive, he is almost certainly an inexperienced defendant, and an inexperienced defendant is, to our common knowledge, a defendant who shows greater likelihood of being an innocent one than does the defendant who is completely experienced, because experience and guilt have a way of going together. While it is true that a man may be innocently accused time after time, it is not quite so likely. Thus, if he is not asked whether he wishes counsel, we are in the curious position of so shaping our rule as to be most unbending toward the more deserving person.[28]

Where the defendant has a right to have counsel provided, it is a largely unanswered question whether this right applies only to

27. 287 U.S. 45 (1932).
28. The argument that a court should be affirmatively under a duty to inform a defendant of his right to have counsel provided is, it is submitted, exactly parallel to the admitted obligation of a court to warn a defendant who offers to plead guilty of the consequences of the plea. If, quite rightly, we are solicitous of warning him of his rights there, it is difficult to see why we should not be solicitous to warn him of his present rights. It is illogical to make one warning compulsory and not to require the other at all.

the trial itself, or also to posttrial motions, or even to review proceedings. Only a few states have answered this question fully in the affirmative.

3. If, then, a defendant, either with or without having been expressly informed of his rights, asks that counsel be provided for him, and indicates that he is himself indigent and so unable to secure such aid for himself, what method should be used to secure it for him? Several have been employed, but none is entirely satisfactory. One device, the most obvious of all, is for the court simply to designate a member of the bar to serve as his counsel. This is within its power. Membership in the bar is a privilege, and, being a privilege, it may carry with it certain duties. Only those who are willing to live up to these duties are entitled to retain the privilege. One of the duties is the obligation to aid in the smooth operation of the courts. This not only entails certain conduct in the courtroom and behavior in the cases involved, in order to secure the smooth running of the court machinery, but it may also involve obligatory service in the capacity of that court officer called "defense counsel" if so designated. When this service must be gratuitous, it is simply counsel's misfortune. This method of meeting the problem is one widely employed, but it has proved far from satisfactory.[29] It will scarcely work in courts where the judges are elected and regularly come up for re-election, as the designation of an unwilling lawyer is hardly a way for a judge to make friends for himself.[30] Furthermore, the resultant service will probably be grudging and unwilling. As a consequence, it is more than likely that the court will limit its designations to inexperienced lawyers who have been unsuccessful in attracting clients and therefore have plenty of time on their hands, and a desire for some advertising, or to inexperienced young attorneys who wish to broaden their field of knowledge. In any event, it spells out service for the defendant that is not too satisfactory.

29. In addition to the objections listed in the text, this method does not provide for the direct cash expenditures that may be needed to make an adequate and competent defense. Appointed counsel can hardly be expected to pay them out of his own pocket.

30. It is, therefore, not an accident that this method is more frequently used in the federal courts, where the judges are appointed for life.

The awareness of these disadvantages has led to the adoption of a slightly different device. Under this attorneys will be designated by the court, but more or less with their own consent only, and the matter will be made more attractive for them by means of fees paid to them, not by the indigent defendant, but out of the public funds, with compensation very often set by statute at so-and-so much maximum per such-and-such number hours of service or such-and-such type of case. Such fee service, it was thought, and to some extent correctly so, would get somewhat better counsel for the defendants, because there was the prospect of compensation. But this system, too, has not worked to complete satisfaction. If the fee is a very small one, it tends only partially to meet the objections to the feeless system. There will still be unwillingness, though perhaps not so extxreme. If, on the other hand, the fee is raised high enough to be attractive, there is the risk of running into a different kind of danger—not a danger necessarily always encountered (such an asumption would be grossly unfair) but sufficiently possible so that it cannot be disregarded. The very fact that the fee has become a desirable one, and that it thereby becomes a distribution of patronage by the assigning court, may lead to assignments of improper nature. This is an extremely dangerous situation. At its best it may cloud the judge's judgment as to who is the right person to appoint, and at its worst it may result in a state of affairs where there is a division of the fee with the assigning judge. In that event it may even lead as a final step, with a completely dishonest judge, to a situation in which the judge will see to it that, however little personal attention attorney John Doe gives to the case, John Doe's client will get every break conceivable. And so it soon becomes known that, if one is represented by lawyer John Doe, he can count on having the judge on his side and therefore has little to fear. Again it should be said that such a state of affairs would be most rare. But the possibility is there.

These unsatisfactory considerations have led to a third method that is being used in a small minority of jurisdictions throughout the United States. This is the so-called "public-defender system." Under the theory of the public-defender system it is as much the duty of the public, of the body politic, the state, to secure the acquittal of innocent defendants as it is to secure the conviction of guilty ones. True, the body politic is the plaintiff in a criminal case, and in that sense, as plaintiff, it occupies a partisan position. But the state is not, or at any rate should not be, like other plaintiffs, anxious only to win. It should be anxious to have justice prevail. And under our accusatory system of justice, with the court occuping only the position of umpire, it may be necessary, in order to secure the proper outcome of the case (viz., the defeat of the state where the state should be defeated), to help the defendant by means of counsel. Hence it is entirely logical that this function be taken over by a public official.[31]

There is also a great deal to be said for the public-defender idea from the practical side. In a trilogy of rather unsatisfactory solutions to this problem it is not a question of finding the perfect answer; it is a question of finding the least imperfect one. It may well be that the public-defender system fills the role of the one least to be criticized. It does not have the objection of inexperienced and unwilling counsel or the phenomenon of possibly selfish interest. Thus the two big objections to the other methods are removed. With their removel we are probably justified in saying that it becomes the most promising method. On the other hand, there are difficulties connected with it which are sufficiently great so that, while in theory they can all be met, it will prove a difficult task to do so.

For one thing the public defender will almost inevitably find himself in a situation where he has so many cases as to make it extremely difficult for him to give adequate service. This is so because, by and large, the defendants in criminal cases are not prosperous citizens. If there is any doubt as to the soundness of the adage that crime does not pay, its proof can usually be found in the persons filling the role of defendant. Of course there are

31. This step has been taken in three widely separated places—Baltimore, Chicago (viz., Cook County), and Los Angeles. In New York City a form of halfway step between the assigned counsel, on the one hand, and the public-defender system, on the other, has been worked out and is very largely used in that, to a much greater extent than in Chicago, the function of defending indigent defendants is turned over to and accepted by private charitable agencies of the legal-aid type. Thus the function of defending is retained in private hands. On the other hand, it is not a system of feeless volunteers, because under the legal-aid system generally the charity that operates the system has a paid staff.

prosperous defendants. But in the main they are either indigent or close to the line.[32] The overwhelming quantity of work thus carries with it cutting down the amount of time that can be devoted to a given case. With that there may arise serious doubt as to the adequacy of the service that the public defender is able to render. For practical reasons the obvious solution of giving him a larger appropriation, so as to enable him to have a larger staff, is largely merely a theoretical one. Thus this is a difficulty that not merely cannot be met by the honesty and sincerity of the public defender but may even be increased by these qualities.

Another difficulty, though of a less frequent and less serious nature, may be in the relationship between the public defender, on the one hand, and the prosecuting attorney, on the other. So long as counsel fill the partisan role that in the theory of our criminal law they are supposed to fill, there is a measure of desirability in not having defense counsel and prosecution counsel on too intimate a footing with each other. The public defender's relationship may too easily become a warmer, friendlier one with his opponent than it is with the transitory clients whom he happens for a moment to be representing and whom he will probably never see again. It might, of course, be argued that this danger works both ways: if the public defender is friendly with the prosecuting attorney, the prosecuting attorney is friendly with the public defender. And if this means that the latter is considerate of the former, it also means the converse. But, quite apart from the fact that justice would hardly gain from such a give-and-take, this is not the equalized way in which their relationship would work out. It is more likely to be a one-way form of courtesy, operating in the direction of the public defender's giving and the state's attorney taking, and not the other way around. This is so because normally the prosecuting attorney is an incomparably more powerful figure locally than the public de-

32. In Cook County approximately two-thirds of the criminal cases were formerly defended by the public defender and now about one-half are. It is true that the public defender will take a defendant's affidavit as to his own indigence as sufficient proof. He will not attempt to investigate whether he really is indigent. But the reason why the affidavit is taken as sufficient is that it has been found in the overwhelming majority of cases that the claim was true and that the cost of adequate investigation was greater than that of an occasional undeserved defense.

fender. He is an elected official. He cannot be deprived of his office during his term. He is not only legally a powerful, independent officer; he is a politically powerful figure. Thus directly or indirectly he can call the tune. The public defender, on the other hand, is employed, not for any fixed term, but at the pleasure of the county commissioners, who, however powerful they may be as a group, are certainly individually comparatively minor figures. (In Cook County he is selected by the local bench.) In consequence their subordinate, the public defender, will also fail to have comparable stature.

THE PROSECUTING ATTORNEY

The prosecuting attorney is a comparatively new figure as a public official. When the criminal law took its shape in England, as was stated in other connections previously, there was no functionary whose duty it was to prosecute criminal cases. Instead, when a crime occurred, the normal procedure would be to employ counsel specially to act as prosecuting attorney for that case, just as any other client would secure a barrister to represent him.[33] It was only by gradual degrees and in comparatively recent times that more and more the prosecuting of cases was taken over in England by a public official who did that and little but that. We, however, have had such an official much longer. The title given him varies, with "state's attorney"[34] and "district attorney"[35] being the most common. But, however known, he is of interest to us in his capacity of prosecuting attorney and will be so referred to here.

The prosecuting attorney has very great powers, both de facto and de jure. It has already been pointed out that in the list of de facto powers must be included a great share in deciding whom the grand jury will indict. Where informations may be filed, he even has de jure the power to launch criminal proceedings. The point for present consideration is the measure of his power to

33. Thus, as has already been mentioned, even so late as in the nineteenth century the noted barrister, Sir Edward Marshall Hall, was almost as often employed by the prosecution to act as prosecuting attorney as he was employed by the defense to act as defense counsel.
34. E.g., in Illinois.
35. E.g., in the federal courts and in New York.

terminate a case once it has been started. Here, too, there has already been comment on what is at least a related topic, that is, his partial compromise of criminal cases, by agreeing to waive part of the charge and to accept the defendant's plea of guilty to a less serious crime comprised within the more serious one. Can he go further? Can he entirely and permanently terminate a case? De facto he certainly can. The old maxim applies that "you can lead a horse to water, but you can't make him drink." You can lay a case on the desk of the prosecuting attorney, but, if he fails to act, it is, practically speaking, impossible to make him prosecute.[36] In fact, the case is terminated then and there.

The prosecuting attorney's right de jure is scarcely less. With only one qualification, he can at any time enter a nolle pros[37] in a case, thereby ending it as fully and effectively under our double-jeopardy doctrine as if the case had come to a formal verdict of not guilty.[38] (It follows from this that, if the nolle were entered under circumstances not involving jeopardy, it could be recommenced by him.) The reason for qualifying the sweeping statement just made is that in some states the consent of the court must be obtained before the nolle is entered.[39] Theoretically, it is said, that should be so, because the order dismissing the case is an order of the court, and the court should not be put in the position of having to give an order without first considering and approving the action, even though normally it will follow the wishes of the prosecuting attorney. Other states somewhat more realistically allow the nolle to be entered as of course, recognizing that in any event his is the only decision that really

36. This is not literally and entirely true. The local law may provide that, on a showing of bias or adverse interest or involvement of some sort on his part such as to make him an unfit person to prosecute, a special prosecuting attorney may be appointed (in some states by the local court and in others by the governor).

37. This is the name commonly given to a motion to dismiss a case. The corresponding verb is "to nolle." The terms arose from the opening words in the Latin form of the motion to dismiss.

38. It must be recognized that courts have frequently made loose statements to the effect that "after a jury is empaneled, the case cannot any longer be nolled." Closer reading will, however, disclose that what is really meant is—a very different proposition—that he cannot nolle the case and then later on change his mind and recommence it. In other words, jeopardy has attached.

39. This is the view taken in Federal Rule 48(a).

counts.[40] Thus it seems perfectly safe to say that in the main, either in fact or in law, there is no important limitation on the prosecuting attorney's power to terminate a case.

Another aspect of the prosecuting attorney's power to prevent a prosecution involves the legal effectiveness of his promise of immunity to someone in return for turning state's evidence.[41] If, in violation of his commitment not to do so, he nonetheless wishes to go ahead, can he do so? The question is not likely to arise, since he will scarcely be inclined to go back on his assurances and thereby shut off the flow of future testimony by future possible state's witnesses. Indeed, it is entirely possible that a prosecuting attorney may find it desirable even to accord a considerable degree of importance to promises that (let us say) some high police officer may have made to an accused person. Nor is the accused person in much greater danger if the prosecuting attorney goes out of office and his successor comes in, since the newcomer will hardly wish to become known as a welcher, even though the promise was not his own. If, however, the highly unusual situation arose, then, under the common-law view generally prevailing, the prosecuting attorney could go back on his promise. The trial court might very probably then do what little it could to protect the victim of the double-dealing, so far as it had any discretion. But as a legal matter it was possible to initiate and carry through the prosecution. An increasing minority of states, however, have come to regard the promise of immunity as an actual defense, to be raised under a plea of not guilty.[42] The whole question, however, is more one of substantive, than of procedural, law.

40. Federal Rule 48(b) contains an innovation on the common law in that it permits the court, of its own motion, to dismiss proceedings if the prosecution has at any time been guilty of unnecessary delay in getting the case to trial.

41. Such a promise may take the form of agreeing to dismiss proceedings begun against the witness if and after he has performed his part of the bargain. If so, and if the promise is kept, the effect of the dismissal will, of course, be exactly as great as that of any other dismissal. The assumption here made is that (with or without proceedings having been begun against the witness) there has been a promise of immunity and that, despite the promise, the prosecuting attorney is nonetheless contemplating proceeding against him or refusing to dismiss.

42. In a few states the prosecuting attorney is even given the power, in specified crimes, to force immunity on an unwilling witness, in order that he may

Is it proper for a prosecuting attorney to receive the aid of outside counsel (under the cloak, perhaps, of appointing to his staff a special assistant state's attorney designated merely to help him prosecute a given case)? If our vision of a criminal proceeding rises no higher than to regard it as a form of sporting event, our answer would often be affirmative. Such special assistance would probably be highly skilled and might by aiding an inexperienced prosecutor create a more even contest. But even a more constructive viewpoint might lead to the same conclusion. Society's interests are not served where the prosecuting attorney is clearly overmatched by defense counsel. Therefore he is, in general, allowed to accept such special help.[43] Yet there can be a danger in allowing the practice; at least in theory the prosecuting attorney is more than a mere partisan. His discretion should be exercised, and his decisions arrived at, on more than merely partisan grounds. The assistant will almost surely be completely partisan and by his special skill may easily become the really dominant figure, actually superseding the prosecuting attorney. This would be particularly likely where the "assistant" was full time on the staff of some trade group that was specially concerned with the repression of specified offenses. How far his dominating position would be socially undesirable is a debatable question, but for better or for worse it is a probable consequence of which we should be aware. As a result in some states it is held[44] that before such special assistance may be accepted the permission of the court must be secured and that this permission will not be granted if there is danger of oppression. In general, the compensation for the special assistant will be allowed to come from the interested private parties, but there is authority for the view that the only compensation that counsel so appointed might receive must flow from county and not from private funds.

---

no longer be able to refuse to testify on the ground of self-incrimination. Such a power is especially useful in crimes like bribery, where the facts are normally known only to the participants.

43. It should go without saying that he has complete power to refuse such proffered help.

44. For this view see *Hayner* v. *People*, 213 Ill. 142 (1904).

SOME GENERAL COMMENTS ON THE TRIAL

As already stated, no attempt is being made in this chapter to give an inclusive comment on the trial procedure but only to mention those matters in which criminal law presents special features. This remark applies particularly to the present section. Inclusiveness should, therefore, not be expected here.

The defendant has the right, if he wishes, to be present at every moment of every stage of his trial, from the arraignment to the judgment and the pronouncing of sentence.[45] If he is kept away, or if any step is taken without notice to him, he is deprived of his right, and, without regard to whether in fact any harm was occasioned to him, a conviction will be reversed. He may not even waive this right so far as the arraignment is concerned. In other words, he must then be present to indicate how he wishes to plead. At all the later stages[46] he may, according to the generally accepted view, waive his presence, and, if he is free on bail, his voluntary absence will constitute a waiver. A few states hold that in a felony proceeding he must be present throughout and cannot waive this right. Under such a view it follows, of course, that he cannot during the trial be accorded freedom on bail, since, if he was thus free, he could at will put an end to the trial at any time he chose.

The defendant's right to be present rests on the belief that only thus can he be sure that his defense will be adequate and complete. Another right is accorded him for much the same reason—the constitutional right to confront all the witnesses who testify against him, so that he may hear their testimony and cross-examine them as to its truth.[47] Furthermore, the witnesses are less likely to lie when they must do so in his presence. Yet it may be obvious that in a given case, by the time the trial takes place, a

45. The right does not extend to the proceedings on review in an appellate court.

46. There is authority for the view that in a capital case he must be present at the rendition of the verdict and subsequent proceedings.

47. The right of confrontation does not, however, extend to the proceedings where the court is determining the amount of punishment to be imposed or whether probation is to be granted. Here the court may hear, and make use of, reports and investigations based on information obtained from persons not called into the courtroom.

witness in failing health may be dead, or there may be a reason
to fear that he will be unobtainable in court because of illness or
absence from the state. In such cases the defendant is often permitted to protect himself by means of depositions.[48] It has been
urged that there is almost equally great[49] need for the prosecution to protect itself by taking depositions in the same manner as
the defendant may. Nor would this be in violation of the constitutional guaranty of confrontation, since we assume that the
defendant would be allowed to be present and to cross-examine.
Yet so far the prosecution has not been given this privilege.
Along similar lines it ought to be the privilege of either party,
on a second trial, where a witness who testified at the first trial
is no longer available, to use the written record of his testimony
at the earlier trial. This, too, would in no sense be a deprivation
of confrontation, since it took place at the first proceeding.

At one time parties to litigation could not take the witness
stand. Neither the plaintiff nor the defendant could testify, on
the ground that their incentive to lie was so great that their testimony was valueless—an attitude that placed scant value on cross-
examination as a means of disclosing falsehood. The problem did
not arise in criminal cases, so far as the plaintiff was concerned,
since the plaintiff is the people, and therefore there was never
any objection to the victim's testifying. But the doctrine did operate to prevent the defendant from testifying. No matter how
complete and satisfying an explanation he could give, he was not
allowed to be a witness. The obvious and gross unfairness of this,
in many instances, led to the now almost universal[50] permission
to take the stand in his own behalf, if he so desired. If he chose
so to do, he was like any other witness and was subject to the
same cross-examination as any other witness. He was subject,
too, to the same inquiry as any other witness as to whether he
was a person whose testimony could be relied upon as truthful

48. So provided in Federal Rule 15. A deposition is a proceeding whereby,
on notice to the other party and an opportunity given him to be present and
cross-examine, specified written questions are asked the prospective witness
and his sworn answers are set down in writing.
49. Not fully as great need, since in the case of an absent witness the government's facilities for securing his return would usually be much greater.
50. The lone exception is Georgia.

or, on the other hand, was one in whose word no trust could be placed—an inquiry which, of course, opened a possible door to many pieces of extremely unfavorable information about him. He was, however, given his choice whether to speak, with such possible consequences, or to remain silent.

So that this might be as nearly as possible a matter of genuine and free choice, it was also usually provided that there could be no adverse comment on his silence, if that was his choice,[51] and the defendant could ask the court to instruct the jury not to draw an unfavorable inference.[52] There has, however, been sharp disagreement with this view and insistence that such comment ought to be permitted.[53] In support it is asked why the jury should not take the silence into account. In daily life we should most certainly do so. In any event, how can we in fact prevent the jury from doing so? The only real effect of the prohibition on comment is that in the excitement of the concluding argument the prosecuting attorney may, perhaps inadvertently, make a remark which is of no practical significance but which will be seized on as grounds for reversal by a higher court. This view has, however, prevailed in only a few jurisdictions.[54]

This is not the only type of argument that is held to be unfair. There are numerous others. A very important one involves reference to other crimes alleged to have been committed by the defendant.[55] Plainly such a fact is highly prejudicial to the accused

51. The statement in the text does not fully apply in the case of comment by the court. This will be discussed below. As to comment by the prosecuting attorney, this is now permitted in a few states. Nor does this constitute a deprivation of due process.

52. The asking of such an instruction might, however, be highly ill advised as further directing the jury's attention to his silence.

53. This position is forcefully maintained in an article by Judge Frank H. Hiscock in 26 Col. L. Rev. 253 (1926).

54. See n. 51 above. An additional argument that could be made for this position is that it may in any given case be most difficult to draw an exact line between fair argument and improper comment. Certainly the prosecuting attorney may urge the strength of this case, the credibility of his witnesses, how numerous they are, etc. Similarly he may urge the contrary facts on the defense side. Where will such urging become a covert way of calling attention to the fact that the defendant did not testify? It will always be a hard line to draw but much more so in the heat of trial argument.

55. The points here made apply, of course, also to means other than argument to bring such prior criminality to the knowledge of the jury—for example, by the questions asked of a witness.

and may easily distract the jury's attention from the only issue before them: Is he guilty of the offense charged? Any such argument and information are improper if their purpose is merely to prejudice the jury against the accused. But it may also be that the information as to previous criminal charges and possibly even the conviction on them does throw light on the present case. The situation then is an entirely different one. It is, from the defendant's point of view, highly unpleasant information, but that is no reason why it should not be as admissible as any other pertinent evidence is. Thus crimes showing a pattern of conduct may throw light on the defendant's present guilt.[56] If he has taken the witness stand, a showing of conviction of an offense involving falsehood may aid the jury in deciding how much faith to put in his testimony. If the second or subsequent conviction of a given offense involves more serious punishment, his history becomes a pertinent matter. In all these ways his prior record of criminality may be a legitimate matter of inquiry and hence of comment. This is not true where the only purpose is to arouse prejudice.

For the same reason, and in the same way, appeals to the racial or religious prejudices of the jury are improper. It is improper to assume as facts matters that have neither been shown in evidence nor been judicially noticed. Similarly it is improper for the attorney either directly or indirectly to put himself in the position of a witness and in his argument in effect himself to testify by hinting that he has information not available to the jury. If he has such information, he should withdraw from the case, let an assistant replace him, and then take the witness stand like any other witness. It is, or should be, improper for the prosecuting attorney to refer to some of the consequences that will follow a verdict of guilty as against one of not guilty, such as, for example, that on a verdict of guilty the defendant may appeal the case to a higher court but that on a verdict of not guilty it is impossible for the prosecution to appeal. Such a consideration

56. Where and where not there would be sufficient pattern has been decided along highly capricious and unpredictable lines. But it is such damning evidence that it should be clearly informative, in order to outweigh its prejudice-producing tendencies. Where the line will be drawn can only be determined by examining the cases in any given state.

might induce a jury to shirk its responsibility and try to pass it on to the higher court. For similar reasons it is improper for a prosecuting attorney to refer to the kind of punishment that may be given to an accused person and to suggest that, if he is acquitted, the defendant goes free but that, if convicted, there is a likelihood of freedom on probation. This, too, stimulates the likelihood of a verdict of guilty without any concomitant certainty on the jury's part that he really is guilty. These constitute the most frequently found types of improper arguments. There are, no doubt, others where merely inflammatory considerations are brought out, considerations which have no bearing on the defendant's guilt but which are very likely to influence the jury. All alike should be banned.

What are the consequences of such an impropriety? The court's rebuke of the offender and direction to the jury to disregard the remarks may be sufficient to undo the damage.[57] On the other hand, so harmful an idea may have been implanted as to be incapable of real cure. Then a fresh commencement before a new jury would be required. It is a question of degree and is largely left to the discretion of the trial judge, with reviewing courts rather hesitant to substitute their opinion for his.

The sequence of closing arguments is that the state is allowed the final word. This is in recognition of the fact that the burden of proof rests on it.[58]

The defendant and the public alike have a right to insist on a public trial, although, of course, the preservation of decorum may require occasional limitations.[59] This is in the interest both of the defendant and of the public, which has a concern in the working of its courts. There is probably a carefully limited discretion, however, in the court to exclude specified persons or groups where advisable. This includes mobs and persons for whom it would be harmful or offensive to hear certain testimony. Like-

---

57. It is difficult entirely to escape wondering whether the law is wholly realistic in believing that a jury can be freed from the effects of an improper argument by being told to disregard it. Is it not almost as likely that it will be driven home even more effectively?

58. Minnesota alone gives the conclusion to the defendant.

59. It is under this qualification that the court can forbid such conduct as the taking of pictures.

wise the embarrassment of a witness may call for some exclusion. In all these cases the exclusion is proper only to the extent needed, both as to persons shut out and as to length of time in force.

THE JUDGE AND HIS PARTICIPATION

There will be no attempt to touch on those matters in which the situation as to the judge and his participation is the same as in civil cases, for example, his absence or incapacity. Sufficient comment has already been made on his share in selecting the jury. His role during the course of the trial, in ruling on objections, etc., is the same as in civil cases. May he participate in questioning witnesses? In the continental European systems it is normally the judge and the judge alone who does the questioning. Partisan counsel do very little, and then only when the judge accords them that privilege. They may suggest questions that they would like to have asked, but they do not themselves normally do the questioning. Thus our system of partisan counsel questioning is the diametrical opposite. This does not mean that the judge has no right under our system so to participate. On the contrary, it is possible to say sweepingly that all our common-law jurisdictions would agree that in theory at least the judge has the right to participate in the questioning procedure. But such qualifications may be put on the right as will in practical effect largely destroy it. He may not, by his manner of questioning, do more, in indirectly indicating his opinion on the facts, than he is allowed to do locally by direct comment on them. Thus, if we are in a state[60] which permits him to comment on the evidence, considerable latitude in witness questioning would also be felt proper. But if we are in a state where no comment is permitted, questioning by him would almost always be felt to be objectionable, as it would almost certainly carry with it some disclosure of his own views.

But, regardless of what the local view is as to the propriety of his commenting on the evidence, there is in one respect at least a strong argument to be made against widespread judicial taking-over of the questioning function. If numerous questions are be-

---

60. This will be commented on below.

ing asked by him, there is always the possibility that the judge, like partisan counsel, may ask an improper question. In this event it puts the victim of the impropriety in a very difficult position. He is asking the judge to rule on his own impropriety, and, if he raises the point, the judge may or may not be willing to go through the embarrassing procedure of admitting his own fault. If he does admit it, there is the risk of having antagonized the judge. If the judge rules that his own question was a proper one, he may have partly dissipated the judge's friendship, and, in addition, the jury will draw unfavorable inferences. Hence the only wise course to take may be to say nothing and allow the improper question to be answered—not a desirable solution.

When the evidence is all in and the concluding arguments have been made, it becomes the duty of the judge to give his instructions as to the law to the jury. It may be that at one time he was under no duty to do so but could send the jury out to deliberate without any instructions, but, if this was ever the case, it is without present-day significance, as instructions are always given. It is frequently required, however, that the instructions given must be in writing, so as to make available to a reviewing court exact information as to what the jury was told was the law. The failure to give a particular instruction can usually be complained of only if the party wishing it drafts it in correct form and asks that it be given.[61] It is also often required that such a requested instruction be submitted in written form. In any case other than an extremely simple one the giving of completely "correct" instructions (viz., instructions with which the reviewing court is in full agreement) is very difficult. Furthermore, the device of finding instructions to be "incorrect" is a very useful one for a reviewing court to employ if it wishes to reverse. It is, therefore, no wonder that more cases are reversed for errors in instructions than on any other ground.[62]

61. This does not apply to an instruction informing the jury of the presumption of innocence and that it must be convinced of guilt beyond a reasonable doubt. It is usually held that this must be given, whether it is asked for or not.
62. Lester B. Orfield, *Criminal Appeals in America* (Boston: Little, Brown & Co., 1936), p. 206. There is, however, often room, as stated in the text, to suspect that the alleged "error" in the instructions is merely a convenient peg on which to hang a reversal which the reviewing court thinks in fact called for, but for which it is perhaps unable to assign a wholly orthodox reason.

May the judge, as part of his instructions, comment on the evidence, weigh the worth and meaning of the testimony of the witnesses, and indicate what, in his opinion, is the truth? Under the earlier common law he might do so. Under a fear of too auto-cratic a judicial control, however, he was gradually deprived of this right, until in some three-quarters of the states it was im-proper for him to give any indication of his own opinion. In re-cent decades a trend in the other direction has set in, but it is still only in the minority (and in the federal courts) that he may do so. The argument against giving him this authority rests in the tremendous weight that the jury will give to his views and the assumed undesirability of such weight in view of the fact that the judge is perhaps subject to influence and that he is per-haps not a fit person to have such a degree of responsibility—a sad commentary on our elective process and the kind of officials whom it assumes we choose to act for us. It is also, as indicated above, a curious survival of the fears aroused, three hundred years ago, by autocratic royal judges in England.[63]

Against this there are certainly some very definite advantages for allowing judicial comment. By no means an insignificant one is the saving of time due to the speedier arriving at a verdict, thanks to the way in which the judge may have simplified the process for the jury by stripping aside the brushwood of incon-sequential matters. In the same way his helpfulness may reduce the number of jury disagreements. With criminal cases becoming constantly longer and more involved, the problem facing a jury is growing to be often a more and more burdensome one. The jurors are being called upon to keep in mind simultaneously a mass of evidence that it may have taken days or weeks or even occasionally several months to lay before them, and the task for them, therefore, is a much greater one than it used to be. Un-aided by judicial comment, it may prove beyond their powers, as shown by the greater number and frequency of irrational ver-dicts that clearly disclose a jury beyond its intellectual depth, or, if not irrational verdicts, then an increasing frequency of

63. Paradoxically in England the judge has retained the right. Indeed, more, for, unlike counsel, he may even comment on the defendant's failure to take the witness stand.

juries unable to agree, resulting in the discharge of the jury and the need to try the case all over again.

Furthermore, the power to comment and hence, in a sense, the duty to do so certainly give the judge a more responsible position during the proceedings and therefore are likely to make him more attentive than can be expected if his function is confined to more or less routine rulings on objections. This greater responsibilty in turn should attract to the bench a grade of man not tempted by the role of a mere umpire. The argument that the jury will abdicate its authority and allow the judge to decide for it takes no account of the fact that an able jury would be quick to resent the comments of a domineering judge who presented his views too forcefully. As for a jury so weak as to have no mind of its own, but subservient to every suggestion, it would be better, it would seem, to have such a poor group of jurors swayed by the judge than by the last word of the more effective partisan speaker. Normally in daily life we find that it is much better to reach a result with the aid of experience, either one's own or that of an adviser, than to reach it without experience or the guidance of an experienced adviser. There is no reason to suppose that this is in the least degree less applicable to a jury.

There is another respect in which the authority of the judge has found little or no challenge. This is in his power to direct a verdict of not guilty when the evidence is not sufficient to sustain a verdict of guilty. Historically the power to direct a verdict grew out of the power to set aside a verdict. If a given verdict would certainly be set aside, it was elementary economy of time to permit the directing of the contrary verdict. Since there was no doubt of the right to refuse to receive a verdict of guilty, it carried with it the resultant power to direct the verdict of not guilty.

Much more difficulty has been occasioned by the converse proposition. May the court ever direct a verdict of guilty? There is no power to set aside a verdict of not guilty, hence the logical basis on which the power to direct rests is not here present. For this reason and the further one that the directed verdict of guilty might be argued to be a deprivation of jury trial, it is generally held that it is improper unqualifiedly so to direct. There is a tendency, however, to permit what comes rather close to it; that is, where the state's case is undisputed by any evidence offered by the defendant, to point out this fact and that under the law the jury has no choice but to convict.[64] Even here some courts hold that it is necesary to include some such words as "if you believe" the state's witnesses, as there should be an acquittal if they are not believed by the jury.

THE JURY'S VERDICT

The instructions having been given to the jury, it will then retire to see whether it can arrive at a verdict. The common law required unanimity on the jury's part, and this is still generally true. In some states there was, however, a tendency to provide by statute that, in less than capital cases, less than unanimity was necessary. For example, ten out of twelve might suffice for any other felony, and eight for a misdemeanor. Such statutes have met various fates on the constitutionality issue as to whether they constituted a deprivation of jury trial. In recent years, with the increase in jury waivers and the decrease in jury trials, the issue has tended to attract less attention. If a jury, after extended deliberation, reports that it is unable to agree, it is proper for the judge to urge on it the importance of reaching an agreement and the inconvenience to all concerned of having to go through a new trial before another jury and may then send the jurors back to deliberate further, provided that there is no hint or indication that any particular verdict is desired. It is, however, improper to coerce a jury into finding a verdict,[65] and if, after a second period of deliberation, the jurors again report inability to agree, it is

64. If in violation of its moral duty the jury nonetheless acquits, there is nothing the court can do about it. The verdict stands.

65. This was not always so. Under the earlier common law it was entirely proper to force a jury to reach agreement. If the jury did not readily do so, then pressure could be applied. The favorite method was to inform the jurors that they would be retained until they agreed and that in the meanwhile they would be furnished with bread and water only, and only on alternate days, with fire in the jury room to keep them warm only on the days of no food. The bleak prospect of a future consisting only in the alternation of a warm day and a fed day usually led without much delay to agreement.

generally regarded as coercion to retain them still longer. They must be discharged, and, unless the prosecuting attorney is willing to drop the case, it must begin afresh before a new jury.

When the jury reports with a verdict, the latter must be responsive and complete.[66] (What these terms call for will be explained shortly.) If it is not both responsive and complete, the court should call the inadequacy to the attention of the jury and instruct it to deliberate further and to bring in a verdict that will be adequate. If this is not done, there is no basis on which to rest further proceedings, and the error of receiving an improper verdict may necessitate a new trial. Reviewing courts have, however, been somewhat more lenient in construing verdicts and in drawing inferences than they have been in the case of faulty indictments.[67] But a wise trial court should not depend on the reviewing court to help it out. It should refuse to receive a verdict that is not clearly responsive and complete.

In order to be responsive, a verdict must answer with a "Yes" or a "No" the question, "Is the defendant guilty of the offense charged?" The jury cannot validly find him guilty, or not guilty, of some offense not included in the charges. There is, however, one apparent but not real qualification to this statement. Where the offense charged consists of a smaller, less serious, offense plus aggravating circumstances which, all together, create the offense charged, it is entirely possible that the jury may be entirely satisfied that the defendant is guilty of the smaller offense and yet have a reasonable doubt as to the further, aggravating circumstances. In that event a verdict would be properly responsive which found him guilty of the smaller offense. But of course this applies only where the smaller offense is comprised in the greater

66. The modern custom of providing juries with blank forms covering all the possibilities which under the instructions given them by the court are open to them has cut down the chance of improper verdicts. But this custom is not everywhere followed. Situations will continue to come up where the wording of the verdict raises serious doubts as to what it was that the jury really found and what its conclusions really were.

67. So, e.g., where a jury has failed to indicate that the defendant was found guilty but has proceeded to specify what punishment was to be imposed, the finding of guilty has been inferred.

one charged.[68] This relaxation in the full strictness of the rule
has proved a great procedural convenience.[69]

Where the crime is one that can in its nature be committed
only by two (or more) persons, and not by one alone,[70] it is held,
with doubtful logic, that a finding of not guilty as to one defendant necessarily signifies that the other, too, is not guilty. This
would be true if the acquittal necessarily meant that the wrongful act had not been proved. But the acquittal may rest on the
jury's not being convinced that the acquitted defendant was a
participant. The automatic acquittal of both where one is freed is
in fact an outgrowth of the trend, noticeable in many parts of
the criminal law, around 1800, to shape every debatable doctrine
in the defendant's favor.

It is not enough that the verdict be in answer of the questions
addressed to the jury (viz., responsive). It must be a complete
answer. If the indictment contains more than one count, there
should be a finding as to each one. A general finding of "guilty,"
without specifying on which count or counts, will, it is true, be
valid where the counts merely present the same transaction in

68. On a charge of assault with intent to kill, or of assault with a deadly
weapon, the defendant could be found guilty of simple assault. Murder is the
unlawful killing of a human being with malice aforethought. Manslaughter is
exactly the same as murder except that the element of malice aforethought is
absent. A jury, convinced that all the elements of murder except malice aforethought have been proved beyond a reasonable doubt, may well bring in a verdict of manslaughter. Robbery is larceny from the person by means of assault
or battery. If the jury is convinced that there has been a larceny but is not
convinced that there was any assault or battery in connection with it, a larceny
verdict is proper. The larceny of an automobile involves the doing of certain
acts that are comprised in the smaller offense of "tampering with an automobile." If the tampering is with a certain evil intent, it is larceny of the automobile. It is possible for the jury not to be satisfied of this intent and therefore
to confine its verdict to that of which it is sure (viz., the tampering). Many
other examples could easily be given.

69. At one time (but no longer today) it was held that, where the larger offense charged constituted a felony, the jury was not permitted to bring in a
guilty verdict of a smaller, comprised offense if the latter was merely a misdemeanor (viz., it was not proper to cross from one grade of offense to the
other). This limitation was entirely logical at a time when a person accused on
a felony charge had less rights than one on a mere misdemeanor (see, e.g., the
material on right to have counsel). To permit crossing to the lower might thus
indirectly deprive the defendant of a defense right. With the disappearance of
the reason for the restriction, the latter, too, has disappeared.

70. E.g., bribery, adultery, and conspiracy.

varying language. But where the counts deal with different trans-
actions, such an unspecific general finding is invalid.

There are other respects in which the verdict may fail to be
complete. With increasing frequency juries are called on to do
more than merely find as to the issue of guilt. They may be
given the responsibility of setting the punishment or (less drasti-
cally) may be permitted to make more or less binding "recommendations" as to it. Again, the punishment to be imposed on
a second (or subsequent) conviction may be different or more
severe. If so, the prosecution may show such previous convictions,[71] and as a consequence it is necessary for the jury to speak
not only as to the defendant's present guilt but also as to whether
it is true that he has been previously convicted. Or the degree
of the crime (e.g., larceny) may depend on the value of the
property taken. If so, this must be specified in the verdict. All
these are supplementary duties that may arise in the event of
a conviction. But an acquittal, too, may carry some with it.
Probably, if the acquittal was based on the insanity of the defendant at the time of the alleged crime, the jury will be required so to state, in order that any necessary steps may at once
be taken to commit him to a mental hospital. The jury may
even be required to make a finding as to whether the defendant
continues to be insane or has recovered his sanity. These are the
principal, but no doubt not inclusive, examples of findings, over
and beyond that of guilt or nonguilt, needed to make a verdict
complete. Here, too, a trial court that is adequately performing
its duties should refuse to receive a verdict lacking in one or
more of these requisites.

Assuming now that the verdict is responsive and complete,
at what moment does it become irrevocable, so far as the jury
is concerned? It might well have been set at the moment when
the jury foreman announces the verdict or, if written, hands
it over to the court. In all but four states, however, the court

71. This showing of other crimes committed by the defendant is not objectionable, because it is pertinent here and is not merely to create prejudice. It
has been suggested that a fairer way to handle the present problem would be
to exclude any reference, at the trial, to such prior criminality. If, and only if,
this ended in a verdict of guilty, the jury would then for the first time be
shown the evidence as to the defendant's prior convictions and be asked to
pass on whether he is, or is not, a second (or subsequent) offender.

may, or at the request of either party must, poll the jury. That is to say, each juror in succession is asked whether this was and is his verdict. If all answer in the affirmative, the verdict is received and has become final. If one or more answer negatively, the court may discharge the jury or may order it to retire for further deliberation.[72]

One matter in connection with the verdict remains for consideration—the sealed verdict. This is a device to minimize the inconvenience to all concerned in case a jury should arrive at a verdict in the middle of, or at the beginning of, a recess of court, say, a week end. To keep the jury together in enforced idleness after its work is done would be highly objectionable to the jurors and would make for even greater unwillingness on the part of citizens to perform their duty to serve as jurors. Yet it would be almost equally inconvenient for the judge, the counsel, and the defendant (if out on bail) to remain in close attendance all this time, lest the jury wish to report. The sealed verdict is a compromise to meet the needs of both sides so far as possible. The device usually rests on a statutory basis, but, as these statutes are fairly uniform, considerable generalization is possible. With the consent of both parties the court may in advance authorize the jury to place its verdict in a sealed envelope, leave it with a designated officer (such as the bailiff who is guarding them), and then disperse, remaining, however, under strict instructions not to discuss the case with anyone.

At the convening of court the jury will reassemble, and the sealed verdict will then be opened and read. The jury may then be polled in the usual manner. This brings to light a basic weakness in the device. If the verdict, on being read, turns out to be defective, or if, on the polling, a juror denies that it is his verdict, the usual recourse of sending the jurors back for further deliberations is not available. Their having mingled with the outside community creates too great a risk that outside influences may have been brought to bear on them. Only one course of

---

72. Once the verdict has been received, it is final, so far as the jury is concerned. The hostility toward allowing an ex-juror to impeach his verdict (by alleging that some impropriety occurred during the jury deliberations) and hence the almost universal refusal to hear him to this effect are identical in criminal and civil cases and so will not be considered here.

action, therefore, is possible—to discharge the jury and have a new trial. It is this consideration that has led to the view that it is wise to restrict the use of the sealed verdict to comparatively minor cases that are likely to be fairly brief, so that, if there is a need for a new trial, there will be the minimum of inconvenience. Probably the terms of the local statute will expressly limit it to misdemeanor trials. But, even if the terms of the local statute permit its use for more serious offenses, the court in the exercise of its discretion is hardly likely to give the necessary permission.

XIV

POSTTRIAL MOTIONS—ERROR
CORAM NOBIS

IF THE defendant has been acquitted, the case is ended. The present discussion therefore assumes a verdict of guilty. There are now two motions that the defendant can make. He can make either or both, as the grounds on which they respectively rest are not overlapping. These are the motion in arrest of judgment and the motion for a new trial.

MOTION IN ARREST OF JUDGMENT

A motion in arrest of judgment asks that no judgment be pronounced against the defendant because one or more specific defects appear on the record of the case.[1] The defects which are regarded as so serious as to warrant, even at this late stage, the termination of the present proceedings[2] vary somewhat from state to state. All would agree that, if it appeared on the record that the case was one in which the trial court had no jurisdiction (viz., one that the court was not authorized to adjudicate), the judgment should be arrested; it should not be necessary by appeal proceedings to secure the inevitable reversal. Many include the defect that the indictment[3] does not state a complete offense.[4]

1. It should be remembered that the word "record" is here used in its highly technical, narrow, legal sense. It includes, therefore, only the bare recital of the legal steps that have been taken: the finding of the indictment (which is set out in full in the record), the arraignment and the pleas, etc., the fact that a trial was held, and the wording of the verdict that the jury found. It does not include the proceedings within the trial, e.g., the selection of the jury, the evidence that was admitted or excluded, the questions that were or were not allowed to be asked, the instructions to the jury that were given or refused, and all the infinite mass of circumstances that occurred during the trial and may be claimed to have affected its fairness.

2. Whether new proceedings can be begun will be considered below in speaking of the effects following a successful motion.

3. Throughout this discussion, where an indictment is referred to, it should be understood that an information is included.

4. These two grounds, and no more, are specified in Federal Rule 34.

Others add a verdict of uncertain meaning or one convicting the defendant of an offense that was not included in the charges against him. A few include any substantial defect that appears on the face of the record.[5]

In deciding whether few or many defects may be available, it should be remembered that in any event all these defects will be available in the review proceedings before a higher court. If the defect is one that is regarded as sufficient, it is not necessary that the defendant, if he had an earlier opportunity to raise it, must have availed himself of it.[6] He may raise it now for the first time. This is, of course, a great procedural advantage, since it means that the defendant may remain silent on the defect, hope for an acquittal, and, if disappointed, still have his contention in reserve.

If a defendant has an adequate ground to make the motion but fails to do so, the court should have (and is generally regarded as having) the power of its own motion to arrest the judgment. The motion must be made within a specified number of days after verdict. Federal Rule 34 specifies five days but introduces flexibility by allowing the court, if it sees fit, to grant more time.

If the motion is sustained, the defendant is discharged, but new proceedings may be begun at the point necessary in order to be free from the defect in question.[7] The defendant cannot contend that this is double jeopardy, because he by his motion in arrest of judgment has contended that these proceedings are utterly invalid, and he obviously cannot claim them to be invalid and at the same time valid as jeopardy.

It has been argued that the motion in arrest of judgment should be abolished. Defects in the verdict, it is argued, could be added to the matters that can be raised in a motion for a new trial. As for the other matters, the defendant, it is maintained, is sufficiently protected by his present ability, unlike the

---

5. Illinois is in this group.

6. E.g., if it is claimed that the indictment does not state a complete offense, it is not necessary to have already raised the contention by a motion to quash.

7. If this was because of a defective verdict, it will, of course, be necessary to have a new trial, since the verdict cannot be referred back to the jury, as it will meanwhile have been discharged.

condition that once prevailed, to raise them before a higher court.

As has already been stated, the motion for a new trial can be made only by the defendant and not by the prosecution; its defeat is final so far as the trial court is concerned. The court may, of its own motion, grant a new trial.

The grounds on which the motion can rest range over an extremely wide area but are characterized by one point of identity: all are defects that do not appear on the face of the record. The Model Code attempts to list them,[8] specifying (a) that the defendant was not present at a time when his presence was requisite; (b) that the jury received evidence outside the courtroom; (c) that the jury separated during its deliberation; (d) that a juror was guilty of misconduct; (e) that the prosecuting attorney was guilty of it; (f) that the court had erred in a ruling; and (g) that the court had erred in its instructions. Long as this list is, it soon turns out not to be inclusive. Thus it fails to mention mob dominance during the trial and (extremely important) newly discovered evidence. It is, in fact, impossible to list in advance all the improprieties that may find their way into a trial, and so, far more realistically, Federal Rule 33 simply says that a new trial may be granted "if required in the interest of justice." The answer lies in the purpose of allowing such a motion—to correct a defect without requiring the defendant to go to the cost and trouble of raising it before a higher court.[9]

The time within which such a motion might be made has always been sharply limited. It could be made as a matter of right only prior to the judge's pronouncing judgment and sentence, although the judge might permit it to be made until the end of the term of court. This left it largely dependent on the judge's speed in pronouncing judgment. Today the tendency is

---

8. Sec. 365.

9. It may be required that the defendant have made an objection at the time of the impropriety, when conceivably the court could still correct matters. But even here the court may at the time of the motion have come to feel that the impropriety was so serious that the effort to correct it was not, or would not have been, successful and so may grant the motion.

to allow a fixed number of days after the verdict.[10] (There are special provisions where the ground relied on is newly discovered evidence. This will be described shortly.)

One of the most important grounds for asking for a new trial is the discovery of new evidence of a nature favorable to the defendant. But, to justify the awarding of a new trial, the evidence must meet certain tests. It must not be merely cumulative evidence, simply telling the same story from the lips of more, and different, witnesses than previously told the story. It must be new evidence in the sense that its content is different. It must also meet the requirement that it was not previously known to the defendant or such as should by the exercise of reasonable diligence have been known to him. He will not be permitted deliberately to hold back available evidence in the hope of acquittal, and then, if disappointed, be allowed to play his cards over again. Finally, the evidence must be of sufficient persuasiveness so that the judge feels that there is reasonable probability that a different result would have been reached had that evidence been available. Only when the trial court in the exercise of a fair discretion feels that all three requirements are met will it grant a new trial on this ground.[11]

It will be evident that new evidence meeting these exacting requirements will hardly ever be discovered within the short time limit described above for making the motion. More probably it will only come to light six months or a year or two later. Under the old common law, with singular harshness, there was no longer anything that the court could do about it. Only the pardoning power could act. Now, far more fairly, statutes are frequently found providing that for this ground a new trial may be granted for a much longer time—even for a specified number of years.[12] It might, arguably, have been even wiser to remove the time limit entirely, but such cases would be so highly

10. Federal Rule 33 gives five days but leaves the court free to allow a longer time.

11. Whether an order granting or denying a new trial on this or any other ground is appealable see Lester B. Orfield, *Criminal Appeals in America* (Boston: Little, Brown & Co., 1936), p. 513.

12. Under Federal Rule 33 for two years; under the Illinois statute for five years.

exceptional that there seems little disadvantage in letting the pardoning power take care of them.

If a new trial is granted, it should be (and substantially is) as though the first trial had never been held so far as its results are concerned. Thus where on the first trial the defendant is convicted of a less serious degree of offense than he might have been, on the second the issue is opened anew; and it should be possible to convict him even of the more serious degree, though this is not uniformly the view held. Where at the first trial the defendant was convicted on some counts and was acquitted on others, there is a sharp difference of view as to whether the new trial reopens the issue on the acquittals or only on the convictions. Apparently the latter is the prevailing view. In actual fact, however, in many instances where a new trial is ordered, none in fact takes place, and the case is dropped, either because the defect is one that will probably recur or because both parties have agreed to some other adjustment of the matter.

WRIT OF ERROR CORAM NOBIS

To a very limited extent the common law made somewhat more provision for the correction of injustices. Where facts existed which affected the regularity of the proceedings the court retained the power to reopen the case. What will be regarded as "affecting the regularity of the proceedings" has received no clean-cut answer.[13] The reopening of a case in this manner is under what is known as a "writ of error coram nobis." It represents a fumbling and unclear effort to strike a vague compromise between the conflicting goals of protecting defendants by keeping the courts open to them and, on the other hand, of securing some finality to court action. This unsatisfactory uncertainty as to the scope of a convicted person's rights, where he claims he has not in fact had due process, has led in some states to attempts to produce a more definite state of affairs by means of statutes setting up definite provision for postconviction hearings.[14] Detailed dealing with this problem falls more appropriately into a seminar on civil rights.

13. See hereon Orfield, *op. cit.*, pp. 522 ff.
14. See hereon *Jennings* v. *Illinois*, 342 U.S. 104 (1951), and cases there cited.

XV

JUDGMENT AND SENTENCE—CORREC-
TIONAL TREATMENT

Assuming now that no motion in arrest of judgment or motion for a new trial has been made or that, if made, it has been overruled, it then becomes the duty of the judge to pronounce judgment and sentence.[1] If the offense is a felony, the defendant must be present at this stage. A judgment is the court's formal pronouncement, entered on the record of the case, that, a trial having been held, such-and-such a verdict was brought in and that as a consequence of these proceedings the court finds that the defendant is guilty of such-and-such an offense. From this it should be apparent that the judgment must correspond to the verdict, just as the verdict must correspond to the charges at the trial, and these in turn to the charges in the indictment. There cannot be a valid judgment finding the defendant guilty of an offense not specified in the verdict.[2]

After—and usually immediately after—the judgment has been

1. The text, of course, assumes a verdict of guilty. If the jury has acquitted the defendant, a judgment of not guilty would follow at once, and there would be nothing further to be done.

2. Let us assume that the verdict finds the defendant guilty of the full offense charged, in one of those situations where the jury might have found the defendant guilty of a smaller offense that is included in the one charged, and also assume that the judge believes that a verdict of guilty of the smaller offense would have been supported by the evidence, and hence proper, but that the full offense was not shown beyond a reasonable doubt. Does the judge, in an analogous manner, have the power to pronounce judgment of guilty of only the less serious crime? Will this be regarded as a judgment corresponding to the verdict? Or must he set aside the verdict and order a new trial as the only way to limit the conviction to what he considers proper? The majority (but not all) of the few cases that have considered this problem have denied him the power thus to reduce the judgment (even though, as has been indicated, a corresponding power is granted to the jury and to the prosecuting attorney by accepting a plea of guilty to such lesser offense). This seems a needless and unfortunate limitation on his authority. In a few states statutes have conferred this authority on him. See, for the minority view, *United States* v. *Linnier*, 125 Fed. 83 (1903).

pronounced, it is the duty of the judge to pronounce the sentence.[3] The sentence is the court's formal declaration of the consequences, as to the defendant, of the judgment just pronounced. Thus it is apparent that the two—judgment and sentence—are logically wholly separate steps by the judge. Yet they are so closely connected in time that they have tended to coalesce. Indeed, reviewing courts have even held that, where the court recites a verdict of guilty and then proceeds to pronounce sentence, it would be proper to infer a tacit judgment. It will, of course, be obvious that the sentence must correspond to the judgment, in the sense that the former may impose on the defendant only such consequences as are provided for the crime that the judgment speaks of. If, however, a court erroneously pronounces a sentence imposing consequences not provided for, the result will merely be a resentencing in proper terms. There is no need for a new trial.

Assuming that a court has a choice of punishments and, by sentencing, has exercised that choice, may it thereafter reconsider and resentence, imposing increased or decreased punishment? Yes, within sharply defined time limits. There is agreement that the power to increase exists up to, but only up to, the time when the convicted person is handed over to the executive authorities (e.g., the prison warden) to commence undergoing punishment. Some states apply the same limitation to a decrease.[4]

3. This is not strictly accurate. Formerly in all felony cases the judge, before pronouncing sentence, was required to ask the convicted defendant whether he had anything to say as to why sentence should not be pronounced against him. This proceeding was known as the "allocution." It is still required in all capital cases but, in most states, not in other felonies. Illinois follows this majority view, but Federal Rule 32(a) requires it generally. No allocution is required in misdemeanor cases. The matters that the defendant might state in the allocution were limited and obviously would not include an attempt to reopen the question of his guilt. He might claim (1) that he had become insane since the verdict was rendered (the law will not punish a person unable to understand what he is being punished for and why he is being punished, and, if such be the case, the punishment must be deferred until he is able so to comprehend); (2) that he has received a pardon for the offense in question; (3) that he is not the person against whom there was a finding of guilt and a judgment; and (4), if the defendant is a woman and the sentence may be death, that it be deferred because of pregnancy.

4. E.g., Illinois.

Others permit a decrease even thereafter, provided that it occurs within the same term of court.[5]

DETERMINING THE PUNISHMENT

Except for a few comments in connection with sentencing, nothing has up to now been said as to who determines what the punishment shall be and how wide a choice may be made. These matters will be considered here along very broad lines. The history of our law shows constantly increasing flexibility—a constant increase in the degree of adaptation of punishment to the needs of the individual convicted defendant—in other words, the individualization of punishment. At first punishment was wholly fixed in nature.[6] A given sentence automatically followed a given judgment, and the ideal was to have the punishment fit the crime, not the criminal. Gradually some measure of choice came in, with exile—transportation from England to one of the colonies—one of its early manifestations. Subsequent development has consisted in the constant increase both in the number and in the scope of mechanisms of flexibility. The order in which these are here discussed is not to be taken as necessarily reflecting either their importance or the sequence in which they arose.

The legislatures have attempted to retain for themselves some share in the individualization of punishment by the enactment of habitual-criminal laws, providing that on a second (or subsequent) conviction the punishment is to be more severe than on first conviction. Such provisions are still popular, but far commoner are provisions permitting the period of imprisonment (or the amount of the fine) to be set at any figure between a specified minimum and a specified maximum. The responsibility of so setting the duration (or the amount) of the punishment was at first intrusted to the judge. As part of the Jacksonian dislike of authority and confidence in the ordinary citizen's adequacy to do any job, there was for a while in the nineteenth century a tendency to transfer the measuring-out of the punishment from the judge to

5. Federal Rule 35 presents a wise variant of this in substituting for the term of court a flat sixty days within which there may be a decrease.

6. Even at a fairly early date, where the punishment was by its nature capable of variation in quantity (e.g., imprisonment), there might be some small discretion given to the sentencing judge as to the quantity.

the jury.[7] The objection that such a statute was unconstitutional because it assigned the punishment-measuring function to an agency other than the court, whereas it inherently belonged to the court as part of the sentencing process, was met by the reply that the jury is itself a part of the court, that the change merely meant transferring this function from that part of the court (in the large sense of the word) which is called the judge to that part which is called the jury, and that the measurement of punishment is still left in the hands of the court in the larger sense. The question of the wisdom of the change depended on the balancing of two practical considerations. On the one hand, there was the judge's greater experience with problems of this sort; on the other, there was the (probably) greater willingness of the jury to convict if the consequences to the defendant were within their control. In some states a compromise was attempted by authorizing or requiring the jury to make more or less binding recommendations to the judge. In still others the jury was given the task in a few specified crimes, while leaving it to the judge in general.[8]

In recent decades the tendency to involve the jury in the punishment-fixing function seems to have come to a complete stop. Even in the situations just described, where the judge had to share with, or hand over to, the jury the fixing of punishment, he retained indirectly the possibility of a great voice in it. It may be that the judgment based upon the verdict finds the defendant guilty on a number of different indictments that were all tried simultaneously or finds him guilty on more than one count of the same indictment. The judge in the sentence may specify whether the punishments set by the sentence are to run consecutively or concurrently. The difference to the defendant is obvious! It is within the judge's discretion, and the reviewing court will not interfere. Such litigation as has arisen in this area deals rather with the interpretation to be put on a sentence which

7. Of course, if there were a waiver of a jury and thus an intrusting of its functions to the judge, this function too would go to him.

8. Thus in Illinois the jury sets the punishment in (and only in) kidnaping, rape, manslaughter (imprisonment up to a maximum of fourteen years), and murder (imprisonment for not less than fourteen years or for life or a death sentence).

fails to indicate clearly, as it should do, whether service is to be consecutive or concurrent.

This brings us to the two most important mechanisms of individualizing punishment—probation and parole. First, as to probation. Probation consists in allowing a convicted person to remain at liberty under supervision and, perhaps, subject to his meeting certain conditions and requirements, with the end result that, if he behaves in a satisfactory manner, he will be discharged and so freed from having to undergo punishment. Where it may be granted (which will be considered shortly), it is for the judge to determine whether to grant it or not. Its constantly increasing use rests on a growing realization of a number of facts. One is that imprisonment and the resultant close association with experienced wrongdoers will probably have a harmful, instead of a helpful, effect on the incarcerated person. Another is that, if there is to be the best chance of rehabilitation, there should be the minimum amount of destruction of roots that the defendant has in the community—familial, social, and economic. It has also been urged that probation is much cheaper to administer than is incarceration in an institution. This argument, while valid, is easily the one of least importance. A probation system ought not to be thought of as necessarily something cheap. A good system must be provided with funds sufficient to accomplish its purposes. The essential is adequate, rather than cheap, supervision.

In a few states the courts asserted that the common law, unaided by statute, gave them the authority to release on probation.[9] They correctly asserted that it had always been regarded as proper to defer the carrying-out of a death sentence to allow time to seek a pardon or to inquire into the sanity or pregnancy of the defendant. As more opportunities were given to the defendant to have his conviction reviewed in a higher court,[10] the need and frequency of such procedural delay steadily increased, and such postponements inevitably became part and parcel of

9. In the discussion here and elsewhere no distinction will be drawn between (a) suspending the imposing of a sentence and (b) imposing sentence and then suspending carrying it into effect. As a result, the comment somewhat oversimplifies some of the problems.

10. As will be described in the next chapter.

the procedure of adjudicating the case. From this purely procedural power to postpone the courts then claimed the power
to postpone for a much longer time and for an entirely different
purpose (viz., the purpose of reforming the wrongdoer). The
logic of this inference seems doubtful, to say the least, and most
courts have refused to make it. Instead they have maintained
that legislative action, specifically creating a probation system,
was necessary.

But whether legislative action is necessary, or whether the
courts as a common-law matter have this power, it is far preferable to rest upon a statutory basis, for at least two reasons.
For one thing, the power to postpone is not the power to discharge. A mere common-law foundation inescapably brings the
dilemma of a perpetual probation hanging over the defendant's
head or a discharge that would clearly seem to invade the pardoning power. For another thing, a probation system calls for
funds, personnel, and adequate machinery to run it. This in turn
calls for statutory aid. For these reasons probation must in fact
rest on a statutory basis.

Only a few of the most important points can be made as to
what such a statute should provide. Normally the defendant
must make application to the court to be put on probation, and
very often specified kinds of offenders (e.g., those with a record
showing some prior conviction) are made ineligible. Again, certain offenses may be excluded from probation.[11] Both of these
factors (and the former especially) should, of course, be given
most serious consideration by the judge. It seems questionable,
however, that they should absolutely tie his hands. The nature
of the offense in particular may or may not bear on the chances
of the defendant's reforming. If we lack confidence in the judge's
capacity to weigh these factors, we lack confidence in his ability
to do the job at all.

If the judge's decision to grant or withhold probation is to be

11. The classification of nonprobationable offenses is often arbitrary, to say
the least. Larceny is sometimes made noneligible if the property taken exceeds
a specified value—probably an irrelevant matter in determining the chance of
reform of the offender. In one state (Illinois) until recently robbery with a
gun was probationable, while voluntary manslaughter—committed, probably,
under an emotional stress that would never be repeated—was not.

made on adequate grounds, there must be provision for an administrative agency to make a preprobation investigation of the offender and a report on what it has found.[12] Only then can the judge act advisedly. Unfortunately, not only are such reports often not available to the judge; too often he will show a discreditable unwillingness to abide by such information, in preference to his own preformed favorable or unfavorable prejudices. Opinion is divided, however, as to whether this report should or should not be disclosed to the defendant.[13] On the one hand, to make it available may poison the relations between the offender and the probation authorities and may draw out to impossible lengths the procedure of determining whether or not to grant probation, owing to criticism of reports that in the main would be accurate and impartial. On the other hand, to keep it from the defendant may put him at the mercy of an unfavorable report whose inaccuracies he could easily demonstrate.

The court may, and frequently does, impose various requirements and conditions on the probationer, which he must agree to observe. These include such obvious requirements as that he make steady payments by way of restitution to the victim, that he take a job and work faithfully, that he refrain from evil associates, and that he stay sober. Such conditions will not arouse controversy.

There are two others, however, that have caused more discussion. One, which is probably unquestionably within the power of the court but where there is considerable disagreement among social workers as to its advisability, is the condition sometimes imposed on traffic violators that they must participate in a personally conducted tour through a hospital, where they are forced to view the victims of traffic accidents. A more frequent, and even more controversial, condition is that the probationer serve a limited period of time in the institution of confinement from which he is supposedly being saved by probation. May such a brief period of incarceration be imposed as a preliminary

12. Federal Rule 32(c)(2) specifies, in a way that can serve as a model, what information such a report should include.
13. It has already been pointed out (chap. xiii) that the defendant's right to have witnesses against him confront him does not apply here.

to probation? This is a great deal more doubtful, both practically and logically. It completely disregards the basic assumption on which the case for probation rests—the undesirability of subjecting the defendant to the experience of being locked up. Logically, by imposing punishment and then terminating it, it comes close to trenching on the executive's pardon power. But despite these considerations the practice is followed in numerous states.[14]

There is likewise a difference of view as to whether probation, once granted, may be withdrawn arbitrarily or whether, though initially a matter of grace, once conferred, it has become a matter of right, to be lost only after a hearing. Whatever view may be stronger on purely theoretical lines, it would seem that the rehabilitative purposes of probation can be effectively served only if the probationer can feel that he has been granted a certain status and that he cannot be arbitrarily deprived of it.[15]

The greatest disappointments in probation, however, have been due not to any of the problems just described but to the inadequacy with which it has been administered, and this in turn has stemmed largely from the niggardly financial support that it has received. Inadequate preprobation investigation has led to unwise decisions, and inadequate supervision has led to relapse into crime. At worst probation in a given area may be a dead letter because its costs must be paid locally, while the cost of incarceration in a penitentiary, though much higher, will come out of state funds. In an atmosphere of this sort it is obvious, too, that the selection of the personnel will be governed much more by doling out jobs to the politically deserving than by considerations of fitness. It has been suggested that improvement might be looked for if, instead of having each court administer its own locally supported probation system, the function were to be centralized and made a state one. Probably this would mean a real improvement. The difficulty, however, is to accomplish the change. No government entity willingly gives up power, and the local judges, asked to surrender the management

14. In a number of states a statute expressly authorizes a brief incarceration period (e.g., in Illinois).

15. Discussion of this topic and of its counterpart in revocation of parole will be found in an article by Henry Weihofen, in 32 J. Cr. L. & Crim. 531 (1942).

of the local system, have been no exception. Approval of state grants-in-aid has been more than easy to get, but there has also been uniform resistance to any provision giving the state the slightest degree of authority to insist on the wise spending of such funds by supervising in any way the selection of probation officers and seeing that they satisfied minimum standards of efficiency.

But state-wide administration presents other advantages besides the hope of better selected and supported personnel. Our county lines are today far too constricted to constitute boundaries for work of this sort. There are far too many instances where men live in one county, work in another, and must constantly travel through a third. Supervision must be equally unhampered. Co-operation between different parts of the state (and even with other states) would be easier in case a probationer desired to move. Uniform policies could be adopted. Co-operation with the state parole system would be simplified.[16] The experience of the few states that have made the change to state administration confirms these forecasts.

The other great mechanism for individualizing treatment of the convict is parole, or, more properly, the indeterminate sentence. Under the indeterminate sentence neither the judge nor the jury nor any fixed provision of law specifies at the time of the conviction exactly what punishment the convicted person is to undergo. The law merely specifies that on conviction of such-and-such an offense the defendant shall be sentenced to the penitentiary for not less than a specified number of years and not more than another specified number.[17] When, within this minimum and maximum, he will actually be released is thus left wholly undetermined for the time being.[18] That question is left to the future determination of an administrative agency usually known as a parole board. It is the task of this board to determine when

16. Under the federal system one organization supervises both probation and parole.

17. A variant in which the court may, within these limits, set more narrow ones will be considered later.

18. Obviously such a sentence, with its set minimum and maximum, is not in strict language wholly indeterminate. No state, in that sense, has a completely indeterminate sentence. But there would seem to be no danger of a misunderstanding from the slightly inaccurate language.

within that period he is to be allowed to go free. The foundation on which the case for indeterminate sentence rests is that the protection of our social structure is the paramount consideration. Such protection is to be secured by training X to be a better person in so far as that is possible, or by keeping X out of circulation just as a dangerous animal might be, if that is what social protection calls for. The incarceration must, then, be as long as the protection of society makes necessary. There should not be the obligation to release him a day sooner than the need indicates. By the same token neither society's nor his own interest (in so far as it may be followed consistently with the safety of society) justifies keeping him incarcerated any longer than is necessary for this protection.

But both theoretically and practically it is obvious that it will be an immensely difficult task to determine when that moment of safe release arrives. If we ask the jury or the judge to make the determination at the trial stage, we are asking that it be done at a time when a task that is always difficult is at its absolute height of difficulty, because the emotional elements—hysteria, rage, fury, excitement—are at their height. We are asking that it be done at a time when the information available to the performer of the task, be it the judge or the jury, is likely to be at a minimum. And we are asking that the task be done without any possibility of correction if it is later found that the date was set too far in the future, long after the person had become a safe risk, or too soon, so that social protection is by no means achieved at the release date of an individual who continues to be a menace to society. Finally, we are asking that the task be done at a time when one of the major factors involved must, in its very nature, be as yet unknown—the effect of incarceration on the prisoner himself.

All these difficulties are inescapable if the measure of punishment is to be set at the trial stage. In all other fields of life we know that it is much better to act on hindsight rather than on foresight. The same is true here.[19] The indeterminate sentence

19. Even the economic situation at the time of release, the possibility of getting an honest job or the probability of unemployment, is a vital factor. If judge or jury can unerringly forecast this years in advance, they will have a bright financial future.

is simply the adoption of the view that it is better to decide the date of release in the light of all this information than to guess at it months and years beforehand.[20] The case for the indeterminate sentence, however, is even stronger than this. Not only does it enable us to make a decision that is vastly more realistic, because it is based on hindsight, but it even allows us to reopen this much less dangerous decision, where the more difficult one could not possibly be reopened, because part and parcel of the indeterminate sentence structure is the fact that the person so released will only be released on parole. That is to say, he will be released under supervision, with a watch kept over him to see whether the decision that he was a safe object for release, a safe risk for the community to take, was in fact founded upon a correct appraisal of him. If, in the light of his behavior, it is found that the release was premature, matters can be corrected by his reincarceration. Finally, the very fact that there is supervision not merely serves the above purpose but, as an equally valuable by-product, probably will make his ultimate going-straight a greater likelihood because, during the crucial period of re-establishing himself and of striking new roots, there will be much more hesitation about returning to the old ways if the parolee is aware of day-to-day supervision.

This constitutes the logically unassailable case for the indeterminate sentence and its inseparable partner, release on supervision—the combination that constitutes parole. Is it, however, in its real working tied to so many defects that its purposes are in fact wholly defeated? It will here be contended that the answer is "No," that the criticisms directed against it are superficial or mistaken, and that, given a fair trial, it has brilliantly justified itself. We shall then consider, however, some typical shortcomings in its administration and the really constructive steps that can and should be taken in such situations.

Parole, it is asserted, may be appropriate for the first offender or the otherwise promising one. (Who will disagree?) It is out

20. We do not demand of the doctor when he sends us to the hospital that he irrevocably commit himself as to the exact day of our discharge. Yet the doctor, whom we are perfectly willing to accord uncertainty in this matter, is dealing with well-known diseases, as against the judge and the jury, who are dealing with relatively unknown factors. The doctor is dealing with a future that is measured in terms of weeks or a month. The judge and the jury are dealing with time spaces of as many years!

of place, it is said, for the recidivist with many failures against him. The illogic of this position is curiously unclear to many people. It might well be argued that the recidivist should never be released—a harshness of view that is less and less likely to prevail.[21] But, if we are going to release him, surely he of all persons is the one against whom we should most carefully guard ourselves. To release him on definite sentence only is in effect to say, "Here is a person so dangerous that society must insist on his freedom without supervision—so dangerous that there must be no possibility of reconsideration!" If parole is peculiarly appropriate for the first offender for his sake, it is peculiarly appropriate for the repeater for society's sake.

Another unsound argument often made against parole is that it is nothing but a system of licensed and encouraged leniency—a system whereby offenders are treated so mildly as to do away entirely with the deterrent effects of punishment. It is not appropriate at this point to reopen the question of the effectiveness of deterrence. All that needs to be said is that the parole system as such does not connote anything in the way of either excessively lenient punishment or excessively severe punishment. It is entirely consistent with the system as such that the period served in the institution before supervised release is a longer one than would prevail under definite sentence, or is a shorter one than would so prevail, or is approximately the same. Parole as such does not suggest necessarily anything in the way either of severity, on the one hand, or of leniency, on the other. A given parole board may have a tendency to release individuals more speedily than prevailingly judges or juries in that particular state, if they set a definite sentence, are likely to do. Another board may be so constituted as to be slower to release individuals than judges and juries in that state would. The system of release has no necessary bearing on it.[22]

21. About ninety-five out of every one hundred persons sent to the penitentiary will ultimately come out.

22. Some years ago in Illinois a vicious attack was made on parole. It was contended that it was nothing more than a licensed form of exemption from any real punishment. No attention at all was paid to the fact—plainly demonstrable though it was—that on the average the time actually served inside the walls of a prison had proved to be longer than the time so served before the days of the indeterminate sentence, rising from something over four years to five years and seven months.

It is also maintained that the records of parolees after release demonstrate the failure of the system.[23] This calls for rather extended consideration. Their allegedly poor performance is, it is asserted, shown by statistics that some high figure—say, 15 per cent—of all on parole in a given year are guilty of violations. Actually such a figure would prove little or nothing. "Violations" are whatever the local rules declare to be violations[24] and may mean much or nothing. Hence they may be made common or rare. Further, their "frequency" depends equally on the energy with which parole agents seek them out and report them. The less attention paid to the violations rate, probably the better. Much more significant is the percentage of parolees who, while on parole, are convicted of a new crime. Here the figure apparently is about 5 per cent. Unquestionably this looks high, and it is high when compared to the performance of the population as a whole. But the only comparison that is meaningful is that of the performance of persons released on parole with the performance of persons released by another mechanism, say, the definite sentence. This would constitute a comparison that is significant —not a comparison of the general law-abiding community performance as against that of a selected group that has demonstrated its lawbreaking tendency. On this basis the record of parolees probably compares very favorably with that of definite releasees, although fully reliable statistics are difficult to obtain.

But what has contributed most to the widespread belief that parole is so often unsuccessful is that parole failures are in their very nature almost always newsworthy, because sensational and dramatic. The successes are uninteresting and unexciting. The man from Mars might, on reading our papers, believe that every train was wrecked, every plane fell in flames, every marriage ended in divorce. We are not misled ourselves, because our own personal experience tells us of the trains and planes that arrive safely and the homes that are happy. But when it comes to parole most of us are men from Mars, taking the front-page story as

23. This "argument" is often strengthened by simply referring to every ex-convict, in the event of subsequent misconduct, as a "parolee."

24. E.g., such absurd rules as forbidding being outdoors after nine-thirty or setting foot inside a motor-powered vehicle. These are actual—not imaginary—regulations.

our sole information. But parole is in an even worse position than are these other human undertakings in this regard. After all, the railroads, the airlines—even the happy celebrators of a golden wedding—are not averse to having their success publicized. They may not receive much publicity, but they get some and are happy to get what they can! But parole labors under the further handicap not only that its successes are undramatic and so would never get into the newspapers but that part of the reward which an ex-convict is entitled to have for going straight is the very fact that his case should not be publicized. Only in the form of dry statistics may their achievements be broadcast. And any human activity can be made to look bad if only its failures are allowed to be known! It is small wonder that the public labors under a distorted viewpoint and one extremely difficult to correct.

There are, however, in all but a few states glaring faults in the administration of the system that urgently call for correction. In part these concern the parole-granting authority—usually a board —and in part the supervising agencies. They will be considered in turn. In too many instances the board's membership is determined by political considerations. Appointment is a reward for a deserving person who has to be provided with some sort of job after a successful political campaign. Not only would the board be selected in this way but its term of office would be only as long as the governor who appointed it stayed in office himself. Chronic inexperience would be the normal condition. What is needed is longer terms for board members—say, six years—staggered so that at no time will the membership be wholly or mainly green material.

Turning now to the way in which the board functions, a frequently encountered criticism is that it is influenced in its decisions by political considerations. Realistically, however, the tendency is to overemphasize the danger of political influences in the actual disposition of cases. While, of course, that danger may exist, with a politically appointed body too ready to decide specific cases on political considerations, on the whole the danger of politically influenced decisions is less than is generally assumed, for the very practical reason that the average person coming before a parole board simply does not have any political influence to bring to bear. If he had any at his entry into the penitentiary, it will have been pretty well dissipated by the time he comes up for parole. Gang loyalty is a short-lived flower. Corruption, too, is a much smaller danger, in board efficiency, than the incompetency and inexperience already mentioned. This latter factor in particular means that the board during much of its incumbency will not yet be influenced by the background of information, small as it is, which is being built up as to parole performance, favorable factors, unfavorable factors, etc., but is likely to be influenced by its emotional reaction to the job it is doing. Such emotional response, regardless of whether it goes in the direction of leniency or in that of harshness, is a poor foundation on which to build a wise decision.[25]

There is also a great spread between the ideal and the usual reality in the matter of parole supervision. Two shortcomings are common, and both ought to be curable. The first is the chronic one in so many fields of public activity, namely, that the personnel is selected on the basis of political expediency. The job of parole agent is given to a political hack who has something coming to him, and he performs his task with the diligence and the efficiency that might be expected in view of his background and his knowledge as to why he got and why he presumably will retain the job. There will not be effective parole supervision unless we have parole agents adopting that as a career and selected with a view to their personal fitness for the work and assured that they will be retained in their position so long as that effective performance continues. This is an ideal that has been attained in a number of states,[26] but only in a small minority. Too often what is miscalled "parole" is in fact release without effective supervision.

Allied to this shortcoming is that of the assignment to a given parole agent of an impossibly large number of cases. While the number of cases that may safely be assigned to an agent of course varies from area to area, and differs between city and country,

25. Statistical information as to parole performance is slowly building up, much in the same manner in which insurance companies have through many decades built up mortality tables.
26. Notably New York and California.

it has been said that on the average the absolute maximum load per agent should be fifty cases. Yet in many cities the load is, or recently has been, as high as two hundred. There have been instances of a load of five hundred! Again one can say that only the name, not the reality, of parole can then exist, to the undeserved discredit of the real thing.

In a few states a modified form of the indeterminate sentence has been adopted under which the trial judge is required in his sentence to specify a minimum (not less than the statutory minimum) and a maximum (not more than the statutory maximum) that the convict is to serve. A judge convinced of the value of parole could set his two figures far apart—as far, if he wished, as the statutory ones themselves. But one bent on destroying the system could also easily accomplish his purpose by putting his minimum and maximum so close together that in effect there is no chance for effective supervision.[27] The result may mean the tacit refusal of a parole board under such circumstances to parole these individuals at all, in view of the short time available for supervision.[28]

One final mechanism of flexibility remains to be mentioned. We are becoming increasingly aware that the problem of crime is concentrated most largely in the age group above juvenile-court range and below twenty-six years. Under the leadership of the American Law Institute, model legislation has been drafted

27. This statement rests on the assumption, true in most but not all states, that supervision cannot extend longer than and beyond the maximum time that the parolee could have been kept in prison.

28. E.g., in states with well-developed parole systems, like New York and California, about 80 per cent of releases are on parole. In Illinois the figures were almost as high until the adoption of this type of statute. Now they are reversed, with the huge majority being released without supervision. It is ironical also that, whereas one of the principal arguments for the change in Illinois was the supposed excessive leniency of parole boards and the shortness of time, therefore, that society was protected against wrongdoers, statistics show that in 1939, before the changes went into effect, only 2 per cent of the releases from the Illinois State Penitentiary comprised persons who had been in the penitentiary less than three years. There were none released who had been in the penitentiary less than two years. By 1945, even if the maximum time allowed under the judge-set maximum were served, 77 per cent would be released in less than three years. This trend has continued since. In other words, short periods of incarceration have increased from 2 per cent to 77 per cent under a law designed to increase severity!

(and adopted in a few states)[29] making special provision for the trial and correctional treatment of persons in this age range. One such model act sets up a special court for them—known by some such name as the "adolescent court"—geared to, and sympathetic of, their special problems and needs. Another act, of even more importance, would create a "youth correction authority" (viz., a small board or commission) to whom offenders of this type would be committed instead of to an institution or prison. This authority would then have the full responsibility of determining what kind of correctional program each person would be subjected to and for how long. Its choice would be largely untrammeled and might range from close confinement to nearly complete freedom. Great use would probably be made of many small institutions, each with its own individual work and rehabilitation program.[30] Such a development holds out many hopeful possibilities.

We turn now to a final matter concerning the determination of what the punishment is to be—the extent to which we allow ourselves experimentation and innovation in the kind of punishment that will be imposed. At one time many different punishments were used, of which imprisonment was only a minor one.[31] In addition, and far more important, there were the death sentence, torture of various kinds, mutilation of one sort or another, exile, and numerous varied ones, such as the stocks, the pillory, and the ducking stool, to name only the principal ones. Of them all we have preserved only three[32]—death, imprisonment, and a monetary punishment in the form of a fine. To make sure that such shall continue to be the state of affairs, we have normally also imbedded in our state constitutions a provision forbidding cruel and unusual punishment. In some states the word "and" does not appear, but the word "or" takes its place. Such a provi-

29. Notably California.

30. In this the model act is based on the famous English Borstal System of small prisons. For a description of them see William Healy and Benedict Alper, *Criminal Youth and the Borstal System* (New York: Commonwealth Fund, 1941).

31. Imprisonment as a recognized punishment is a comparatively modern development. Its use in the Middle Ages was rather of a political or extralegal character.

32. In two states flogging has never gone into disuse.

sion is now understood as forbidding not only innovations, in the form of wholly new punishments never previously used, but also the return to punishments that at one time were in use but that at the adoption of the constitution had fallen into disuse. It is an interesting question as to how wise such a constitutional prohibition really is. No doubt we can agree that brutalized punishments, such as public ones, floggings and many others, are distinctly unwise and that we are well rid of them.

It is, however, a very real question as to whether we have attained the ultimate of wisdom in this field any more than we have in other fields, and it is by no means certain that the last word in constructive punishment (if, indeed, punishment is constructive) has been said when we have hit on the magic three of death, imprisonment, and fines. Even here something may conceivably remain to be learned.

Like the constitutional guaranty of jury trial, this one, too, presents some questions as to its scope and extent. One of these consists in the problem of differentiating between a new means to achieve an old (and legitimate) end, on the one hand, and an entirely new punishment, on the other. Granted that a new punishment cannot be imposed, does that forbid us from imposing an old punishment by new means? Traditionally the death sentence was carried out by one or the other of two means, hanging and beheading. Is it still proper today to execute by means of beheading, or is this a means to the end that has so thoroughly disappeared in this country that we can say that it is a different punishment? What of such novelties as electrocution or lethal gas? It has been said that these are not different or new or unusual punishments; they are merely new ways of accomplishing the same end. But a new method of killing that constituted an additional punishment in and of itself (say, flaying alive) would be improper. There may, however, be a real difficulty in distinguishing between that which is merely a new means (and therefore legitimate) to achieve the same end and that which is an end in itself and is unusual and therefore forbidden.

A closely allied difficulty is where to draw the line between an increase in the quantity of punishment that amounts only to degree and where it is so great as to become a change in kind. It is easy, and inadequate, to say that the quantum is a matter for legislative discretion. But exactly where the boundary line is crossed between the legitimate increase that the legislature may decide upon and one that makes it an entirely new punishment is something that is incapable of precise formulation.

For a fairly brief period in the early decades of the present century there was considerable enthusiasm for the adoption of laws providing for the compulsory sterilization of offenders who fell within a specified description. That description might include anyone who committed a crime over and above a certain grade of severity or one who committed any one of a specified list of crimes. For all such, either in the discretion of the court or without alternative, there would be compulsory sterilization. Naturally such statutes were at once attacked on the constitutionality ground. Some, but not all, were upheld on the ground that they were eugenic measures, intended not by way of additional punishment but as social protection of a highly necessary sort, and that the mere fact that the protective measures which society had to take were unpleasant did not necessarily make them punishment. In other states it was argued that such statutes were punitive in nature, because they did not apply to all persons having a given defect but only to those who had a given defect and who had been convicted of crime and that the sterilization, being a consequence of a conviction, was therefore a punitive consequence.

The whole subject, however, has in recent years lost considerable of its interest, partly because in certain states where the law was passed it never was much more than a dead letter. Even more important, later thinking has given rise to considerable doubt as to the effectiveness, in any event, of a supposed eugenics law like this. Is criminal conduct a hereditary manifestation? England during the reign of Henry VIII had thousands of death sentences carried out every year. At that rate England should have been completely cured of criminal propensities by the elimination of this unworthy stock by the next generation, yet that was not the case. Virginia and to a less extent Australia were the points of destination for thousands of transported offenders sent out from England. On the same argument, Virginia ought today to be the most crime-ridden state in the Union. It is not, nor is Australia particularly bad. Certainly this puts a large burden of proof on those who believe that criminality is inheritable.[33] Even if that burden can be carried and certain individuals can be positively pointed out as the breeders of sure criminals, it is discouragingly likely that we shall be able to segregate these black sheep only after the damage has been done and their offspring-producing activities have passed their peak.

33. Of course many aspects of social inadequacy—such as the inability to earn a living—may be due to inherited handicaps, but that is another thing. No one is advocating sterilization for mere social inadequacy, even if its existence makes for difficulties that may lead to criminal conduct.

XVI

APPELLATE REVIEW

THE trial court having concluded its activities in the case, as described in the preceding chapter, the judicial branch of government was, at one time, completely through with the case. The trial court was not only the first but also the final court. It was only by degrees and very slowly that the possibility of having a conviction reviewed in a higher court was gradually developed.[1] Today this change has been completed, and the defendant, defeated in the trial court, has exactly as broad an opportunity of review as has the plaintiff or the defendant in a civil case. Just as in chapter xiii, "The Trial," so here, too, there will be rigidly excluded from discussion all those matters in which the criminal procedure is like the civil. As a consequence there will be no treatment of the meaning of such terms as "writ of error," "bill of exceptions," or "appeal." The mechanics and the scope of review will be largely omitted, and only a few matters peculiar to criminal review, and of importance, will be dealt with, in random rather than in logical order.

Since reviewing courts will not ordinarily decide matters that have become merely moot, the defendant who has already served his time in the penitentiary and has been released before the reviewing court considers his case and decides it will normally find his appeal dismissed. Similarly if he has paid his fine without protest, the case will be ended. To take care of the possible injustice of such a situation, states generally have provided by statute for the possibility of a stay of execution (viz., a delay in the undergoing of punishment). Such statutes usually provide that, where there has been a conviction and where the accused person informs the trial court that he proposes to appeal, the trial court may, if it believes that there is good ground for his appeal,

1. After considering review at the instance of the defendant there will be comment on the possibility of review in behalf of the prosecution.

stay the imposition and the carrying-out of punishment.[2] If the appeal is from a sentence of death, the stay is, of course, a matter of absolute right. If there is no stay, the defendant does not have the right to be present at the review proceedings. That right terminated with the trial court.

The matters that a reviewing court will consider are, as already indicated, much the same as in a civil proceeding. As to alleged defects in the trial procedure, it has already been stated that it will usually demand that the defendant must have raised an objection at the time the defect occurred and when, therefore, corrective steps might have been taken. The defendant cannot by his own remissness prevent the curative steps from having been taken and now complain of the fact that they were not. Strictly speaking, however, the remissness is not so much the defendant's as that of his counsel, and it is, therefore, rather interesting to observe that reviewing courts have shown a growing tendency to consider errors, even though not objected to, in those cases where the defendant was represented by counsel assigned to him by the trial court. It would, after all, be rather harsh to hold him for the shortcomings of an aid whom he did not select. Even more liberally, a few courts have been willing to inquire into the general efficiency or inefficiency of counsel and to open the door where they found that, though the defendant had chosen him, he had obviously made an extremely poor choice.

Statutes are fairly common providing that there shall not be any remanding or reversal of a case merely because unsubstantial error has been committed but that there shall be such a reversal or remanding only where there is substantial error. If the error is not substantial, the case shall be affirmed. This is a recognition of the fact that in a long-continued trial it is almost inevitable that the trial court will make certain rulings that the reviewing court disagrees with; and, where there is a disagreement between the trial court and the reviewing court, that constitutes an error, because that is error which the reviewing court does not agree with! Such statutes, however, can in the nature of things be little

---

2. Whether he may remain free on bail during his appeal was discussed in the comment on bail (chap. v).

more than pious exhortations to reviewing courts, because the latter necessarily have the last word. It is still for them to declare what errors are substantial and what errors are not. Some have been exceedingy technical in finding an error to be substantial. Others have found it easier to co-operate with the avowed policy of the law and have declared that it was part of the responsibility of the defendant to show that the error was a substantial one.

Like the defendant, the prosecution originally had no appellate review, but, when the former gradually gained it, this was generally not true of the latter. Accordingly, it may safely be assumed that the trial-court proceedings are final for the prosecution unless, in any given state, this has been changed (usually by means of a statute).[3] The arguments for at least some measure of appellate review are numerous.[4] Without such review, there may be a lack of uniformity of interpreting the law in various parts of the state. If the point is of such a nature that only the prosecution is aggrieved by it, no opportunity would arise to secure harmony by means of a higher court pronouncement. More serious yet, the fact that only one side can appeal may easily, though unconsciously, affect the rulings of the trial judge. On the one hand, to favor the defendant is a sure way to eliminate all danger of an embarrassing reversal, hence the risk that he will receive more than his due. On the other hand, with a judge of a different bent, he may get less, since the judge may feel that to resolve a point in the prosecution's favor does not carry the finality that the opposite ruling would. In either event, then, factors would intrude that have, or should have, no bearing. Furthermore, the more responsibility is assigned to the judge, the more attentive in the nature of things he will be and the higher the type of person who will be attracted to a judicial career.

Against such review it is argued that it is unfair to ask a defendant, victorious below, to defend that victory in a second court. This, however, is begging the question: If review is permitted, he has not yet gained the assumed victory. Along the

3. We have already seen that the prosecution may not receive a new trial and also that a verdict of not guilty cannot be set aside. Thus even at that level of procedure it occupies an inferior position.

4. They are well presented in an article by Justin Miller, "Appeals by the State in Criminal Cases," 36 Yale L.J. 486 (1927).

same lines it is also asserted that it would make possible the continuing harassment of acquitted defendants by forcing them to continue to defend themselves. To this several answers can be made. The right to appeal might be restricted to situations in which in the opinion of the trial judge or a reviewing court judge there was reason to believe that the appeal might be successful. Furthermore, in the states where appeal is possible, there has not, in actual experience, been any indication of a prosecution tendency to persecute by frivolous appeals. On the contrary, busy prosecutors have been much more inclined to let the matter drop rather than to go out of their way to advertise to the public that they failed to achieve success in the trial stage. They have usually found it much more pleasant to let sleeping dogs lie.[5]

In many states, therefore, statutes have been enacted which accord to the state some right of appeal, but the extent to which this right is accorded varies enormously from state to state. In Connecticut, at one extreme, the state has almost as great a right to appellate review as the defendant has, while in other states

5. A piece of legislation which once had a vogue for a short time sought to compromise and to secure the advantages both of state appeal and of no state appeal by providing that the state might have a broad and inclusive right of appeal (particularly where there was nonuniformity of interpretation), but the higher court's decision, whatever it might be, was not to affect the defendant in any way whatsoever. In other words, the question was to be reviewed and considered by the higher court purely for the purpose of guiding the future, and the decision would be without any effect on the litigation which occasioned bringing up the case to the reviewing court. Such statutes did not prove a success. Several were quickly snuffed out on the constitutional ground that they were attempts to force a court to decide a mere moot question, not affecting any matter in litigation. (The constitutionality problem is dealt with in an article by F. G. Munson, "The Decision of Moot Cases by Courts of Law," 9 Col. L. Rev. 667 [1909].) Even where they survived this ordeal, they have not accomplished their purpose. Prosecuting attorneys who have lost below have been highly reluctant to advertise their failure, for the sake of a reversal that will not affect matters in any event. Even a decision in his favor would not clear up anything for that particular prosecutor, except for the unlikely event that he confronted exactly the same problem a second time during his term in office. That would hardly appeal strongly to a busy man. Even in the exceptional case which may be carried up, a reviewing court can effectively determine what the law is only when it has the help of a sharply contested issue, with each side presenting its arguments as forcefully as it can. It is obvious, however, how much an unconcerned defendant will spend to contest litigation of no interest to him. Or how much crusading zeal his probably unpaid counsel will display. The resulting opinion almost necessarily will reflect the inadequate argumentation behind it.

only specified situations give the state that right.[6] The one in which it is most widely given is the quashing of an indictment.[7] Such statutes have been attacked on the ground that they subjected the accused to double jeopardy, and this is the view taken by the United States Supreme Court, where a federal statute sought to grant limited prosecution appeal.[8] To this it is answered that jeopardy necessarily attaches only when the proceedings have been brought to a termination, and the granting to the state of the right of appeal merely means that such a termination has been deferred to a later time (viz., when the review possibilities on both sides have terminated).[9] The United States Supreme Court, though not sharing in this view, has decided that it is not so untenable a one as to constitute a denial of due process and has thus left the states free to go as far as they choose in this matter.[10]

6. The Model Code (sec. 428) would give the right very broadly. It lists as appealable the quashing of an indictment, the order of a new trial, arrested judgment, any ruling in favor of the defendant where the defendant was nonetheless convicted and is himself appealing, and a sentence which was illegal considering the crime on which the defendant was convicted.

7. In this situation, and in this one only, the state may appeal in Illinois.

8. *Kepner* v. *United States*, 195 U.S. 100 (1903).

9. The constitutional law problem is dealt with in a comment in 37 Mich. L. Rev. 103 (1939).

10. *Palko* v. *Connecticut*, 302 U.S. 319 (1937).

XVII

PARDON

THE foregoing chapters have dealt, in the main, with the activity of the judicial branch of government in a criminal case, although the executive branch has received some attention (mainly the police and the prosecuting attorney). In this final chapter we consider a participation by the executive which may enter the case at any stage, before, during, or after prosecution, although usually it takes place only after successful prosecution and after the judicial proceedings have come to a full and complete end. This participation consists in the executive's power to pardon.

Historically in England the king as the autocratic head of the government always had the power to pardon. But though it rested originally on his being above the restrictions of the law, it survived because it filled a very necessary function. In many instances the law had remained static, whereas notions of justice and fairness had radically changed. An excellent example is in the defense of self-defense, where, when the law first took shape, this was absolutely no defense whatsoever to a person's guilt but where views of moral justice, as against legal justice, very soon decided that it should operate in favor of the accused. The pardoning power therefore was necessary to bring the operation of the law into conformity with the changing social need.[1] It was also necessary because, as we have seen, the procedural inadequacies of the old law gave no adequate right of review to convicted defendants, and therefore there was nothing that could be done judicially in favor of one who had been unjustly convicted. Thus a power arising out of wholly different reasons survived

1. To the modern mind another solution would seem more obvious and easy: why not change the law by statute? But it must be remembered that the notion of the legislature as a law-changing mechanism has only won acceptance at a comparatively recent date.

239

because of the wholly different uses later found to be served by it.

By an entirely natural process in the American colonies the royal governors, as the king's representatives, assumed and exercised the same power. From them, by the same natural development, it went to the state governors for state offenses and to the President for federal ones.[2] Thus, in the absence of any provision otherwise in a state constitution, the full, untrammeled power still resides in the hands of the governor, and any effort on the part of the legislature to reduce that power or to interfere with its exercise by procedural devices would be unconstitutional as an attempt by one branch of the government to interfere with another branch. But it is frequently the case that state constitutions do in some respect modify or restrict the pardoning power of the executive, or, if the constitution does not itself so modify or restrict the power, it may confer authority on the legislature to do so.

Such restrictions take one or the other, or possibly both, of two forms. They may provide, or may authorize legislation providing, that the governor's power to pardon shall be shared with some other agency of government. Thus a pardon may in certain instances call for the joint action of both the governor and this other agency. A notable example of this is the provision of the California constitution whereby a governor who wishes to pardon one previously convicted of a felony must obtain the concurrent action of the California Supreme Court. More frequently, the constitution may contain a provision, either itself specifying, or authorizing the legislature to specify, the procedural steps that must be taken before the governor may pass upon an application for a pardon. Those procedural steps often take the form of setting up a board of pardons (which may very likely be identical with and made up of the same persons who constitute also the state's board of parole). All applications for pardon and all proposed pardons must go to it for consideration and recommenda-

2. So literally, in fact, has this development been adhered to that in quasi-criminal cases (viz., the violation of city ordinances) the mayor as head of the executive branch of the city government has, at least in some instances, been held to have the same power.

tions before the governor may act. Whether he will then follow the recommendations or disregard them is for him to decide.[3]

The pardoning power is not restricted to a flat choice between a complete pardon and a complete refusal. The pardon may be a conditional one, that is, conditioned on the recipient's living up to specified requirements of conduct, and not becoming absolute until the conditions have been met. Or the pardon may be a partial one, cutting down the amount of punishment that is to be undergone. This partial pardon is usually called a "commutation of sentence." But it is not usually possible under the guise of "commutation" to change the nature of the punishment. Who is to say whether a change from, say, a year in prison to a $10,000 fine (or, for that matter, vice versa) is a decrease, or an actual increase, in punishment? One person's evaluation may differ entirely from that of another person. The governor cannot, under the guise of commutation, force on a convict what may in the latter's opinion constitute an increase in punishment.[4]

The foregoing sentence suggests a question which at one time raised considerable doubt. May the convict refuse a pardon, or does it take effect without reference to his acceptance or approval? (Though acceptance is so likely that we can take it almost for granted, there have been instances of endeavors to reject a pardon.) It was at one time contended that acceptance was necessary. This position rested, in the main, on two arguments.

The first was the extremely legalistic argument that a pardon is an instrument under seal and is therefore a deed or akin to a deed. A deed becomes effective only if there is delivery, and the person to whom it is offered may prevent the delivery by refus-

---

3. Usually a governor will welcome some such provision as this. The issuance or denial of pardons is one of the greatest burdens of his office, and to discharge it adequately calls for a huge expenditure of his time. To have considered and responsible recommendations is a great and welcome relief. Thus what may on paper be only a procedural device may in operation mean that the governor will quite legitimately turn over much of the responsibility for decisions to the board. In the case of a governor who is less conscientious such a procedural restriction is likewise a very desirable thing, because it will require him to act in the light of publicity. It would prevent such disgraceful performances as that of one governor who in the last twenty-four hours of his term signed several hundred pardons for reasons best known to himself.

4. The exception is the change of a death sentence to one of life-imprisonment. The instinct to keep one's life is so nearly universal that this is an allowable commutation.

ing to accept it. Hence, just as one can prevent a deed from coming into operation by preventing the completion of delivery, so one can prevent the pardon from coming into existence by refusing to accept it.[5]

The second argument, a more realistic and substantial one, was that, since the acceptance of a pardon constituted an admission of guilt, the convict ought not to be forced to make such an admission. What he has done may have been so completely a matter of principle with him that even undergoing punishment is preferable to an admission that he was in the wrong. The weakness of this argument should, however, be obvious. It assumes its own conclusion. A pardon can be an admission of guilt only if it can be refused. If refusal is impossible, the fact that there has been a pardon loses any significance as an admission.[6] The contrary position, that either acceptance or rejection by the convict is immaterial and entirely meaningless, rests on far stronger grounds.[7] According to it, the issuance of a pardon is a determination by the appropriate and responsible official of the government that in the case under consideration it now seems wise and in the social interest to reduce or eliminate further punishment. It is not an arbitrary act of mere generosity. In arriving at a decision as to what is now in the best social interest, we do not and should not consult him for his opinion any more than we did when the original sentence was imposed. His approval or disapproval should make no difference. There is, however, one possible qualification. Where the pardon is a conditional one, imposing new requirements on him, whose weight might be differently ap-

5. If there is any value in pursuing such legalistic reasoning any further, it might be asked whether the delivery is in fact to the accused person or is to the custodian who has charge of the penitentiary in which he is incarcerated. If the latter, then apparently the person who might set the governor's decision at naught would seem to be the warden of the penitentiary, which is, to put it mildly, a rather bizarre conclusion to reach!

6. Compare a proceeding closely related to a pardon—a general amnesty. Its issuance does not, and cannot, constitute either an adjudication of a specific person's guilt or an admission of it by him.

7. After considerable hesitation and doubt, this was apparently the view taken by the United States Supreme Court in *Biddle* v. *Perovich*, 274 U.S. 480 (1927). This has about settled the question.

praised by different persons, it might be argued that his consent
should be a requirement, so as to make sure that the punishment
was not being increased.[8]

Let us now assume that the defendant has been pardoned and
thereafter is again convicted of an offense for which a more serious punishment is provided on second conviction than on first. Is
he to be treated as a first or second offender? Both views are well
supported by authority. The conclusion that he is a "first" offender results from the argument that the pardon has blotted out
his guilt, so that it is as though he had not been convicted before
at all.[9] But here again we have a question-begging answer. The
contrary view maintains that the more serious punishment for a
second offense is not—and, indeed, cannot properly be—a belated
additional punishment for the first offense. It results merely from
the fact that, by having continued in his criminal ways, he has
conclusively shown that he is more of a social problem than was
first supposed and hence needs more punitive (or rehabilita-
tional) treatment. This new evaluation of the extent to which he
constitutes a social menace is not affected by the fact that he was
previously pardoned.[10] He nonetheless needs the more severe attention. While this view seems preferable to the former one, it,
too, is not free from objections. This results from the basically
ambiguous nature of a pardon.

As we have seen, the pardon originally served two entirely

8. It might even be argued (though without support in the cases, apparently)
that, since the only reason that the governor may not change the nature of the
punishment is that he might thereby increase it, a change in nature should not
be objectionable, if the convict consents, thereby conclusively showing that the
change constitutes, in his opinion, a decrease. We have already seen (n. 4,
above) that a change from death to life-imprisonment is permitted, because of
our confidence that the change will be universally regarded as a decrease in
punishment.

9. This view was maintained by an early case in which a figure of speech
was used: the pardon made a "new man" of him. As so often the case with
metaphors, what was first meant merely as a figure of speech soon came, for
many courts, to have independent value of its own, and it was asked: How
could he be a second offender, since he was a "new" man? So far as is known,
no court has ever regarded this "new" man as a candidate for juvenile court
attention!

10. It should be noted that it is on exactly this line of reasoning that many
courts permit the imposition of the heavier punishment even where the "first"
offense was committed in another jurisdiction.

different purposes, and the dilemma has arisen because of the difference between them. One function of the pardon was that of exempting from further punishment a wrongdoer who in the opinion of the pardoning authority had been punished enough. This purpose of the pardoning power presupposed that the pardon was being exercised in favor of a wrongdoer and law violator. The other function of the power was to fill the serious gap in the judicial process, whereby the latter was in great measure unable itself to correct mistakes that had been made in adjudicating a person's guilt.[11] The pardoning power exercised through the executive was the only way in which the unjust result arrived at by the judicial branch of government could be corrected. But in this type of situation the pardon was predicated on the complete innocence of the convicted person and was, therefore, an entirely different thing. The dilemma of whether or not to consider a pardoned offense in the event of a second conviction stems basically from this uncertainty as to what a given pardon should be regarded as meaning. The real way out of the dilemma would be the procedural requirement that the governor in granting the pardon should indicate whether it is for innocence or for sufficient punishment. If the pardon is for innocence, then the defendant should be considered a first offender; if for sufficient punishment, a second one. No single answer is possible. Unfortunately, there is usually no requirement that the governor indicate which type of pardon any given one is.[12] So long as this uncertainty remains, we shall continue in our dilemma.[13]

The same uncertainty as to the meaning of any given pardon has led to a similar disagreement in another, but allied, area. Conviction of a serious offense normally carries with it consequences other than merely imprisonment. The convict may lose his right to vote. He may no longer be eligible to serve in the position of confidence and responsibility that we call "trusteeship," to act as an executor, etc. He may be subject to certain disadvantages

11. E.g., as we have seen, the absence or inadequacy of review possibilities or the discovery of important new evidence after the term of court was over.
12. Iowa is an exception. Code (1946), secs. 248.7 and 747.7.
13. This problem is well discussed in an article by Henry Weihofen, "The Effect of a Pardon," 88 Penn. L. Rev. 177 (1939).

should he be called upon as a witness. What should the effect of a pardon be on these collateral consequences? If they are punitive in nature, the answer would be easy. The pardoned individual should be exempted from them. But in the main they are not considered as additional punishments. Rather, these collateral consequences are merely the reflection of society's belief that this citizen, who has proved himself inadequate in the past, is not a safe risk to intrust with such responsibilities in the future. Shall a pardon modify this appraisal? In exactly the same manner as above the uncertainty as to the reason for, and hence the meaning of, a pardon prevents a definite and satisfactory answer.

INDEX

04